THE POETRY OF W. B. YEATS

The Poetry of
W. B. YEATS

by

LOUIS MACNEICE

with a foreword by

RICHARD ELLMANN

faber and faber

This edition first published in 2008
by Faber and Faber Ltd
3 Queen Square, London WC1N 3AU

Printed by CPI Antony Rowe, Eastbourne

A CIP record for this book is available from the British Library

ISBN 978-0-571-24345-7

To
E. R. DODDS
AN IRISHMAN, A POET, AND A SCHOLAR,
WHO KNOWS MORE ABOUT IT ALL
THAN I DO

And Pan did after Syrinx speed
Not as a nymph, but for a reed.

MARVELL

Foreword

by Richard Ellmann

The poets who went up to Oxford in the 1920's were puzzled whether to consider Yeats a monument or a folly. His occultism embarrassed them as being primitive, and if that was not (since the Dadaists) an adequate slur, primitive in the wrong way. And yet the verse of Yeats was cultivated and subtle, not to be scouted nor easily matched. Even as an older man he persisted in exploring themes such as personal love and general ruin which the younger poets would have liked to reserve for themselves. His behaviour was much less congenial to them than T. S. Eliot's. Eliot was proceeding with stately anguish into middle age and spirituality, while Yeats advanced precipitously, without this American decorum, upon old age and corporeality.

Auden, Spender, and MacNeice all responded to this pressure from their older contemporary. The method of Auden was to brave Yeats by ludicrous deflations of his dicta. When he and MacNeice wrote in Iceland their 'Last Will and Testament', Auden's hand is probably displayed in their joint determination to 'leave the phases of the moon/To Mr. Yeats to rock his bardic sleep.' In the same volume MacNeice more politely registers Yeats's influence in 'Eclogue from Iceland', where the stylization of friends clearly owes something to 'All Souls' Night':

> There was MacKenna
> Spent twenty years translating Greek philosophy,
> Ill and tormented, unwilling to break contract,
> A brilliant talker who left
> The salon for the solo flight of Mind.

MacNeice, like Stephen Spender, moved gradually from qualified to assured, but never easy, admiration of Yeats. When in 1938 he wrote discursively on *Modern Poetry*, he still criticized Yeats for living in a 'largely private world', for being 'utterly individualistic' and 'egoistic'. He acknowledged also, however, that Yeats, after having in youth perpetrated 'luxury-writing', had now come closer to MacNeice's own ideal of a poetry which should be 'functional', which should convoke things, people, and political events.

After *Modern Poetry* was published there occurred the death of Yeats in January 1939 and then the outbreak of war. In this period MacNeice conceived of a book entirely about Yeats, to disentangle his own mixed feelings, probably, as well as for a more overt purpose, to establish the reality of poetry at a moment when it seemed most tenuous. He had not written much of the book when, in January 1940, he went to the United States; he remained until December, completing most of it there. He says in his autobiography, *The Strings Are False*, that as an Irishman he was not sure what part to take in the war; he returned still candidly muddled but certain that he belonged in England. This recognition was not an obvious one: MacNeice was the son of a Protestant rector in the North of Ireland who, astonishingly, favoured Home Rule. Yet much as he loved Dublin and Donegal, MacNeice could not in conscience see from the southern Irish point of view, for he had been educated in England from the age of ten. He felt himself to be an exile from the Irish 'quarrel', and wrote in *Autumn Journal*, nostalgic yet impatient:

> Why should I want to go back
> to you, Ireland, my Ireland?

His book on Yeats was an assessment of a poet whose land he shared but whose convictions he often could not accept.

The Poetry of W. B. Yeats finds nevertheless much to commend. Yeats is celebrated for making a transition from fantasy to fact which yet left much of the fantasy intact. Though not a mystic, MacNeice granted now what he had questioned earlier, that mysticism such as Yeats's was a force in all thought, an assertion of what could be instead of what was. He liked Yeats's Whitmanlike willingness to contradict himself, to speak 'from different poles of his being'. The politics of Yeats, which disturbed Spender in *The Destructive Element* and later critics as well, MacNeice was inclined to indulge. Without denying Yeats an element of folly, he saw that the real political direction was a fastidious nationalism based upon individual freedom and spontaneity. On this point MacNeice's restraint is likely to be vindicated; with his eye fixed on the ennobling of Ireland, Yeats could see no political party that satisfied him, and recklessly snatched at rebelliousness where he found it, conscious that though it might well be wrong-headed, it at least offered the excitement of ineptitude and the possible distinction of failure.

If MacNeice felt as an Irishman affinities with Yeats, Yeats felt them too. He liked or at least rather liked (within the confines of his own perspective) MacNeice's verse, and took an interest in what the young man was doing. In 1936 he attended a performance of MacNeice's translation of the *Agamemnon*, and that year he chose four of MacNeice's poems for his *Oxford Book of Modern Verse*, a greater number than he took from Auden or Spender. All the poems had points of common interest with his own work. The two men seem to have met only once, and on that occasion Yeats held the floor. Without giving MacNeice much chance to speak he shrewdly took note of such qualities as the young man's 'intellectual passion', 'social passion', and 'social bitterness', phrases he applied to him in the *Oxford Book* and in a BBC broadcast on 'Modern Poetry'. While 'intellectual' and 'social' were doubtful words in Yeats's language, 'passion' was a good one; and he did not belittle MacNeice's emphasis on communal plight though he would have preferred less unconcern for the self. After Yeats's death his two sisters, Lilly and Elizabeth Yeats, made light of seeming divergences by publishing a small book of MacNeice's poems at their Cuala Press.

MacNeice's book on Yeats is still as good an introduction to that poet as we have, with the added interest that it is also an introduction to MacNeice. It discloses a critical mind always discontented with its own formulations, full of self-questionings and questionings of others, scrupling to admire, reluctant to be won. Yet mistrust of Yeats is overcome by wary approval, in a rising tone of endorsement. Then at the end MacNeice declares a kind of independence, as if this mode of thinking, feeling, and writing was 'no go', like the merrygoround and the rickshaw, and must be put aside as belonging to the past rather than the future. In the same mood he had just collected his *Poems 1925–1940*, and had prefaced them with the remark that the part of his life they represented was now dead. Moving on, he sensed a dissolution of old relationships, including that with Yeats. His judgements of Yeats's works and acts reveal his own changing needs, but are not for that reason less sharp or relevant. Those aspects of Yeats that remain central in all subsequent critical writings, including the most recent, are descried and delineated by MacNeice: the half-spurned estheticism, the Irishism, the deliberate belief, the sense of responsibility, the appetite for passionate experience, the laboriously invented diction. And by being rigorous, by offering Yeats no quarter, no deference, MacNeice succeeds in imparting Yeats's own energy, in making him muscular rather than august.

Contents

Preface

There is not, to my knowledge—nor do I think there can be – any satisfactory definition of the relationship of poetry to life. I am convinced however, that there is such a relationship and that it is of primary importance; I am also convinced that a poem is a thing in itself, a self-contained organism, a 'creation'—I might almost say, saving the presence of philosophers, an absolute. When Dr Johnson demanded that the products of 'Wit' should be *both natural and new*, he was recognizing these two characteristics of a poem, that it corresponds in some indefinable way to life and that it is at the same time an individual, brand-new *thing*. The literary critic, being unable to assess thinghood, inevitably concerns himself with poetry as correspondence. Such criticism can be valuable but it never rises above what Aristotle called 'bastard reasoning'.

When we talk about the value of anything, we tend to suppose a gulf between this abstracted value and the thing which is valuable. This seems to me wrong. When a rose hits me in the senses, it is the rose that hits me and not some value separable from the rose. Idealist philosophers in talking about their Absolutes and Universals have made them vulnerable by hypostatizing them, whereas the only invulnerable Universal is one that is incarnate. We still tend to think that, because a thing is in time, its value can only be explained by an abstraction from the thing of some supposedly timeless qualities; this is to explain the thing away. That a rose withers is no disproof of the rose, which remains an absolute, its value inseparable from its existence (for existence is still existence, whether the tense is past or future).

A poem (which, we must never forget, is a physical organism) is in the same category. For this reason all literary critics are falsifiers in that they try to disintricate the value or essence of a poem from the poem itself; they peel away the onion. Thus in my book, *Modern Poetry*, I overstressed the half-truth that poetry is *about* something, is communication. So it is, but it is also a separate self; in the same way a living animal is an individual although it is on the one hand conditioned by heredity and environment and the laws of nature in general and on the other hand has a function outside itself, is a link in a chain. In *Modern Poetry* I also denied that the poet is properly a mystic and argued that the poetic is a

15

normal human activity. I still hold that the poet is a distinct species from the mystic, but I should like to correct the emphasis here, although I shall have occasion to repeat these points later. Mysticism, in the narrow sense, implies a specific experience which is foreign to most poets and most men, but on the other hand it represents an instinct which is a human *sine qua non*. Both the poet and the 'ordinary man' are mystics incidentally and there is a mystical sanction or motivation for all their activities which are not purely utilitarian (possibly, therefore, for *all* their activities, as it is doubtful whether any one does anything purely for utility).

Life—let alone art—cannot be assessed purely in terms of utility. Food, for example, is useful for life but what is life useful for? To both the question of pleasure and the question of value the utilitarian has no answer. The faith in the *value* of living is a mystical faith. The pleasure in bathing or dancing, in colour or shape, is a mystical experience. If non-utilitarian activity is abnormal, then all men are abnormal. It was because I did not think of men as essentially utilitarian that I maintained that poetry is a normal activity, that 'the poet is a specialist in something which every one practises'.

In writing about Yeats and his poetry I have inevitably concerned myself with 'facts'—with what Yeats was writing *about*, with the life and ideas from which his poetry came. These facts provide certain clues to his poetry but the poetry cannot be summed up in them. I would repeat that a poem is about something but that a poem also is. The critic being impotent to convey this thinghood of a poem, no one need expect that critical discussion of poetic values can ever convey *the* value of a poem itself, for every poem is unique and its value inseparable from its existence. The background of a poem, its origin, its purpose, its ingredients, can be analysed and formulated, but the poem itself can only be experienced. All that the critic can do is lay stepping stones over the river—stones which are better forgotten once the reader has reached a position where he is in touch with the subject of criticism.

L.M.

September, 1940.

NOTE

The poems by Mr Yeats quoted in this book are reprinted by permission of Mrs Yeats and of Messrs Macmillan & Co. Ltd, and the Macmillan Company, New York, the publishers of his works.

CHAPTER I

Introductory

We impose on one another, and it is but lost time to converse with you whose works are only Analyticks.   BLAKE

I

If I were making a general anthology of shorter English poems, I should want to include some sixty by W. B. Yeats. There is no other poet in the language from whom I should choose so many. This being so, I feel it would be merely academic for me to discuss at length whether Yeats was or was not a great poet or to spend much time trying to rank him. I am not interested in ranking poets and I am not even very much interested in greatness *per se*. The poets who interest me are the poets whom I like re-reading. I like re-reading Yeats more than I like re-reading most English poets. This is why I undertook to write a book about his poetry; I wished to find out why Yeats appealed to me so much and I hoped also to present Yeats sympathetically to others. Poetry nowadays appears to need defending. I would not attempt however to defend poetry itself; that poetry is good seems to me axiomatic; if you do not accept this axiom, we have no common ground for argument. In a world, however, where the vast bulk of criticism is destructive, I feel that to express and, if possible, to explain one's admiration for a particular poet is something worth doing.

It is perhaps especially worth doing at this moment when external circumstances are making such a strong assault on our sense of values. I had only written a little of this book when Germany invaded Poland. On that day I was in Galway. As soon as I heard on the wireless of the outbreak of war, Galway became unreal. And Yeats and his poetry became unreal also.

This was not merely because Galway and Yeats belong in a sense to a past order of things. The unreality which now overtook them was also overtaking in my mind modern London, modernist art, and Left Wing politics. If the war made nonsense of Yeats's poetry and of all works that are called 'escapist', it also made nonsense of the poetry that professes to be 'realist'. My friends had been writing for years about guns and frontiers and factories, about the 'facts' of psychology, politics, science, economics, but the fact of war made their writing seem as remote as the pleasure dome in Xanadu. For war spares neither the poetry of Xanadu nor the poetry of pylons. I gradually inferred, as I recovered from the shock of war, that both these kinds of poetry stand or fall together. War does not prove that one is better or worse than the other; it attempts to disprove both. But poetry must not be disproved. If war is the test of reality, then all poetry is unreal; but in that case unreality is a virtue. If, on the other hand, war is a great enemy of reality, although an incontestable fact, then reality is something which is not exactly commensurable with facts.

Yeats all his life was a professed enemy of facts, and that made my generation suspicious of him. It was a generation that had rediscovered the importance of subject matter: a poem must be *about* something. Further, a poem must be about something *real*, and 'real' was often taken to mean contemporary. By these standards much of Yeats's poetry was vicious. In his later books, however, there was enough contemporary subject matter to permit of the discovery that Yeats had become a 'realist'.

Most arguments nowadays about realism rest upon unwarranted over-simplification. The champions of realism are suffering from a reaction against Pure Form, against Art for Art's Sake. It was quite right that a poet like W. H. Auden should reassert that a poem must be about something. It was right to go further and maintain that great poetry cannot be made out of subject matter which is essentially trivial. But it was a mistake to take subject matter, as some of the 'realists' seemed to, as the sole, or even the chief, criterion of poetry. It was a mistake to fancy that criticism could ever devise a sliding scale which would assess the value of a poem by simple reference to the objective importance of its subject matter. The believers in Art for Art's Sake had gone too far in asserting that poetry can be judged without any reference to life. But the realists went too far in the other direction. A poem does not exist in a vacuum, but a poem at the same time is a unity, a creation. Criticism based on the assumption that a poem is a mere *translation* of facts outside itself is vicious criticism. The facts outside a poem, the facts which occasion a poem, are no longer the same facts when they have been fused into a poem. Or, looking at it in another way, one can say that the facts which occasion a poem are far too complex to be fully ascertainable by the critic. No poet writes a poem merely about a house; any poem he writes about a house is also a poem

18

about himself, and so about humanity and life in general. The realist critic tends to diagnose subject matter crudely and naïvely. Was Pindar really only writing about foot-races and boxing matches? Was Rilke really only writing about a panther in the Jardin des Plantes? Was Wordsworth really only writing about villagers or celandines?

This book will be largely taken up with a discussion of Yeats's subject matter during various periods of his life. I shall try to show what were Yeats's dominating ideas, his prevalent likes and dislikes, at different periods. Unlike the believers in Art for Art's Sake, I consider that such a study will make his poetry more intelligible and more sympathetic. I do not, however, think for a moment that knowledge of the subject matter will provide a key to any one poem *qua* poem, and, while I admit that in Yeats's case, as in the case of many other poets, an improvement in his poetry seems related to an extension of his subject matter, I would make the proviso that this relationship cannot be rigidly formulated; and, further, that there are few poems in the world which can be taken exactly at their face value. Few poems are exactly what they appear to be; you cannot say 'This is a love poem' or 'This is a nature poem' or 'This is a piece of satire' and leave it at that. Again, if the critic, as critics must, should abstract various aspects of poetry and discuss it say under the headings of matter and form, or again should subdivide form into such categories as rhythm, diction, imagery, it must always be remembered that these are only convenient abstractions from an indissolubly blended whole. It is an outrage to a poem to think of it as such-and-such matter *plus* such-and-such form, or even as a matter *put into* form. Form must not be thought of as a series of rigid moulds. All matter is to some extent *informed* to start with; and the very selection of matter is a formalistic activity. On the other hand artistic form is more than a mere method or convenience or discipline or, of course, décor. Just as one cannot, by the furthest analysis, completely deformalize matter, so one cannot completely desubstantialize form. Musical form, for example, is in a sense a *thing*. Artists use form not merely to express some alien matter but because form itself is a spiritual principle which calls for expression in matter. The relationship between form and matter is like a marriage; matter must find itself in form and form must find itself in matter.

The 'realists', to excuse their acceptance of Yeats, pointed to a poem like Easter 1916, and argued that this is a good poem because it is about an important event in contemporary history. Such events, we can agree, made a welcome entrance into Yeats's later poetry. Such subject matter confers an advantage both on the poet and the reader; on the poet because a contemporary event such as the Easter Rising in Dublin is likely to produce in him that emotional tension which can do half the poet's work for him; on the reader because, being himself acquainted with and probably moved by that event, he is already halfway to an understanding of the poet's reactions to it. We cannot, however, infer from this that a poem about such an event is necessarily a better poem or a more important or even a more realistic poem than a poem about something far less contemporary or far more obscure or private. We can say at the most that many poets—including, I think, Yeats—are more likely to write well, that is with clarity, strength, and emotional honesty, when they are writing about something which has moved them *and others* in their own time than when they are writing about something which belongs more exclusively to their own private mythology. We can say also that most readers are more likely to react poetically to material which they know themselves than to material which they have to take on trust from the poet. And the poet in turn, who tends to adjust his sights by the presumed knowledge of an imaginary reader, is more likely to shoot truly when he knows that there are many real readers who have knowledge of the matter which he is treating.

Realists of a narrower school sometimes take realism to imply photographic verisimilitude or scientific objectivity. On their criterion *Easter 1916* is not a realistic work, or at any rate it is much less realistic than say *The Plough and the Stars* by Sean O'Casey. And on the average it will be found, on their criterion, that poetry is less realistic than drama and drama less realistic than the novel. Does this mean that poetry is less successful than these other forms in attaining its object? Or does it mean that it has a different object?

I would say that poetry *has* a different object and that it is certainly further from realism than the prose drama or the novel, if realism is used in the constricted sense mentioned above. I would suggest however that the poet's business *is* realism, if it is admitted that the reality which he is trying to represent is further removed than the novelist's is from the reality of the scientist or of the photographer or of any one who is engaged in recording facts which do not include himself and are not modified by his own emotional reaction to them. I do not think we can say that the poet's reality is therefore less real than the scientist's—unless we are prepared to say that hunger is less real than bread. The poet's reality is not less real; it is merely different. Can we see if we can define it a little further?

INTRODUCTORY

Poetry, I think, cannot be assessed solely in terms of itself; it must be referred back to life. But to what life? The great difference, I would say, between the scientist and the artist is that life for the scientist means something outside himself, neither affecting him nor affected by him, whereas life for the poet is essentially *his* life. However objective a poet's method may appear to be (for it is in no way unpoetic to be scientifically knowledgeable or to be an exact recorder), the poet, even in selecting the material, which he may afterwards record with a superficially scientific frigidity, is governed by personal motives. Mr T. S. Eliot in our own day has repeatedly preached 'impersonality' as a virtue of poets. But by impersonality he means something different from the impersonality of the scientist. Mr Eliot in his own poetry avoids saying 'I' but he would admit that the poet's world is a world coloured by himself, complicated by his own emotions and re-arranged on a principle which is anathema to the scientist. When Mr Eliot attacks 'personality' in poetry, he is really attacking the kind of anarchist individualism which characterized the Romantic Revival. Sophocles for example was not impersonal in the sense that he wrote without emotion or presented a world uncoloured by emotion; he was impersonal in that he wrote within the conventions of a tradition and an outlook shared by most of his public. In this narrowed sense of the word, the personal poet is a law to himself, judging the world entirely by reference to his own emotions. Whereas the impersonal poet, in the narrow sense, though he need not be unemotional or inhuman, does not impose his emotions upon the world but rather (though this is a clumsy and loose distinction) accepts them *from* it.

I prefer to use the word 'personal' in the wider sense and to call any writing personal which is conditioned by the writer's own emotions— whether these emotions are peculiar to himself or sanctioned by a community or a tradition and whether the writer himself is conscious or unconscious of the effect that his emotions have upon his presentation of facts. In case it should be thought that I am subscribing to a Wordsworthian doctrine of poetry, I must explain that when I say that poetry is a personal activity because it is conditioned by the emotions of the poet, I am not using emotion in the narrow Romantic sense of intense emotion, nor do I wish to abstract emotion from the poet's self in opposition to intellect. The poetic self—like any human self—is ipso facto emotional and intellectual at the same time. Emotion can be subordinated to intellect, or vice versa, but the two elements are always present. Every poet does two things, though he may be more conscious of one than of the other and though his success may be due more to one than to the other. He reacts emotionally (though such emotion may be strong or weak, conscious or unconscious) to his subject matter and he selects and arranges that subject matter—consciously or unconsciously—in order to square it with some intellectual system of his own. But even this distinction is too crude, for these two moments of the poetic activity are inseparable like the positive and negative elements in electricity. Even before the artist has started his art-work proper he is not only reacting emotion- ally to his subject but he is also automatically systematizing it. I agree with Croce that the artist is functioning artistically from the very first moment he thinks or perceives his subject; I do not however agree that his subsequent expression of it is of merely secondary importance. When the artist goes on to express his subject in his proper medium, he is not only systematizing, he is also still developing his own emotional reactions. (Thus Wordsworth's 'Emotion recollected in tranquillity' is a half-truth which is more true of some poets than of others but is never entirely true of any poet. Other critics have made out a case for 'Tranquil- lity recollected in emotion'.) Speaking roughly, one can say that one poet has an intellectual bias (writes 'deliberately'), and another an emotional bias (writes 'spontaneously'). You may feel emotionally towards a thing because it occupies a special place in your system or you may give it a special place in your system because you feel emotionally towards it. The 'spontaneous' love poet lets love do his system-making for him; the Pro- vencal troubadour or the Latin elegiac poet selects love as a theme because it is a convenient frame-work. (Some poets have gone further and have deliberately set out to be passionate *in their lives*, motivated not by passion but by a *belief* in it. In the next chapter I shall suggest that this was a habit found among the English poets of the Eighteen Nineties.)

These generalities, although it is hard to express them with the requisite subtlety and precision, are really truisms. I have had to try to express them before going on to the particular criticism of Yeats. The literary critic's judgements are never more than approximately true. To make his points he has often to over-stress them. Sometimes, especially when I am taking —or refusing to take—Yeats at his word (his own statements about poetry are usually unqualified), I may seem to be forgetting that a poem— or a poet—is a complex unity, that is, complex *but* a unity (or a unity *but* complex). I may seem to make a facile use of such concepts as 'emotion', 'personality', 'system', 'belief', using them with an unwarrantable rigidity. For this I apologize in advance. The final justification of a poem is the poem itself. In shedding a little of what I hope is common sense upon poetry I do not imagine that I am offering an adequate appreciation of it. All I hope to do is to make it easier for certain readers to appreciate certain poems when they come to them or come back to them. Thus in reading Yeats it seems to me to be helpful to know who Yeats was, who were his friends, what were his literary influences, political opinions, and social prejudices. These things were not the cause of his poetry but they were among its conditions.

Critics often tend to write as if a condition were the same thing as a cause. It is very helpful to the reader to know the poet's background, but no poems can be accounted for merely by reference to that background. I labour this point because this book will be largely concerned with background and because I do not wish continually to make the qualification: 'But this is not the whole story.' If indeed we knew *all* the conditions behind a poem, these conditions might be taken collectively as the cause of it. Further, there is just one condition which is constant whenever people write poetry and which therefore, being acquitted of the relativity of the others, might be justly regarded as a cause in itself. This is the urge to expression itself. It may be argued that this urge is itself conditioned by psychological factors within the poet. I agree, but it is the urge that is the first principle; the psychological factors merely canalize it.

This primary urge is something which the critic can say little about; he ought however to remember that in the last analysis all poetry or artistic creation presupposes it. Too much criticism is founded upon the fallacy that all activity is utilitarian. Animal activity is presumed to mean the instinctive employment of means to ends; specifically human activity is presumed to mean the rational employment of means to ends. This utilitarianism begs two questions: the question of the value of the end and the question whether any activity can be pursued merely as a means and not to some extent as an end in itself. People often speak as if the sole motive for all actions whether of animals or human beings, were the wish to go on living. This is an inadequate explanation and not even a truly utilitarian one. One has merely to ask '*Why* should they wish to go on living?' and one introduces a question of value which has nothing to do with utility; food may be useful because it keeps you alive but what is life useful for? The answer is that, if life is desirable, it is not desirable because it is useful but because it is good in itself. But, if this is so, it cannot be regarded as a mere ideal terminus governing the various activities of living but itself beyond them; these activities *are* life. This being so, all these activities

23

themselves involve the question of value. It would be absurd to contend that either animals or human beings do all they do because that is the best way of keeping alive. Life for living creatures is not something which you merely have or have not; it is something plastic; it *is* what you make it. The sense of values governing this conscious or unconscious creation of life (presumably unconscious among the lower animals, partly conscious among human beings) is not utilitarian; it can only be described as mystical.

In previous writings about poetry I have offended certain readers because I have grouped the poet with ordinary men and opposed him to the mystic proper. I do not withdraw from this position. I think that human activity begins at a stage below thought with an urge which I can only describe as mystical; at this stage the individual does not distinguish the forces within him from the forces outside him; he does not know what he is driving at and he is not, I suspect, even properly conscious that it is *he* who is driving at it. The stage of thought, on the other hand, is a stage of distinctions and of consciousness of the ego. The mystic proper transcends these distinctions and once more merges the ego in the cosmos. Ordinary civilized men live most of their lives in the intermediate stage—the stage of distinctions and egoism. The poet is found among them because the poet's job is to be articulate and man cannot be articulate unless he makes distinctions; the logical outcome of mysticism is silence. On the other hand the poet shares the paradoxical position of the ordinary man. The paradox is this: man lives by egoism, by making distinctions, but he derives his driving force from a stage below distinctions and he derives his ideals from a stage above them. The ordinary man, that is, has his sub-self of animal and his super-self of mystic proper (if I admit that animal activity is in a sense mystical I must be sure to add that human mysticism is founded upon, even though it may transcend and appear in opposition to, human rational thought). The poet is not necessarily either more animal or more mystical than the ordinary man, though he may be either, as he may also be more rational. The poet must have in one respect or another a heightened consciousness or sensitivity; he is not a creature apart from ordinary men, he is an ordinary man with specialized gifts.

Some critics of recent years (for example the Abbé Brémond in his book *Prière et Poésie*) have stressed—I think, overstressed—the mystical aspect of poetry. That some poets have been inspired by direct mystical experience cannot be denied. It is also, I suggest, a fact that poetry as such has a mystical sanction in so far as poetry can be described as an end in itself.

But this is not the whole description of poetry because every poem is by its nature a compromise. A poem may be a bridge to the Unknown but it is a bridge essentially constructed in terms of the known. Those mystics proper who have written poetry, have had in so doing, when trying to express the ineffable, to descend from the mystical plane; they start from a sense of mystical union, a fusion of subject and object, and have to translate this into the language of a world where subject and object are separate and clearly defined. The normal poet, on the other hand, starts in this world of distinctions and approaches the mystical plane from below and, as it were, incidentally. The poet's medium is language and the purpose of language is the making of distinctions. Therefore, though the poet may transcend the world of distinctions, he can only do this by a kind of bluff, by pretending at least to recognize that world. In most poets this is not even a conscious pretence. They regard themselves and their poetry as *of* that world and, in so far as they approximate to a different world, they do it, as I have said, incidentally and unintentionally.

Yeats himself often spoke as if the function of poetry were mystical and sometimes tried to give the impression that he himself had mystical experiences, in the proper sense of the word. Some critics, taking him at his own valuation, have described him as a 'mystical poet'. This is an incorrect description, if the word is being used in the narrow sense. Yeats was no mystic in the sense that certain Christian and Hindu saints, or his own friend, A.E., were mystics. Yeats believed in mysticism (a belief which itself perhaps is mystically conditioned) but he does not seem to have had, in any unusual degree, direct mystical experience. The lack of such experience, in my opinion, was not necessarily a liability. If we compare Yeats's poetry with A.E.' s poetry, we may even come to think that it was an asset. If I may borrow a simile, which Yeats himself used in another application, he was like Lancelot who nearly saw the Grael. He believed in the Grael, *divining* its presence (to use Plato's metaphor), he made great efforts to achieve direct vision. But it was perhaps just because he lacked this direct vision that he was able to write poetry. Would not Lancelot have been able to give a better account of the Quest than Galahad? Galahad, I feel, would have forgotten the road in the goal achieved and have lost his human feelings in that superhuman experience.

Yeats in his critical writings stresses the religious aspect of poetry but he tends to think of the poet as priest rather than saint. Poetry is a mystery cult, a ritual. Yeats has for this reason often been accused of mumbo-jumboism. I shall have several occasions to discuss the difficult question of his sincerity. I have no doubt that he often practised his ritual merely for ritual's sake. At the same time I think that his addiction to ritual can be referred back to an original intuition of some intangible reality and that his final answer, if driven to defend himself, would be that of the Irishman[1] arguing about transubstantiation who, when asked 'How can bread be God?', replied 'What else would it be?'

II

Most literary critics must find themselves repeatedly on or over the verge of self-contradiction. This is because criticism implies the application of standards of a certain rigidity; if the critic relaxes his standards too far, he is lost in flux. But if he does not relax them, he is certain to be unjust to the particular subjects of his criticism, to be guilty—if only on a small scale—of the sin of Procrustes. Absolute fairness is unachievable when a work of art is being judged either by a theory of art or by reference to other works of art. Yet these are the only ways in which a work of art can be judged, judgement being less direct than experience. The direct experience of a work of art is the important thing; judgements *about* it are only made in order to rationalize one's appreciation to oneself or to others (if to others, the critic may also hope to lead them indirectly to the direct experience).

Artists are often—very often—damned for failing to achieve something which they never attempted. The critic's view of art is essentially static; the artistic process is essentially dynamic. The critic tries to fit a particular artist into a niche in history as if history were a long corridor with all its niches there already. The artist on the other hand would never have become an artist if all he had to do were to walk down a ready-made corridor. History for the artist is something which is evolving and he himself is aiding and abetting it.

Professor Collingwood in his recent *Autobiography* criticizes the old static conception of a logical judgement accepted by nearly all philosophers. He wishes to substitute a concept which contains two simultaneous moments, the moments of question and answer; a judgement, that is, cannot be regarded merely as an answer to a question outside itself. We can apply this principle to works of art. In any work of art the artist is simultaneously putting his own question and making his own answer to it. We must therefore in literary criticism be careful not to write as if we

[1] Quoted by Stephen MacKenna.

were solving a popular Quiz—as if there were a stock set of answers to be turned up to a stock set of questions. And I must, if I am an artist, be especially careful not to read my own questions into another artist's complex of question-and-answer. This does not mean that, in order to assess another artist, I must forget my own artistic experience. On the contrary. He may be answering quite different questions from mine but the question-answers which he evolves are the same kind of organism, and result from the same kind of activity, as my own question-answers. Therefore, as the only artist whom I know from the inside is myself, I shall be able to approach another artist more sympathetically in the light of my own experience *provided* I do not assume that his experience is merely a reflection of my own.

If it is granted then that my own experience is likely, unless I am careful, to distort my judgement but is also the ground for my sympathy with others, it follows that there are certain artists whom I am more qualified to appreciate than other artists. In considering any poet I begin by asking: What is there in this poetry that appeals to *me*? Was this poet aiming at anything which I can understand? Were his world, his ideals, his methods, at all similar to mine? If I find any considerable similarity, I must proceed to assess the differences. If the differences far outbalance the similarities, I am not a suitable person to judge that poet. If, on the other hand, the poet seems to be *very* similar to myself in temperament, method, and background, I may again not be the right person to judge him; familiarity breeds a certain obtuseness, whereas a certain amount of strangeness is stimulating to criticism. I feel that in Yeats I have met a poet who is strange enough to excite my interest but is near enough to me myself to preclude my misrepresenting him too grossly. People who know my own expressed views on poetry might consider me unqualified for writing on Yeats, whose expressed views are so often the opposite of mine. I hope to show later that this discrepancy between our views is not of cardinal importance.

Poets are commonly grouped together, or opposed to each other, according to rules of thumb. To use Professor Collingwood's principle once more, they are assessed not by the way in which they answered their own questions but by an abstraction from the question-answer complex of a bare question or a bare answer; this is then relegated to some critical category in company with other bare questions or answers all of which are taken to be like each other because all alike have been spirited out of their bodies. Many imputations of 'realism' or 'escapism' are due to this superficial habit of fastening on something in a poem which can easily be labelled and then making your own label the differentia of the poem.

The superficiality of this method is to some extent exposed by time— even by a short lapse of time. Yesterday's 'realists' are denied that title to-day and yesterday's anarchist falls into his place in the perspectives of orthodoxy. I will take a notorious example which is pertinent to the present moment. In 1914 Rupert Brooke, like most of his fellow English poets at that time, was regarded—and regarded himself—not as a poet's poet, like the poets of the Eighteen Nineties, but as a normal human being sharing the emotions of normal human beings and professing to speak intelligibly on their behalf. Brooke did not profess to divorce poetry from life; the Nineties poets—and Yeats, as we shall see, among them—did. Brooke in the eyes of his contemporaries was no mere escapist or aesthete. He could have been described as a 'realist' for two reasons—first, that in his poems he made use of contemporary (and even sordid) properties, secondly, that he said not what aesthetic fashion demanded but what he himself wanted to say and, further, what many of his more normal contemporaries wished to have said. But does either—or do both—of these characteristics constitute realism? I think we have to deny it if we consider Brooke's five war sonnets written in 1914.

Brooke was here treating a public contemporary subject of great importance—as the 'realists' say one should; and he was writing in tune with a large public—as the 'realists' say one should. He was voicing emotions and ideas which were widely shared by many honest everyday people and by many sensitive intellectuals. And he himself was writing with perfect sincerity. But is the result realism? When Brooke describes the British soldiers entering the Great War

> 'as swimmers into cleanness leaping,
> Glad from a world grown old and cold and weary . . .'

it seems to us to be anything but realism; what is more, it seems to us bad poetry. But it is difficult to explain why it is bad. Whatever we may say about Brooke's poetical gifts, the reason we object to this poem lies in the sentiment. The sentiment, from our point of view, has been completely disproved by subsequent facts; Brooke was completely misrepresenting war. But that does not invalidate the sentiment as a sentiment. It was an honest and powerful sentiment and so it was natural for a poet to express it. I have already denied that a poet is subject to the same criteria as a scientist. A poet writing about his beloved is within his rights if he thinks and calls her beautiful, even though 'objectively' she may be ugly. And he is within his rights if he uses hyperboles to express his affection even though those hyperboles, taken literally, are nonsense. Why then should we condemn Brooke while acquitting the love-poet?

It is difficult to answer this precisely. We have to remember that poetry is a compromise, or even a series of compromises. The poet's approach is personal; he does not aim at an objective, scientific truth. But at the same time he is not a solipsist. Poetry is not a mere reflection or a mere imitation of life but it has an essential relationship to life. This relationship I cannot define and have never seen satisfactorily defined. If poetry is good because of its self-coherence as poetry, at the same time it cannot be good if it does not correspond in a certain way to life. And an analysis of this concept 'life' reveals another compromise. A poem, though an individual thing, derives from and has to be referred back to life, which means, in the first instance, the life of the poet. In the same way the life of the poet, though also an individual thing, derives from and has to be referred back to the life outside him. Now a poem is ill-balanced either if it is too far removed from life or if it is too slavishly subordinate to it. In the same way an individual is ill-balanced either if he attempts autarky or if he merely surrenders himself passively to the life outside him. This intimate connection between a poem, its author's life and the wider life beyond the author (a life which expands in concentric circles through both time and space) establishes certain conditions for the truth, and therefore for the value, of poetry; I am not maintaining that the value of poetry consists in its truthfulness to life but only that a poem is vitiated if it relies upon a falsehood to life. On these premises I would argue that Brooke's war-sonnets rely upon an essential falsehood whereas the lover's praises of his beloved do not. That a lover should consider an ugly woman beautiful is, as we say, 'true to nature'. If it is a falsehood, it is not a falsehood which inevitably impedes action and leads to disillusionment; on the contrary it promotes action and may well lead to happiness and aid the proper functioning of society. When on the contrary Brooke regards a war like the Great War as a wonderfully romantic new birth, he is doing more than merely transposing personal values, as the lover does. The lover's transposition of values is not self-contradictory; on the contrary it helps him to self-realization. Brooke's pæans to war *are*, on analysis, self-contradictory; they are a sentimental falsification that, unlike the lover's, has no profound natural sanction. The fact that many of his contemporaries agreed with Brooke does not vindicate his poems. It merely widens the basis of the lie; it would have been hard for a man with Brooke's background to write a good poem about war in 1914.

If we now turn to Yeats, we find that he also at times—and also from sentimental motives—misrepresented the world in which he was living. But it seems to me that there is an important difference between his approach and Brooke's. Brooke, under the mask of realism, flatly asserts that something which is bad is good; what is more, he trumpets his mistaken belief in the manner of one who wishes to convert others. Yeats, who repudiated realism and does not use the tone of a crusader, may present certain facts coloured or distorted by his own partisan feelings but he allows the reader to see that this presentation is founded on an 'as if'. Thus Yeats in his homage to Ireland treats her as if she were a mistress or as a symbol of spiritual realities. He implies tacitly—and sometimes states overtly—that there may be a discrepancy between the fact and the ideal. Whereas Brooke allows for no discrepancies. In any case I would say that Ireland was far less misrepresented by Yeats than the Great War was by Brooke. Both Yeats and Brooke grew up in a romantic, individualist tradition. Yeats tried to hitch his romantic individualism to Irish nationalism, Brooke tried to hitch his to the cause of the Allies in the Great War. Brooke's attempt was doomed to complete failure, Yeats's was only doomed to partial failure. Irish nationalism was a clumsy vehicle for Yeats's ideals but it was a vehicle of sorts. The Great War was a mere negation of ideals.

Yeats avoided the pitfalls of poets like Brooke partly because he kept his poetry within a comparatively narrow range. He was orientated towards Ireland, towards a simplified past, towards certain specialized doctrines. He repudiated general knowledge, world ideals, science, and internationalism. That is, he kept his questions comparatively simple and so was less likely to make hopelessly inadequate answers. On the other hand his questions were not, as is sometimes assumed by his detractors, comparatively trivial ones. Unless it is maintained that no one can ask a question of importance if he lives in a backward country and finds the advanced thought of other countries uncongenial. Yeats's limitations may have prevented him writing the greatest kind of poetry but they enabled him to write perhaps the best poetry of his time. Those who take the whole modern world for their canvas are liable to lapse into mere journalism. It is my own opinion, though it was not Yeats's, that the normal poet includes the journalist—but he must not be subservient to him. The normal poet—witness the Elizabethans—should not be afraid of touching pitch. But the pitch is so thick on the world thoroughfares nowadays that a poet needs exceptional strength not to stick in it. Yeats avoided the world thoroughfares. It would be a disaster if all poets were to imitate him. In his own case the great refusal was justified.

Many people, however, exaggerate Yeats's 'escapism'. He was neither so simple-minded nor so esoteric nor so dilettante a poet as he is often represented. I have met people whose attitude is: 'Yeats was a silly old thing but he was a *poet*.' This is a foolish attitude. No silly old thing can write fine poetry. A poet cannot live by style alone; nor even by intuitions alone. Yeats, contrary to some people's opinion, had a mind. He had also extraordinary force of personality. It is impossible to explain him by merely murmuring about Beauty.

Mr Sturge Moore had occasion to remark to me that Yeats belonged to the company of mystics, that throughout his life his sole object was to break through the so-called real world, the world of Here and Now, to some eternal world of Platonic essences behind it; the bridge to this eternal world was poetry. He quoted as Yeats's text, from which he never swerved, a line from one of his earliest poems—'Words alone are certain good.' I have already stated that I do not consider Yeats a mystic proper, but I agree that throughout his life he continued to think that words—though perhaps not words alone—are certain good. Now A.E., who was a genuine mystic, uses words very differently from Yeats, who uses them with the precision of a dandy. In A.E. they are merely ancillary to a hardly expressible spiritual meaning—a meaning which he would impair if his words were too precise. For Yeats on the other hand the spiritual meaning is impotent until it is clothed in words. He would agree with Shelley:

> Language is a perpetual Orphic song,
> Which rules with Daedal harmony a throng
> Of thoughts and forms, which else senseless and shapeless were.

The emphasis which Yeats himself put upon style has misled people into thinking of him as primarily a stylist; just as his talking about mystical subjects has made other people think him a mystic. One has to be careful not to accept literally what Yeats says about himself. I hope in this book to prove that Yeats, granted his limitations, was a rich and complex poet, who often succeeded by breaking his own rules and who turned his own liabilities into assets. A man is conditioned by his time and his place.

INTRODUCTORY

I shall therefore begin by indicating Yeats's two main backgrounds—the Irish background and the background of the English Aesthetic Movement; they were, it will be seen, complementary to each other. Ireland moulded Yeats's thoughts as a child, but it was the London of the Eighteen Eighties and Nineties that influenced his earliest work. For this reason I shall consider the Aesthetes first. Yeats was at the same time of them and not of them; some of their doctrine persisted in his mind to the end but always he applied it his own way.

CHAPTER II

Aestheticism

Nor heed nor see, what things they be . . .

SHELLEY

The world of the fin de siècle now seems more remote than even the world of Shelley. *The Yellow Book* and *The Savoy* seem to us unreal and unsympathetic. We are inclined to treat the art and literature of England in the Nineties as a freak product that is of very little significance in English cultural history. This is a mistake. However we judge these works in themselves, we must recognize that they are the logical outcome of certain trends in nineteenth-century thought and that they lead on to certain twentieth-century developments which are themselves too often explained by a cultural parthenogenesis. Ezra Pound, for example, would not have written his poetry had it not been for the Nineties. The poets of the Romantic Revival had paved the road for 'escapism'—for the doctrine of Art for Art's Sake, and that although they themselves notoriously transgressed that doctrine, filling their poetry with moral preaching, social criticism, philosophy, and other 'impurities'. Tennyson went further, becoming an object lesson for his successors; he wrote impure poetry with his right hand and pure poetry with his left. His successors, Swinburne and the pre-Raphaelites, began to think that the poet should put his right arm in a sling—should cut away from life. Matthew Arnold's attitude was ambiguous; on the one hand he advocated 'criticism of life' but on the other hand he was so sceptical about life that he tried to form art into a religion. Arnold, I suspect, reasoned in a circle. The next great critic, Pater, dropped Arnold's concept of 'criticism'; art was still related to life but only to life in a very rarefied form. Here there seems to be another circle, for this rarefication itself can only apparently be achieved by an artist. Mallarmé went further and professed to raise poetry to the abstract purity of the higher mathematics. But his practice did not, I think, accord with his preaching. Certainly his less daring and less gifted imitators in England in accepting Mallarmé's principles fell into much self-deception.

The fin de siècle poet was inhibited; he tried to parade his inhibitions as freedom. This, like other neuroses, bore fruit but it was unable to bear long or abundantly. There is an excellent study of it and its fruits in Mr Edmund Wilson's *Axël's* Castle. I cannot here discuss its earlier history in any more detail; I merely wish to point out that this neurosis was dominant in poetry when Yeats came of literary age.

Yeats, as Mr T. S. Eliot pointed out in *After Strange* Gods, felt the want of a religion; having no sympathy with any established religion, he looked for a religion in art, thereby following in the steps of Matthew Arnold. But Arnold's art-religion was too Low Church for Yeats, who wanted ritual, incense, candles — and no morality. Thus he writes in his *Autobiographies:* 'I am very religious, and deprived by Huxley and Tyndall, whom I detested, of the simple-minded religion of my childhood, I had made a new religion, almost an infallible church, of poetic tradition, of a fardel of stories, and of personages, and of emotions, inseparable from their first expression, passed on from generation to generation by poets and painters with some help from philosophers and theologians.' He found his sacred books in Pater's *Marim the Epicurean* and Count Villiers de l'Isle Adam's *Axël*.

For Pater, as indeed for Arnold, philosophy was only scaffolding. Its sole function was to help the artist to build the House Beautiful; when the house had been built, the philosophy could be removed.[1] Thus Arnold wrote in 1880: 'most of what now passes with us for religion and philosophy will be replaced by poetry.' Yeats in an essay on The Philosophy of Shelley's Poetry, written in 1900, speaks of 'my one unshakable belief. I thought that whatever of philosophy has been made poetry is alone permanent.' For this attitude he could find a sanction in his idol Blake who, Yeats wrote in 1897, assumed that art had now changed places with religion and practical morality.

The poets of the Nineties took their doctrine from Pater and their models from the French Symbolists. Yeats writes in his Introduction to the Oxford Book of Modern Verse: 'The revolt against Victorianism meant to the young poet a revolt against irrelevant descriptions of nature, the scientific and moral discursiveness of *In Memoriam* . . . , the political eloquence of Swinburne, the psychological curiosity of Browning, and the poetical diction of everybody.' Some of his own very earliest poems were written apparently before he joined in this revolt, for example the

[1] Similarly Yeats writes that in the making of a play the philosophy — the idea behind the play — is gradually eliminated.

suppressed poem *How Ferencz Renyi Kept Silence* which is in the crusading manner of the Romantic Revival—

> 'Therefore, O nation of the bleeding breast
> Libations, from the Hungary of the West.'

But it took Yeats very little time to effect his purge. The new idols were Catullus, the Jacobean poets, Verlaine, Baudelaire. Verlaine, to judge from the essays of Arthur Symons, seems to have been considered the great poet of the day—greater, because more controlled, than Rimbaud, greater, because *purer*, than Baudelaire, who had his moral preoccupations. Morality was dross. Lionel Johnson said that life must be a ritual; his circle seems to have ignored the fact that a ritual divorced from a belief —or from any belief except belief in a ritual—is a vanity.

They did, however, profess one belief and that was belief in passion. Yeats throughout his life harped upon passion, though this passion became steadily less nebulous and earthier. His early cult of passion came from Pater, who had written in his famous conclusion to *The Renaissance*: 'Not to discriminate every moment some passionate attitude in those about us, and in the very brilliancy of their gifts some tragic dividing of forces on their ways, is, on this short day of frost and sun, to sleep before evening.' It is great passions, according to Pater, and especially the 'poetic passion', that give us a quickened sense of life. He is a hedonist of a very specialized kind. The world for him is a flux out of which there emerges an isolated individual receiving impressions: 'Every moment some form grows perfect in hand or face; some tone on the hills or the sea is choicer than the rest; some mood of passion or insight or intellectual excitement is irresistibly real and attractive to us—for that moment only. Not the fruit of experience, but experience itself is the end.' What we want, to use Pater's own word, is 'pulsations'.

Pater however did not push this doctrine to its logical conclusion which would be sheer sensual epicureanism; few people could argue that looking at a picture gives a man either more or stronger pulsations than the act of copulation. Pater therefore, who was himself afraid that the original conclusion to *The Renaissance* might be misinterpreted by the young, modified his cult of pulsations by a code of values which is really alien to it It is obvious that the aesthetic atomism implicit in the passages quoted above—a pulsation been and gone, another pulsation been and gone— is not consistent with Pater's general philosophy which implies that the valuable thing is not any one pulsation or any other pulsation isolated, so to speak, in a vacuum; what is valuable is the relationship between a continuously existent perceiving subject and a continuous and inter-dependent stream of objects.

Pater's inconsistency may be due, as is so often the case, to a crude use of language; his divorce of 'the fruit of experience' from 'experience' is too absolute. If he treats this abstract distinction as representing two things which are really separable, he is then quite right in saying that the end is not the fruit of experience, which in that case is merely something put away on a shelf. But that would be a false abstraction, a facile and mean-ingless divorce. Pater's whole aesthetic attitude implies not a merely passive receptivity but the exercise by the aesthete of deliberate selection. Now the man who selects may be more or less eclectic but his criterion must be something like what idealist philosophers call a Universal. (Even Marxian materialists may be challenged to disprove this. What do they themselves mean when they say that Dialectical Materialism is the *right* philosophy?) The mere sensationalist must live in the flux of the present Pater renounces flux and lives largely in the past; 'She is older than the rocks among which she sits.' He must not be allowed to have it both ways. Either he must renounce his aesthetic atomism or he must admit that aesthetic experience is good independently of the interpretation put upon it. But he cannot make this admission, for it would be, for him, a contradiction in terms; aesthetic experience for Pater implies interpreta-tion.

Yeats, like many of his contemporaries, was enormously influenced by Pater, but while paying him lip service, he never tried to confine himself to this impossible ideal of aesthetic atomism. Yeats was always trying to think of the world as a system, of life as a pattern. Pater had stressed the importance of the moods—the moods that are passionate or receptive. Yeats elevates the mood into a kind of Platonic Form. Suppose a man has an emotional reaction to a pear-tree in blossom. According to the premises of aesthetic atomism all we have here is a particular man reacting in a unique manner for a particular space of time to a particular object; there is no Before or After, there are no affinities transcending the present ex-perience. But according to Yeats what happens is that the man for this short space of time is subject to one of the eternal moods; the pear tree serves as an occasion for the mood's appearance. Yeats quite rightly follows Pater in insisting that any experience is unique, as any individual person is unique, but he does not for that reason suppose a great gulf between one experience or person and all others; on the contrary, experi-

ences and persons are, for Yeats, manifestations—though unique manifestations—of underlying principles. He will not accept the world as a
hailstorm of data which melt when they touch the ground.

Pater supplied Yeats with a belief in the importance of passion, a belief
in the importance of style, a distrust of the vulgar world, and a curious
sort of aesthetic pantheism, a make-believe homage to material objects
which professes to discount their materiality. This last has innumerable
echoes in Yeats. Thus in his early love poems he seems to be looking for
Marius's 'ideal of a perfect imaginative love': 'The human body in its
beauty, as the highest potency of all the beauty of material objects, seemed
to him [Marius] just then to be matter no longer, but, having taken
celestial fire, to assert itself as indeed the true, though visible, soul or spirit
in things.' Marius's assumption leads to a paradox. If the body of the
beloved is a perfect expression of spirit, she has no need to be spiritual in
the ordinary sense; indeed, seeing that all spiritual or intellectual activities
of human beings are to some extent unsuccessful and impure, the more
she undertakes such activities, the more she will tend to sell her own birthright and outrage the pure spirituality of her body. This paradox is implicit
in much of Yeats's poetry, for example in the late poem, *Michael Robartes
and the Dancer*, where the dancer is reproved for hankering for knowledge:

> I have principles to prove me right.
> It follows from this Latin text
> That blest souls are not composite,
> And that all beautiful women may
> Live in uncomposite blessedness,
> And lead us to the like—if they
> Will banish every thought, unless
> The lineaments that please their view
> When the long looking-glass is full,
> Even from the foot-sole think it too.

Similarly in his love-poems proper Yeats repeatedly deplores his beloved's
refusal to observe the rules of the game, to content herself with existing
merely as a beautiful object. Throughout his life his advice to women is to
abjure the intellect and, in particular, political opinions and the critical
reason. Their discipline is to be that of the looking-glass. This doctrine,
while inherited from Pater's aestheticism, can also be related to Yeats's
dislike of democracy, science, and 'progress'.

He has described his association with the English poets of the Nineties in *Autobiographies*. To most people of my generation their mentality seems more than foreign. These poets believed in the priesthood of the poet but were content, and indeed proud, to be priests without a congregation. Mr Edmund Wilson in *Axël's Castle* analyses certain prominent writers of the last fifty years—the French Symbolists, Yeats, Proust, Eliot, and even Joyce—and decides that they were heretics, although magnificent heretics, against the normal traditions of literature; in his last chapter he suggests mat these normal traditions will soon re-assert themselves. I shall try to show that in Yeats's later poems his heresy, in spite perhaps of his own theories, gradually diminished. His early work certainly lacked what Synge later called the *timber* of poetry. It was composed on a theory which was perhaps inevitable in the Nineties but which would hinder, if not finally inhibit, a poet writing in more normal circumstances.

Yeats with his parents and brothers and sisters settled in London at the end of the Eighteen Eighties, when Yeats was a little over twenty. His father, John Butler Yeats, had already predisposed him to aestheticism. John Butler Yeats distrusted the 'questioning intellect' and held that 'Poets must not meddle with opinions'; 'It should never be forgotten,' he wrote, 'that poetry is the Voice of the Solitary Spirit, prose the language of the sociable-minded.' (Note the distinction between *voice*—the stress on expression—and *language*—the stress on communication.) His son entered literary London under the banner of the Solitary Spirit. At that time, as he says, he 'was in all things pre-Raphaelite', (the pre-Raphaelites being the fore-runners of the Aesthetes) and violently opposed to the new realism imported from the art-schools of Paris. In face of this new realism Yeats was blind as he was blind in face of Ibsen. He met other representatives of the Opposition, in particular Henley: 'I disagreed with him about everything, but I admired him beyond words.' Henley hated pre-Raphaelitism. He did not convert Yeats but he probably served to remind him that the world, and even the world of art, is not necessarily two-dimensional. At the same time, however, Yeats met the prince of the aesthetes, Wilde, whose gospel was the gospel of Pater and who, while holding with the rest that life is irrelevant to art, went further than the others in carrying the principles of his art into life; he lived, Yeats writes, 'with no self-mockery at all an imaginary life; perpetually performed a play which was in all things the opposite of all that he had known in childhood and early youth.' At this time, Yeats says, 'My mind began drifting vaguely towards that doctrine of "the mask" which has convinced me that every passionate man (I have nothing to do with mechanist, or philanthropist, or man whose eyes have no preference) is, as it were, linked with another age, historical or imaginary, where alone he finds images that arouse his energy.' I shall discuss this doctrine of the Mask later. At the moment it is important to note the taboo on the contemporary subject.

Within a short time Yeats had met many of the poets of his own generation—Lionel Johnson, Ernest Dowson, John Davidson, T. W. Rolleston, John Todhunter, Arthur Symons. Johnson and Dowson were devotees of Art for Art's Sake, Symons a spokesman for the French Symbolists, Rolleston and Todhunter links with Ireland— all of them like rebels against, or runaways from, the world in which they lived. 'The one conviction', Yeats writes, 'shared by all the younger men . . . was an opposition to all ideas, all generalizations that can be explained and debated.' Yeats was guilty of knowing himself a born explainer and debater.

The paradox of these poets was that they aimed at an artificial simplicity, that they set out deliberately to seem spontaneous. It is amusing to find their attitude—and the influence of Pater—reflected in an early essay by James Joyce (*Homage to James Clarence Mangan*, 1902): 'A song by Shakespeare or Verlaine, which seems so free and living and as remote from any conscious purpose as rain that falls in a garden or the lights of evening, is discovered to be the rhythm and speech of an emotion otherwise incommunicable, at least so fitly.' (Notice here that the prose, as well as the thought, is the prose of Pater. This strain of the aesthete persisted in Joyce. I refer once more to *Axël's Castle*. Yeats and Joyce, as I shall suggest later, probably had more in common than either of them would have admitted.) Yeats says the same thing in a poem, *Adam's Curse*, published in 1904:

> I said, 'A line will take us hours maybe;
> Yet if it does not seem a moment's thought,
> Our stitching and unstitching has been naught.'

In spite of himself Yeats wanted stronger meat than the songs of Shakespeare or Verlaine. He looked for *ideas* in Shelley and Blake. It would seem that the ban on ideas could be lifted if these ideas were irrational. Blake's cult of the irrational, his belief that 'Science is the Tree of Death', were most sympathetic to Yeats. Like the other Nineties poets Yeats hated rationalism and everyday realism; unlike them, he hankered for system. Paradoxically, he set out in cold blood to build up by a process of meticulous selection a system which should be irrational and in defiance of all accepted contemporary systems. I suspect that he was motivated in this by the knowledge that he lacked an academic education.

Mr Edmund Wilson regards Yeats as the nearest English parallel to the French Symbolists, as an offshoot of the same movement. Yeats, however, though he met Verlaine and Mallarmé, did not come in much direct contact with the new French poetry. He knew it mainly through the translations and imitations and expositions of Arthur Symons, who considerably diluted his originals. Symons in his book on *The Symbolist Movement in Literature* (1899), which he dedicates to Yeats as 'the chief representative of that movement in our country', makes many statements or implications about art which agree almost exactly with the tenets of the early Yeats. Thus Symons writes: 'The artist, it cannot be too clearly understood, has no more part in society than a monk in domestic life. . . .' In the same year Yeats was having a controversy in the Dublin *Daily Express* with John Eglinton, who had complained: 'The poet looks too much away from himself and from his age, does not feel the facts of life enough, but seeks in art an escape from them.' Yeats answered, instancing inevitably Villiers de l'Isle Adam, that art is not for the crowd: 'I believe that the renewal of belief, which is the great movement of our time [wishful thinking?], will more and more liberate the arts from "their age" and from life, and leave them more and more free to lose themselves in beauty, and to busy themselves, like all the great poetry of the past and like religions of all times, with "old faiths, myths, dreams", the accumulated beauty of the age. I believe that all men will more and more reject the opinion that poetry is a "criticism of life", and be more and more convinced that it is a revelation of hidden life, and that they may even come to think "painting, poetry, and music" "the only means of conversing with eternity left to man on earth."'

Yeats was peculiar—almost, indeed, self-contradictory—in that he fused Symbolist doctrine with nationalist doctrine. Thus Mr Wilson writes: 'If we do not ordinarily think of Yeats as primarily a Symbolist poet, it is because, in taking Symbolism to Ireland, he fed it with new resources and gave it a special accent which leads us to think of his poetry from the point of view of its national qualities rather than from the point of view of its relation to the rest of European literature.' In taking Symbolism to Ireland Yeats inevitably compromised it, but he compromised it with something which had already a symbolist tendency. Thus Thomas MacDonagh, writing on Irish Literature (published 1916), expains that the Irish literary movement is parallel, although quite differently motivated, to modernist movements elsewhere: 'To us as to the ancient Irish poets, the half-said thing is dearest.' The half-said thing is conspicuous in the early poems of Yeats. His friend Symons wrote: 'Description is banished that beautiful things may be evoked, magically; the regular beat of verse is broken in order that words may fly, upon subtler wings. . . .' Yeats, as we shall see, later modified this practice, but at this period he was avoiding both description and rhetoric, two characteristics of the journalist. A wider view of poetry might have made him less severe upon journalism. Verlaine was no journalist but what about Villon? Verlaine was no rhetorician but what about Shakespeare or Dante or the Greeks? The Nineties poets, if logical, would have had to consider these poets shockingly impure. And the reason for their impurity was patent; they had too much truck with *life*.

'As for living, our servants will do that for us.' This favourite quotation of Yeats's came from his golden book, *Axël*, published in 1890, the year after its author had died. Villiers de l'Isle Adam anticipated Yeats in many respects, for example in a strong bias towards aristocracy. He always remembered that he was a descendant of the Grand Master of the Knights of St John of Jerusalem and his hero Axël is a hypersensitive aristocrat too exquisite for this world. The same snobbery appears repeatedly in Yeats, who writes, for instance, in *Dramatis Personae*: 'Is not all charm inherited, whether of the intellect, of the manners, of the character, or of literature? A great lady is as simple as a great poet.' In the same way Symons writes of de l'Isle Adam himself: 'To the aristocratic conception of things, nobility of soul is indeed a birthright, and the pride with which this gift of nature is accepted is exactly the opposite kind to that democratic pride to which nobility of soul is a conquest, valuable in proportion to its difficulty.' There seems to be a suggestion here that the latter kind of pride is misplaced. In any case, for Yeats and Symons, it is the former kind which provides a model for the artist. Yeats has many poems exalting monied leisure; the aristocracy find truth through idleness.

De l'Isle Adam also, like Pater, hated science—'the oldest offspring of the chimeras'—and was opposed to 'the monstrous paradox of progress'. Yeats agreed with him in both respects and also in thinking that knowledge is merely a process of recognition. Yeats's doctrine of the Great Memory—a parallel to Plato's *anamnesis*—is andis an aristocratic doctrine which dispenses with the services of Science, 'the religion of the suburbs'. Truth, on this doctrine, cannot be reached by induction

(Yeats never forgave Locke for denying innate ideas); we ourselves are a part of the Great Memory and the truth runs in our veins like blue blood. To find this truth we need not work in a laboratory. We shall find it better when the critical faculty is stilled, whether it be stilled by the supervening of trances or by the mere following of an aristocratic routine—for example by 'the discipline of the looking-glass'. It is interesting that Yeats, like Plato, combined his doctrine of anamnesis with the doctrine of re-incarnation, herein following another French Decadent, Gérard de Nerval.

The Nineties poets, in Symons's words, followed the Symbolists in attempting a 'revolt against exteriority, against rhetoric, against a materialistic tradition'. Their differentia of the spiritual world, or of the internal life, was its mystery. Rimbaud had written: 'The poet should define the quantity of the unknown which awakes in his time.' Yeats wrote in 1900: 'The poet of essences and pure ideas (i.e. the poet par excellence) must seek in the half-lights that glimmer from symbol to symbol as if to the ends of the earth, all that the epic and dramatic poet finds of mystery and shadow in the accidental circumstances of life.' Pater already, in urging the artist to cherish sensations and impressions, had implied that the *stranger* these sensations were, the better.

Yeats's essay on The Autumn of the Flesh (later renamed *The Autumn of the Body*) is another exposition of the gospel of Symbolism as preached by Symons. He once more pays homage to de l'Isle Adam as a writer who 'created persons from whom has fallen all even of personal characteristic except a thirst for that hour when all things shall pass away like a vapour, and a pride like that of the Magi following their star over many mountains'. And, praising Maeterlinck too, he describes his own struggle against 'that externality', which a 'time of scientific and political thought has brought into literature'. The new poets, following a movement begun in England by Rossetti, 'speak out of some personal or spiritual passion in words and types and metaphors that draw one's imagination as far as possible from the complexities of modern life and thought.' It was, Yeats goes on, 'with Goethe and Wordsworth and Browning that poetry gave up the right to consider all things in the world as a dictionary of types and symbols and began to call itself a critic of life and an interpreter of things as they are.' It is a good comment on the mentality of the Nineties that it could think of poets like Homer or Chaucer or Villon as esoteric students poring over a dictionary of symbols.

The new poets, however, did not always practise what they preached. And they did not always preach on the same text. Thus Symons himself, in an essay on Modernity in Verse (1897), utters what would have been anathema to Yeats; 'To be modern in poetry, to represent really oneself and one's surroundings, the world as it is to-day, is, perhaps, the most difficult, as it is certainly the most interesting, of all artistic achievements.' He instances two artists, whom Yeats could not appreciate, Manet and Degas, and speaks of 'the finest of modern subjects, the pageant of London'. It is to be noticed that for Symons, however, modern London is not what Elizabethan London was for the Elizabethans—a huge, multi-cellular organism; it is merely a pageant, an artist's scrap-book.

I shall have more to say about the Nineties poets in Chapter IV. The two to whom Yeats was closest were Johnson and Dowson, poets who lived in the Ivory Tower and died because of it. The Tower at this time had many brilliant apologists, in particular Oscar Wilde, who stated in 1891: 'Art never expresses anything but itself'; it was left to the Abstractionist painters of twentieth-century France to refute this by a *reductio ad absurdum*. Wilde—and here Yeats followed him—hated the idea that an artist should express his own age: 'So far from being the creation of its time, it [Art] is usually in direct opposition to it . . . the two things that every artist should avoid are modernity of form and modernity of subject matter.' It is significant that Aubrey Beardsley, while violently opposing (in 1897) 'the Burne-Jones and Morrisian mediaeval business', should merely change one archaism for another, advocating the setting up of 'a wholesome seventeenth-and eighteenth-century standard of what picture-making should be'. The Victorian worship of facts and belief in progress and democracy had brought about a hatred of facts, a belief that art stands aloof from life, is independent of history, and is caviare to the general. 'The master', Whistler had said in 1885, in his famous lecture, *Ten O'clock*, 'stands in no relation to the moment at which he occurs—a monument of isolation—hinting at sadness—having no part in the progress of his fellow men.' Or, to quote Wilde again: 'The sphere of Art and the sphere of Ethics are absolutely distinct and separate.'

In accepting these beliefs Yeats found himself a member of a powerful clique but facing a powerful opposition. His anti-Christ was Ibsen. 'Art is art because it is not nature,' he kept repeating to himself—or so he says —as he watched his first Ibsen play. 'As time passed, Ibsen became in my eyes the chosen author of very clever young journalists, who, condemned to their treadmill of abstraction, hated music and style.' This very perverse view finds a parallel nowadays among those who dismiss Ibsen as a mere period piece, who insist that Ibsen 'dates' because the problem of *A Doll's*

House is one which in our society has been more or less solved. They do not realize that the particular conflict of *A Doll's House* is tragic not because it is particular but because it is a conflict. Yeats similarly was misled by a surface view; he disliked Ibsen because of the modernity of his themes. The Creek tragedians had taken modern themes and disguised them in mythology. With Ibsen it is almost the other way round: he takes the archetypes and disguises them in Here and Now.

Pater had cried out for *strange* beauty; Yeats for a time seemed almost to equate the strange with the beautiful. Naturally he looked back to the Romantic Revival and particularly to Shelley. But where the Romantics had sowed with the whole sack, Yeats tried to apply Pater's tenet that art is the 'removal of surplusage'. Shelley is full of surplusage. Besides the impurities in his content, Yeats must have seen that Shelley was a careless craftsman, verbose and facile, sometimes vulgar in both diction and rhythm. Yeats began by ignoring the Godwin and the Rousseau and the Plato in Shelley; in his essay on the Philosophy of Shelley's Poetry (1900) he spends his time discussing Shelley's *symbols*—caves, underground rivers, towers, the morning star—and attempts to build out of these a Shelleyan *system* (Hamlet, in fact, without the Prince of Denmark). Shelley's influence—or rather the influence of this pseudo-Shelley— was bad for the youthful Yeats, as can be seen from *The Wanderings of Oisin*. If you purge Shelley of his beliefs, you are left with a mass of non- sense writing—

> his scattered hair
> Sered by the autumn of strange suffering
> Sung dirges in the wind . . .

It will be seen in this book that Yeats steadily moved away both from the doctrines of Pater and the Aesthetes and from the Romantic model. This was largely due to his orientation towards Ireland, who was herself accepted for her romantic and aesthetic possibilities, but who gave Yeats something other than he was looking for. By 1906 he was able to write: 'What moves natural men in the arts is what moves them in life'—and he slips in no aspersion on 'natural men'. About the same time, writing on The Musician and the Orator, he attacks Pater for having said that music is the type of all the arts: 'I in my present mood am all for the man who, with an average audience before him, uses all means of persuasion...and but so much music as he can discover on the wings of words.' This tardy recognition of both life and rhetoric can be referred to Yeats's contacts with the theatre. But why did he take to the theatre? His own explanation, given in 1906, was: 'To me drama . . . has been the search for more of manful energy, more of cheerful acceptance of whatever arises out of the logic of events, and for clean outline, instead of those outlines of lyric poetry that are blurred with desire and vague regret.' That is, he now requires both harder form and solider subject matter. The vision of Axël is fading. 'We should ascend', he writes, 'out of common interests, the thoughts of the newspapers, of the market-place, of men of science, *but only so far* [italics mine] as we can carry the normal, passionate, reasoning self, the personality as a whole.' And about the same time he wrote: 'Surely the ideal of culture expressed by Pater can only create feminine souls.' In accordance with this change of heart his own writing became more masculine and athletic and the personality expressed in it fuller and less rarefied. Most of the poets of the Nineties lost themselves in the sands. Yeats escaped because he harnessed the aesthetic doctrine to a force outside itself which he found in his own country.

CHAPTER III

The Irish Background

The faculty of abstracting from the land their eyes behold, another
Ireland through which they wandered in dream, has always been a
characteristic of the Irish poets.   A.E.

Ireland meant to Yeats something very specialized. It is not Ireland as the
ordinary person knows it, yet it is something distilled from that Ireland. It
may be largely a dream but it is truer than many conceptions of Ireland
held by both Irishmen and Englishmen—than the Ireland of the popular
stage and the popular song or than the Ireland of most politicians, whose
vision, as Yeats would have said, is distorted by abstractions. Most Irish
people cannot see Ireland clearly because they are busy grinding axes.
Many English people cannot see her clearly because she gives them a tear
in the eye; only this year (1939) at a London performance of *The Playboy
of the Western World* I overheard people in the audience saying to each
other 'Aren't the Irish *sweet!*'

Yeats's own view of Ireland was not consistent throughout his life and
was itself, it must be admitted, sometimes distorted or blurred by abstractions, by wishful thinking, by sentimentality, by partisanship. In his early
days he tried to equate Ireland with a Celtic Utopia—a land of beautiful
dreams. (Even Thomas Davis had already uttered the warning that Irish
does not necessarily mean Celtic.) During this period his nationalism was
orthodox and romantic. In his middle years some experience of public life
and politics disillusioned him. The kind of nationalism which he admired, represented by John O'Leary, was in a decline. The nationalism
dominant seemed to him to involve a shocking waste of energy and to have
ruined the lives of a number of his friends. It was vulgar; A.E. no doubt
was thinking of its vulgarity when he said that Constance Markievicz
ought to have been born an American. Ireland now seemed the enemy
rather than the patroness of poetry—'the seeming needs of my fool-driven
land'.

During his disillusionment, however, Yeats met Lady Gregory and

J. M. Synge, who restored to him the Ireland of his childhood. Lady Gregory revived his admiration for the Anglo-Irish landowners—for that Protestant Ascendancy Ireland which Gaelic Leaguers deny is Irish at all. He had always, as I have said, a partiality for blue blood; as a child he was impressed by a great-aunt who had 'a little James the First cream-jug with the Yeats motto and crest'. With this went a contempt for the middle classes. Synge on the other hand strengthened his old admiration for the Irish peasantry but under a new aspect. Yeats had previously been fascinated by the Irish peasant because he was a person who knew the fairies. It was Synge who brought home to him the value of their brute vitality, of—in Yeats's words—'all that has edge, all that is salt in the mouth, all that is rough to the hand, all that heightens the emotions by contest, all that stings into life the sense of tragedy'. As I shall point out later, from the time of meeting Synge Yeats's poetry shows far more recognition of physical man.

Till the end of his life Yeats found the two finest types of Ireland in the peasant and the aristocrat. Thus in a very late poem, *The Municipal Gallery Re-Visited* (published 1938) he writes:

> John Synge, I, and Augusta Gregory thought
> All that we did, all that we said or sang
> Must come from contact with the soil, from that
> Contact everything Antaeus-like grew strong.
> We three alone in modern times had brought
> Everything down to that sole test again,
> Dream of the noble and the beggarman.

The Irish statesman whom he most admired was, inevitably, Parnell, who carried around with him, even in committee rooms, an aristocratic solitude. Yeats in his later days exalted beside Parnell earlier Protestant champions of Ireland, Grattan and Swift—and even Bishop Berkeley. His last prose writing, *On the Boiler*, reveals the reactionary ideals which he would have liked to see embodied in his nation: 'The formation of military families should be encouraged,' for human violence must be embodied in our institutions. And Ireland must have a caste system, taking warning from modern democracies: 'the new-formed democratic parliaments of India will doubtless destroy, if they can, *the caste system that has saved Indian intellect*' [italics mine]. Yeats's demands for caste within the nation and for national sovereignty make an interesting contrast with the ideals expressed by A.E. in *The National Being*.

Before, however, Yeats had arrived at his own elegant brand of fascism, he had received from Ireland a violent shock, at the same time horrifying and stimulating. (It is probable that comparable shocks in his private life also served as stimuli to his poetry.) After his early days campaigning with Maud Gonne, he had come to feel that they were poking a dead fire. In 1913 he wrote a poem deploring the lack of daring and imagination in contemporary Ireland, its petty acquisitiveness and its petty piety —

> What need you, being come to sense,
> But fumble in a greasy till
> And add the halfpence to the pence
> And prayer to shivering prayer, until
> You have dried the marrow from the bone;
> For men were born to pray and save:
> Romantic Ireland's dead and gone
> It's with O'Leary in the grave.[1]

Then in 1916 occurred the Easter Rising.

This rising was so unexpected and so unworldly that it brought Romantic Ireland back — but with a difference. The leaders were not of the Parnell type. Oddly assorted with each other, they were nearly all of them men with whom Yeats could have little personal sympathy. Padraic Pearse declared that bloodshed was a cleansing and sanctifying thing. James Connolly, the practically-minded Labour leader, shelved his differences with the nationalists to undertake an adventure which he knew was foredoomed to failure. Apparently he reasoned that the failure would be fruitful. He was right.

The Irish people, who had ignored or disliked the rebels, swung over to their side in mass as soon as the English shot the sixteen leaders. Yeats, however, seems to have been caught in two minds. The rebels were in the tradition of Wolfe Tone — a tradition whose decline he had deplored — but he could not be sure that their sacrifice was necessary —

> Was it needless death after all?

But, however his judgement may have vacillated, he was profoundly affected for the rest of his life by the Rising and by the violent events which succeeded it. Just as in *On the Boiler* he demands that national institutions

1 Stephen MacKenna expressed similar feelings, writing in 1908 about the backward bitterness of present-day Ireland: 'we are for ever punching the air; no one wins because no one fights; only Ireland always loses.'

shall embody human violence, so again and again in his later poetry he seems to imply that individual violence is one of the rights of man. Thus during the Civil War we find him actually envying 'violent men':

> An affable Irregular,
> A heavily-built Falstaffian man,
> Comes cracking jokes of civil war
> As though to die by gunshot were
> The finest play under the sun.

> I count those feathered balls of soot
> The moor-hen guides upon the stream,
> To silence the envy in my thought,
> And turn towards my chamber, caught
> In the cold snows of a dream.

And he repeatedly recognizes the creativeness of violence (see *Blood and the Moon*) and opposes it to the passivity of mere wisdom. In his very last poems he is still harping on this theme:

> You that Mitchel's prayer have heard
> 'Send war in our time, O Lord!'
> Know that when all words are said
> And a man is fighting mad,
> Something drops from eyes long blind,
> He completes his partial mind . . .[1]

I shall discuss later Yeats's political development and the various meanings which he attributed to Ireland. After this very brief and approximate resume I must go back to Ireland as he found it—as it moulded his first thoughts and as it came back upon him in fuller force after his flirtation with London aestheticism. It is notoriously dangerous to generalize about Ireland, but there are certain things which I can point out, either because

---

[1] I have some difficulty in deciding why, if Rupert Brooke's sonnets quoted in the first chapter were bad because of their sentiments, the above lines should be good—as I think they are. Perhaps it is because Brooke is taking it upon himself to welcome a vast mechanical war, which destroys individuality, as the opening of a new and better life for the individual; whereas Yeats from his observation of people who took part in quite a different kind of war—a localized, irregular war which was governed by individuals instead of governing them—makes merely a *comment* (he is not, like Brooke, uttering any slogans) on the effect such violence had upon those engaged in it.

they are patent facts or because I myself have experienced them. Like Yeats, I was brought up in an Irish middle-class Protestant family. I allow for the difference that he spent his childhood in the primitive west, whereas I spent mine in the industrial north.

Among the patent facts are the facts of size. Geographically Ireland is considerably smaller than England; in respect of population it is very much smaller indeed. And other things within the country are smaller than their English counterparts. Incomes are smaller, fields are smaller, cottages are smaller. The large English meadow, like the large English country meal, is a rarity in Ireland. The farmers are mainly small farmers; consequently there is a lesser proportion of hired agricultural labourers. These characteristic smallnesses, while uniting the country against England which is regarded as essentially big, divide it against itself. As in Spain, there is very intense local feeling; a man from the next parish is a foreigner.

Other patent facts are the facts of landscape and climate. Climate cannot be stressed too strongly. I sympathize with Bernard Shaw who wrote in his Introduction to *John Bull's Other Island*: 'There is no Irish race any more than there is an English race or a Yankee race. There is an Irish climate, which will stamp an immigrant more deeply and durably in two years, apparently, than the English climate will in two hundred.' This climate affects the landscape. An Irish landscape is capable of pantomimic transformation scenes; one moment it will be desolate, dead, unrelieved monotone, the next it will be an indescribably shifting pattern of prismatic light. The light effects of Ireland make other landscapes seem stodgy; on the other hand, few countries can produce anything more depressing than Ireland in her grey moments. Yeats's best-known landscapes were Sligo and Galway and he deliberately set out to match his verse to them. I do not think it fanciful to maintain that he succeeded, that there is something palpably in common between the subtle colour and movement of his verse and that western landscape which is at the same time delicate and strong.

It is harder to predicate characteristics of the Irish themselves than of their country. I would risk the stock generalization that the Irish are born partisans. Whatever they are supporting, they support it violently and— usually—bitterly. This violence is as common in the north as in the south. With it there goes a vigour of speech and a colour of phrasing uncommon across the water. In reading Yeats's *Autobiographies* I noticed an odd paradox: Yeats, as a little boy in the west, read Orange songs and fancied himself dying facing the Fenians; I, as a little boy among Orange-men, imagined myself a rebel against England.

I would risk another generalization, namely that the Irish are born puritans. This is too often overlooked and can be related to the preceding; Irish politics could very plausibly be explained as sublimation. Most Irish writers are conditioned by this puritan background. Thus George Moore is often the naughty little boy self-consciously breaking the rules; Synge is the man whose respectable antecedents have given him a taste for 'all that is salt in the mouth'. Yeats himself began writing in the belief that the body corrupts and, converted late in life to the opposite belief, began to parade his sensuality like a released prisoner conscious of his freedom.

But, as I said, it is unsafe to generalize about Ireland or the Irish. Their character could best be expressed in a set of antinomies, which would require an analysis that I cannot give here. We could say, for example: *The Irish are sentimental* (see any popular song book) but we could also say: *The Irish are unsentimental* (*see John Bull's Other Island*). Or again: *The Irish genius is personal* (see Yeats passim and the popular English conception of the Irishman as a 'character') and *The Irish genius is impersonal* (see almost any translations of early Irish poetry). Or again: *The Irish are formal* (witness the conventions of the peasantry, the intricacies of Gaelic poetry, the political technique of Mr De Valera) and *The Irish are slapdash* (witness the way they run their houses). Or again: *Ireland is a land of Tradition* (think of the Irishman's notorious long memory) and *Ireland suffers from lack of Tradition* (see Yeats's well-founded strictures in *Dramatis Personae*). Such antinomies could easily be multiplied. Yeats himself in an essay on The Celtic Element in Literature (1902) shows that he is conscious of this dialectic: 'When an early Irish poet calls the Irishman famous for much loving, and a proverb . . . talks of the lovelessness of the Irishman, they may say but the same thing, for if your passion is great enough it leads you to a country where there are many cloisters.' The Irish dialectic is best, perhaps, resolved by a paradox: Ireland, like other countries, has obvious limitations; these limitations, if rightly treated, becomes assets. I would suggest therefore as a final antinomy this: *It is easy to be Irish; it is difficult to be Irish.*

It is easy to be Irish because, Ireland being a small country, the Irishman can trade upon the glamour of minorities. If he is in Ireland, all he need do is talk about the country as if it were his family estate; if he is in England, all he need do is talk about being Irish. (One need only, for proof of this, inspect the behaviour of Irish children at English schools.

Yeats was no exception when he went to school in London.) An English-man cannot make capital in the same way out of being English. England is far too over-populated and too complex.

On the other hand it is difficult to be Irish because the traditional Irish aim is to be spiritually self-supporting and in the modern world this is as impracticable—for an individual or for a small country—as to be materially self-supporting. Yeats nominally accepted this aim but in following it practised a good deal of sleight-of-hand. When he borrowed something (say) from India, he would excuse himself by the supposition that India is essentially Irish. And he lacked the logic of the Gaelic League, for all his life he wrote in the language of the alien.

When I read Yeats's account of his childhood I find many things which are echoed in my own or in that of other Irish people I know—in particular, the effects of loneliness, or a primitive rural life; the clannish obsession with one's own family; the combination of an anarchist in-dividualism with puritanical taboos and inhibitions; the half-envious contempt for England; the constant desire to show off; a sentimental attitude to Irish history; a callous indifference to those outside the gates; an identification of Ireland with the spirit and of England with crass materialism.

Even now many Englishmen are unaware of the Irishman's contempt for England. Although brought up in the Unionist North, I found myself saturated in the belief that the English are an inferior race. Soft, heavy, gullible, and without any sense of humour. They had an ugly way of speaking and they had covered the world with machines. They were extraordinarily slow in the uptake. In my eyes they were so much foreigners that when the Great War broke out in 1914 (I was then nearly seven) it was some time before I could make out whether it was the English or the Germans who were the enemy.

Yeats was always conscious that the English were foreigners or, to put the emphasis more correctly, that he was a foreigner among the English. Thus he wrote at the time of the Boer War: 'To transmute the anti-English passion into a passion of hatred against the vulgarity and materi-alism whereon England has founded her worst life and the whole life that she sends us, has always been a dream of mine. . . .' But in trying to avoid the materialism of the Saxon he for some time misrepresented the genius of the Gael. Herein he followed Matthew Arnold who, a thorough Englishman, had been pleased to find in the Celts a 'vehement reaction against the despotism of fact'. This is not borne out by early Irish poetry.

Thomas MacDonagh, who imputes to Standish O'Grady, the founder of the Celtic renaissance, a misunderstanding of the Celt, writes: 'Nothing could be more clear, more direct, more gem-like, hard and delicate and bright, than the earlier lyric poetry. . . .' And Mr Sean O'Faolain in his Introduction to *The Flowering Branch*, writes of these same lyrics that many of them give 'the homeliness and stability of "average" life', while their nature poetry, of which there is a great deal, is entirely free from the 'English sentimental attitude to nature'; far from being pantheistic it is elegantly matter-of-fact. Yeats, though guilty himself of sentimentality and twilight, recognized this fact as early as 1889; in an article on Todhunter in *The Providence Sunday Journal* he wrote of the Saxon: 'He is full of self-brooding. Like his own Wordsworth, most English of poets, he finds his image in every lake and puddle. He has to burden the skylark with his cares before he can celebrate it. He is always a lens coloured by self.'

After this attack on self-brooding it is odd to find the early Yeats practising it himself:

> Beloved, gaze in thine own heart,
> The holy tree is growing there;
> From joy the holy branches start,
> And all the trembling flowers they bear,
> The changing colours of its fruit
> Have dowered the stars with merry light;
> The surety of its hidden root
> Has planted quiet in the night;
> The shaking of its leafy head
> Has given the waves their melody,
> And made my lips a music wed,
> Murmuring a wizard song for thee . . .

Such writing as this was accepted by most of his contemporaries in the Nineties, and is still accepted by some people to-day, as typically Irish.

The old Irish poetry, whose traditions he hoped to revive, was very different, having affinities with Villon rather than with Blake, Shelley, or Wordsworth. I quote from the excellent translations by Frank O'Connor:

> Yes, and the teeth up here,
> Up in the ancient skull,
> Cracked the yellow nuts,
> Tore the haunch of the bull.

> Savage and sharp and huge,
>   They crunched the naked bone.
> And every tittle and joint
>   Was mince e'er the meal was done.

Similarly when in one of these poems a hermit praises his life, his praises are all materialistic—what he has to eat and drink, what he sees and hears around him in the country. This poetry has its hyperboles but it is hard. And its humour, like the Irish humour in all periods, is often cruel:

> Three things seek my death,
>   Hard at my heels they run—
> Hang them, sweet Christ, all three—
>   Devil, maggot and son.

This hardness lasted into the English ballad poetry written in Ireland in the eighteenth century, is found, for example, in the magnificent war ballad so admired by Yeats himself *Johnny, I hardly knew ye*, which represents Ireland more truly than all the songs of Moore.

Yeats did Ireland an injustice when he tried to foist on to her theosophy on the one hand and Nineties aestheticism on the other. But it was Ireland that saved him from becoming the slave of these things. For a little time Yeats, like Lionel Johnson, treated Ireland as the symbol of an aesthete's *Weltschmerz* ; see Johnson's poem which begins:

> Thy sorrow, and the sorrow of the sea,
>   Are sisters . . .

But the tougher Ireland, rediscovered by Synge, dominated in the end and was to receive Yeats's homage in one of his very last poems:

> Sing the peasantry and then
> Hard-riding country gentlemen,
> The holiness of monks, and after
> Porter-drinkers' randy laughter . . .

Before Yeats the best English poetry written by Irishmen had been anonymous. The street-ballads and broadsheets have, in the words of Thomas MacDonagh (echoing Synge) 'the timber and the sap of true poetry', and often, in the words of Padraic Colum, the 'harsh zest of life of people who are below decorum', for example *The Night before Larry was Stretched*. Sometimes, however, they attain a high romantic beauty—

> 'But I will climb a high, high tree,
> And rob a wild bird's nest,
> And I'll bring back whatever I do find
> To the arms I love the best,' she said,
> 'To the arms I love the best.'

This anonymous poetry was one of Yeats's sources and balanced the hot-house products of late Victorian England.

The more self-conscious nineteenth-century Irish poets writing in English were also more vulgar. Thus we get the pineapple sweetness of Moore and the thump and swagger and syrupy self-pity of Mangan. Mangan was a typical figure, the son of a grocer, a down-and-out eccentric, professing to know many languages and a connoisseur of the exotic but a man who had never been abroad, trying with opium and brandy to deaden his sorrows or maybe the sorrows of Ireland. After these there came the professedly political poets of 'Young Ireland', who used, in Yeats's words, 'a method of writing that took its poetical style from Campbell, Scott, Macaulay, and Béranger,' and who were led by the powerful personality of Thomas Davis. Davis in 1845 demanded from Irish poets 'bounding animal spirits' and these are indeed the characteristic of his school—

> In her sun, in her soil, in her station thrice blest,
> With her back towards Britain, her face to the West.

Yeats was lent the patriotic verses of Young Ireland by the Fenian leader, John O'Leary, and they had an enormous effect on him. He writes: 'From these debates [of a young Ireland Society], from O'Leary's conversation, and from the Irish books he lent or gave me has come all I have set my hand to since. . . .' This is a startling admission; there can be few great poets who is their adult years were inspired by such bad poetry. But, though bad, it sprang from impulses akin to his own and so moved him far more than much of the genuine poetry of England. He did not, however, lose his critical faculty and would certainly have agreed with Lionel Johnson's strictures on the descendants of Young Ireland: 'An attention to form and style is apparently an English vice. . . . An Irish poet of to-day may lack a thousand Irish virtues: but if he give a devoted care to the perfecting of his art, he will have at least one Celtic note, one characteristic Irish virtue. . . . Passionate impulse and patient pains are not incompatible. . . .' Johnson goes on to ask: 'Is Ireland to be the only nation which influences from without are bound to ruin and unnationalize: the only nation incapable of assimilating to herself, of nationalizing and naturalizing, the heritage of art and learning, left by other nations?' In the same article Johnson criticizes the usual metric of modern Anglo-Irish verse, those swinging anapaests and dactyls which, while possibly borrowed from the Gaelic, have a very different and much coarser effect in English. With all this Yeats would have agreed. He welcomed the energy of Young Ireland but he recognized that it was running to seed. 'Ireland', he wrote, 'cannot put from her the habits learned from her old military civilization and from a church that prays in Latin. Those popular poets have not touched her heart, her poetry when it comes will be distinguished and lonely.'

Yeats, armed with canons he had taken from the aesthetes, set himself to reorganize Irish poetry, to make it distinguished and lonely. As A.E. says of him, 'He may be regarded as the pivot around which Irish literature turned from instinctive to conscious art.' In reviving Irish literature he revived himself, was saved from spending his time in the adulteration of foreign wines. He may at times have distorted the meaning of Ireland but it was Ireland that gave body to his poetry. His escape from England coincided with his escape from adolescence. His adolescent poetry is his *English* poetry. His early poems still show the undue influence of Keats, Shelley, and Morris. There are worse influences in poems which he suppressed, for instance that of Swinburne whose sensuality is the sensuality of the Englishman trying to be latin. I quote the following, not out of spite to Yeats's memory but to give the measure of his rapid progress in his earliest period of writing and as an encouragement to young poets:

> Afar from our lawn and our levée,
>   O sister of sorrowful gaze!
> Where the roses in scarlet are heavy
>   And dream of the end of their days,
> You move in another dominion
>   And hang o'er the historied stone;
> Unpruned is your beautiful pinion,
>   Who wander and whisper alone.

He himself said that *Innisfree* was his first properly *Irish* poem. It is a poem which owing to its popularity is often nowadays unfairly despised. Thus Mr Stephen Spender writes of it very contemptuously in *The Destructive Element* as a poem which 'calls up the image of a young man reclining on a yellow satin sofa'. Mr Spender can write this because he knows that when Yeats wrote *Innisfree,* he was consorting with the indolent aesthetes of London's fin de siècle. But *Innisfree* actually was a protest against London. I see no reason to disbelieve Yeats's own statement that at the rime when he wrote it, he was longing for County Sligo. And County Sligo is not a Never-Never Land. The poem is a mannered poem and, in a sense, escapist, but the escape which Yeats here hankers for is not merely a whimsical fiction; it is an escape to a real place in Ireland which represented to him certain Irish realities.

An earlier poem, *The Wanderings of Oisin,* his first long poem on an Irish subject, had been in manner and atmosphere still traditionally English. He soon became dissatisfied with it—' with all that over-charged colour inherited from the romantic movement, I deliberately re-shaped my style, deliberately sought out an impression as of cold light and tumbling clouds.' There came a change over both his material and the movement of his verse; these changes I shall discuss later. Mangan had been fulsome, Allingham insipid, though both reflected truly on occasions certain aspects of Ireland; Yeats had found in Allingham's verse, which was regional without being nationalist, a good foil to the Young Ireland poets. It was left to Yeats himself to fuse those elements which had previously only been found in isolation and to do something like justice to his country's rich and delicate complexity. Always a self-conscious artist he owed much of his originality to the deliberate attempt to be Irish, just as other poets have owed it to the deliberate attempt to be modern. In his own words: 'It was years before I could rid myself of Shelley's Italian light; but now I think my style is myself. I might have found more of Ireland if I had written in Irish, but I have found a little, and I have found all myself.'

CHAPTER IV

The Early Poems

Therefore, dear sir, love your solitude . . .

RILKE

Yeats wrote in 1925 that when he had been young, his Muse had been old; as he himself grew older, his Muse grew younger. With this estimate I agree; a study of his development is a study in rejuvenation. His first two important books of poems—*The Wanderings of Oisin* (1889) and *The Countess Cathleen* (1892) show the langour of late Victorian old age. Kipling's Barrack Room Ballads was also published in 1892; Lionel Johnson reviewed it favourably, but Yeats, who perceived the vigour of the ballads, denied that they were serious poetry. One of his idols at this period was William Morris, under whose influence he wished to put the clock back. Very soon he was gearing pre-Raphaelite mediaevalism with the mediaevalism of Ireland, as was indicated in the last chapter. In his own words, written in 1907: 'New from the influence, mainly the personal influence of William Morris, I dreamed of enlarging Irish hate, till we had come to hate with a passion of patriotism what Morris and Ruskin hated.'

The Romantic Revival and the pre-Raphaelite movement were for Yeats supplemented by theosophy. In his 'teens he had, under his father's influence, been interested in contemporary science; his father 'had been a follower of John Stuart Mill and so had never shared Rossetti's conviction that it mattered to nobody whether the sun went round the earth or the earth went round the sun'. Yeats's affections were soon alienated from science by the Odic Force which he discovered in Sinnett's *Esoteric Buddhism*. Having become an esoteric Buddhist he went on to agree with Blake—and incidentally with Nietzsche—that Science is the tree of Death; later he called it the religion of the Suburbs. True religion was opposed both to the narrow-mindedness of the churches and to the nicely calculated less and more of the scientist; it was something revealed to theosophists and *also* to poets. He proposed to the Hermetic Society in Dublin 'that whatever the great poets had affirmed in their finest moments was the nearest we could come to an authoritative religion, and that their mythology, their spirits of water and wind were but literal truth'. He set out accordingly to find literal religious truths in the poetry of Shelley. But these 'literal' truths, as so often with Yeats, continually lapse into symbols. Again, he wishes such symbols to be rigid, but their outlines are continually melting. It is difficult for us, as it was difficult for him, to decide what degree of existence to attribute to such entities. People often discuss how far Yeats believed certain things he said, how far he meant certain statements to be taken literally. It is significant that in later life he explained that what A.E. took literally, he himself took symbolically.

In the same period, as was related in the last chapter, he was introduced by John O'Leary to the movement of Young Ireland. Under O'Leary's influence he dreamed of bringing together the two halves of Ireland, Catholic and Protestant, and decided that for himself personal utterance in poetry depended upon his remembering his Irish background. Being moved by the bad verse of Irish poetasters (see his articles for the *Boston Pilot* and the *Providence Sunday Journal*, 1887–92) he concluded that 'they had moved me because they contained the actual thoughts of man at a passionate moment of life'. For Yeats, hitherto governed by Morris, this was a very important discovery. 'We should write out our own thoughts', he explains, 'in as nearly as possible the language we thought them in, as though in a letter to an intimate friend. We should not disguise them in any way; for our lives give them force as the lives of people in plays give force to their words.'

This discovery marked a divergence from the doctrine of the aesthetes —of Art for Art's Sake. The doctrine of the aesthetes, however, really moved in a circle: Art is the important thing; you must make your life a work of art; if you live like an artist, your life will give you matter for your writing. I suspect that poets like Dowson may have chosen to live in a certain way because that was the *poetic* way to live; Pater had demanded passion. But the great poets of passion, it is safe to say, poets like Catullus and Burns, had let their life look after itself and their art flow out of it naturally.

Yeats's early poems, in any case, do not present his thoughts 'as though in an intimate letter to a friend'. He was writing in the artificial tradition of Rossetti who could write simply but whose simplicity was obviously posed. In his early twenties he had moved with his parents from Dublin to London, being then 'in all things pre-Raphaelite'. He now met two women—Florence Farr (George Moore's lady with the psaltery; see the malicious account of her in *Ave*) who, in Yeats's words, could only express her genius 'through an unfashionable art', and Maud Gonne who could only express hers through a cult of physical violence. Yeats's attitude to Maud Gonne seems always to have had something about it of *Odi atque amo*. He could never quite forgive her diehard opinions and her violence; at the same time her influence saved him from being merely a poet of the salon or the psaltery.

Intellectual London was dominated by Oscar Wilde who in his essay on The Decay of Lying, published in 1891, gave a light-hearted epigrammatic exposition of the doctrines of Pater: 'We have sold our birthright for a mess of facts. . . . Art never expresses anything but itself. . . . So far from being the creation of its time, it is usually in direct opposition to it . . . the two things that every artist should avoid are modernity of form and modernity of subject matter'; and again: 'Start with the worship of form, and there is no secret in art that will not be revealed to you . . . the sphere of Art and the sphere of Ethics are absolutely distinct and separate.'

Yeats, accordingly, started with the worship of form, worried though he was by his own speculativeness, his habit of generalization. The Aesthetes appear inconsistent in their limitation of the concept 'form'. None of these English poets went nearly so far as Mallarmé in attempting to divorce art from life, to make of poetry something as abstract, as purely pattern, as music or higher mathematics. Even Mallarmé had not succeeded in this attempt; his poetry, in spite of his theories, is valuable for the peculiar information which it conveys. The English poets recognized— quite rightly—that they had put something into their poems. So, following Pater, they proceeded to remove the surplusage, to put into their poetry only those elements from life which they considered poetic to start with. This procedure was governed by a fallacy, encouraged by a natural reaction against their Victorian predecessors. If Art expresses only itself, no elements in life are poetic to start with. Whereas, if it is granted that any elements in life are poetic to start with, it will be found impossible to draw a line in the sphere of life between the poetic and the unpoetic. The Aesthetes decided that an object or experience was poetic if it were either intense or strange. Thus they were largely occupied in treating either their own passionate experience (carefully selected and expurgated and made intense or strange to recipe) or carefully selected material from past history or myth or very carefully selected pieces from the contemporary world, bijou bric-à-brac admirable for its colour, its oddity, its uselessness, its flavour of luxury, vice, or decay. Both their diction and their metric were designed to preserve the effect of remoteness, of dreaminess. Dreams themselves are matter from life but they seemed more malleable than the matter of the newspaper and the breakfast table. And these were the days before Freud.

Yeats's early poems are in the Victorian tradition which itself was a development from the Romantic Revival. Tennyson would not have come into being without Keats. Rossetti would not have come into being without Tennyson. Yeats would not have come into being without Rossetti. One of the chief characteristics of this line of poets—in their better poems—is an autumnal, almost a morbid, languor. The Isle of the Lotus Eaters. Keats, Tennyson, Rossetti, each of them had a remarkable eye and an ear for verbal music, but they looked at the world through glasses coloured with self-pity and their music is sultry, overcharged with the emotions accumulated during the summer and waiting for some thunderstorm to freshen them or clear them away. Rossetti is a decadent poet but the seeds of his decadence are to be found in Tennyson and, before that, in Keats. Consider the attitude of these three poets to love. Love, in each case, was perhaps the most important experience of the poet's life; many of their best poems are inspired by it or at least by the idea of woman. This love of theirs is at the same time idealized and sensual—but not with the clear-cut sensuality of Catullus. It is a brooding, self-mortifying love; the poets seem to enjoy the mortification. They like to dwell upon love frustrated—Mariana in the Moated Grange. The lady herself must be more or less unattainable, her setting a mysterious, ominous twilight. Here is no Cynthia clattering on the road to Baiae. So Rossetti, harping on 'the sick burthen of my love':

> But when that hour my soul won strength
>   For words whose silence wastes and kills,
> Dull raindrops smote us, and at length
>   Thundered the heat within the hills.
> That eve I spoke those words again
> Beside the pelted window pane;
>   And there she hearkened what I said,
>   With under-glances that surveyed
> The empty pastures blind with rain.

Every word here is chosen to keep the dream of delight just on the edge of nightmare.

Yeats, falling under the spell of this morbid magnificence, began by writing poems which were similarly dreamy, languid, shot through with *Weltschmerz* and nostalgia. And his life gave him on a plate the theme of love frustrated. These early poems show not only a Victorian individualism (he had no truck, naturally, with the *public* poetry of the Victorians) but that Victorian manner which can be traced back to Keats. Always a deliberate   craftsman, he avoided on the whole Keats's adolescent blunders, such lines as those in *Lamia* —

> Her throat was serpent, but the words she spake
> Came, as through bubbling honey, for Love's sake —

but his better lines have the same appeal as those of the Keats who wrote:

> Where nested was an arbour, overwove
> By many a summer's silent fingering . . .

or more traditionally:

> This still alarm,
> This sleepy music, fore'd him walk tiptoe:
> For it came more softly than the east could blow
> Arion's magic to the Atlantic Isles . . .

The music of the early Yeats is generally sleepy too:

> Although our love is waning, let us stand
> By the lone border of the lake once more,
> Together in that hour of gentleness
> When the poor tired child, Passion, falls asleep:
> How far away the stars seem, and how far
> Is our first kiss, and ah, how old my heart.

This personification of Passion was almost a Romantic cliché. Compare the 'man whom Sorrow named his friend' and Yeats's favourite epithets at this time—' odorous twilight', 'Dim powers of drowsy thought.' Compare also his facile grammatical inversions. In later life, when revising these poems, he removed the inversions, purged the epithets, and modified the Keatsian languor. Thus in the fine poem, *The Man who Dreamed of Fairyland*, for the lines —

> Told where—ah, little, all-unneeded voice! —
> Old silence bids a lonely folk rejoice
> And chaplet their calm brows with leafage dim . . .

the later Yeats substituted:

Sang where—unnecessary cruel voice—
Old silence bids its chosen folk rejoice
Whatever ravelled waters rise and fall
Or stormy silver fret the gold of day . . .

The later version is harder, less 'poetic' in the Romantic sense, less sentimental. Whether the changes are successful is more doubtful, for it is a
sentimental poem and the new appearance of a prose manner—'unnecessary cruel voice'—combined with a grand manner (see the last two
lines) seems to me to disrupt the earlier unity.

His first book of poems, *The Wanderings of Oisin*, contains no political
implications; the Irish poems in it, according to the later Yeats himself,
are not truly Irish—not much more Irish than the Indian poems are
Indian. *Down by the Salley Gardens* is an exception, being merely a trim-
med version of an Irish folk-song. And the fairies which appear in certain
poems here, later suppressed, are trumpery little English fairies, degenerate
descendants of Oberon and Titania. Similarly the Irish ballads in this
collection are, like some of the ballads of Rossetti and Swinburne, the
copybook exercises of an intellectual—

> But Father John went up,
> And Father John went down;
> And he wore small holes in his shoes,
> And he wore large holes in his gown.

The naïve simplicity of this is no more vital nor true to the poet's personality than the simplicity of Rossetti's *Stratton Water*.

As for the long narrative tide poem, *The Wanderings of Oisin* itself, it is
very derivative (he later considered it to be full of the Italian colour of
Shelley) and no more Irish than Tennyson's *voyage of Maeldune*. The
epithets are often clichés and the rhythms are sometimes the more vulgar
rhythms of the Romantics, sometimes feeble—especially when he is
using the rhyming couplets of Morris. Morris's influence can be seen
everywhere in these early poems; in passages which are good Morris, if
not good Yeats—

> When such gray clouds of incense rose
> That only the gods' eyes did not close:
> For that pale breast and lingering hand
> Came from a more dream-heavy land,
> A more dream-heavy hour than this. . . .
> (*The Wind among the Reeds*, 1899)

and in passages which are bad by any standards—

> ... her eyes like funeral tapers.
> Her face seemed fashioned all of moonlit vapours,
> So pale! And sounds of wonder her lips uttered,
> As like a ruddy moth they waved and fluttered.
> To eagles twain that, full of ancient pride,
> Stood lonely, with dim eyeballs on each side,
> ... on their wings the hundredth year
> Scarce left a whitening feather, grey and sere ...

This recalls the recurring instances of bathos in *Endymion*. Keats and Shelley often, even Tennyson occasionally, show a lack of savoir-faire which approximates to bad taste. Yeats, who received the Romantic inspiration largely through the more enervated verse of Morris, ran the risk of being emasculated and crude simultaneously. How dangerous was the influence of Morris is shown by Gilbert Murray's verse translations of Creek tragedy which have made something evasive, languid, and feminine out of an original that was masculine, hard, and direct. Morris, on receiving *The Wanderings of Oisin*, said to Yeats, 'You write my sort of poetry.'

I would not depreciate Morris. Yeats's favourite poem for a period had been *The Man who Never Laughed Again*. Although his own temperament was both speculative and passionate and Morris's poetry was neither, he was attracted by it because it was the abnegation of rhetoric. 'My masters', Morris said, 'have been Keats and Chaucer, for they make pictures.' Rhetoric was the bogey of most English poets about 1890; they acknowledged Verlaine. It was to be a long time before Yeats stopped throttling the rhetorician inside himself. In *Autobiographies* he explains what remorse was caused him in his youth by his own supposedly vicious habit of generalizing. And he admits: 'My very remorse helped to spoil my early poetry, giving it an element of sentimentality through my refusal to give it any share of an intellect which I considered impure. Even in practical life I only very gradually began to use generalizations, that have since become the foundation of all I have done, or shall do, in Ireland.' In his middle period he relaxed his guard against rhetoric and where there had been 'Celtic' whisperings or late Victorian sighs, there came forth an utterance bronze and Roman—

> How should the world be luckier if this house,
> Where passion and precision have been one
> Time out of mind, became too ruinous
> To breed the lidless eye that loves the sun?

For the time being he was content with the making of pictures and music. Picture-making had reached its height in Tennyson who had, however, in the eyes of the Aesthetes, compromised his gift. Let us consider the pictures of the early Yeats. For example:

> And he, of his high kinsman Sorrow dreaming,
> Went walking with slow steps along the gleaming
> And humming sands, where windy surges wend . . .

or:

> See how the sacred old flamingoes come,
> Painting with shadow all the marble steps . . .

or:

> And now I wander in the woods
> Where summer gluts the golden bees,
> Or in autumnal solitudes
> Arise the leopard-coloured trees. . . .

These pictures have the atmosphere but not the precision of Tennyson or Rossetti. Witness Tennyson's

> All day within the dreamy house,
>   The doors upon their hinges creak'd;
> The blue fly sung in the pane; the mouse
>   Behind the mouldering wainscot shriek'd . . .

and Rossetti's

> When the leaf shadows at a breath
> Shrink in the road. . . .

One feels that Tennyson saw the house and Rossetti saw the road a good deal more clearly than Yeats saw any of his landscapes.

Yeats was a maker but not, to any unusual extent, an observer. Visual objects were accepted material for poetry but he uses them just enough to suggest the mood required; he selects his phrases primarily for their music or traditional associations—or sometimes, in later life, for their lack of traditional associations. Thus when, in the poem already quoted he jettisoned 'leafage dim' and introduced 'ravelled waters', he certainly gives us a new picture and 'ravelled' is a correct epithet for a river in spate. Yeats knew it was a correct epithet but he chose it, I suspect, because it is a good hard word which sounds well, a word without associations in this context from earlier poets and with no sentimental aura, a word finally which surprises. His later method was to use straightforward, almost everyday diction, and every so often hit the reader hard with a carefully poised word that is neither the ordinary word nor the 'poetic' word but a word that is both apt and unexpected. His earlier method was to diffuse a poetic atmosphere through a close sequence of poetic touches. In later life, revising these early poems, he reduced the number of epithets by about half.

His second book of lyrics, published in 1892 in one volume with *The Countess Cathleen*, shows an advance—both in competence and integrity. The Hindu themes have gone, supplanted by the ancient Irish heroes—Cuchulain, Fergus, Diarmuid, and Crania. There is more passion and a grander manner—

> Who dreamed that beauty passes like a dream?
> For these red lips, with all their mournful pride,
> Mournful that no new wonder may betide,
> Troy passed away in one high funeral gleam,
> And Usna's children died.

His mystical feelings have now become orientated towards Ireland, the Irish ideal fusing with Shelley's ideal of Intellectual Beauty—

> Rose of all Roses, Rose of all the World!

The Rose, in Yeats's words, was 'a symbol of spiritual love and supreme beauty'—the same (and this is typical of his almost pedantic eclecticism) that was eaten by the Golden Ass of Apuleius in order to regain his human shape; it grows on the Tree of Life which is the pole of heaven and is elsewhere equated by Yeats with the hazel-tree of ancient Irish poetry. In 1892 Maud Gonne was agitating in Paris against the British Empire. Yeats's love poems were nostalgic and autumnal, with a heavy late Victorian odour.

Yeats's third book of lyrics, *The Wind Among the Reeds* (1899), is the culmination of his early manner; after this there was an obvious change in his poetry. Conveniently for literary historians, he ceased to be 'ninetyish' with the Nineties. How saturated with 'Ninetyism' he had been can be seen by comparing him with certain other poets of the period — Symons, Johnson, Dowson. Undeniably they belong to the same school. They have the same properties, the same languid, lingering, or wavering rhythms, the same exclusion of 'unpoetic' material. The Alexandrine was now a popular measure, no doubt under French influence. The Alexandrine as used by these poets, for instance by Dowson, is the measure of some one half asleep —

> Sufficient for the day are the day's evil things.

Johnson, with his classical antecedents, could get a sumptuous splendour out of it —

> Alone with Christ, desolate else, left by mankind —

a line which is strong because of the shifting of the stresses. Yeats also achieves a splendour — overripe — in his Alexandrines, saving them from monotony by the frequent inclusion of additional short syllables —

> O heart the winds have shaken, the unappeasable host
> Is comelier than candles at Mother Mary's feet.

He, too, is very free with the stresses —

> Beloved, let your eyes half close, and your heart beat
> Over my heart, and your hair fall over my breast . . .

There was something hieratic about the Alexandrine of the Nineties, appropriate both to Dowson and Johnson as admirers of the Church of Rome, and to Yeats as a Roman Catholic manqué.

John Davidson mentioned telegraph wires in a poem, but most of these poets studiously avoided anything so contaminating. Their epithets make clear their code of values. Only the beautiful! And beauty for them, as for Pater, seems to imply something in decline, something tired, something — like the hero of *Axël* — too good for this world, something 'wan' in Morris's favourite phrase, something older than the rocks among which he sits. The world-weary epithets recur again and again, as in a forgotten poetess, Olive Custance —

> Pale little princess passionate and shy
> With delicate small hands and heavy hair . . .

Yeats, as I have said, wrote in his old age that when he was young his poetry was old.

His subsequent revisions of these early volumes show his change of attitude. He did what he could to rejuvenate them. Some poems he dismissed entirely but these are those adolescent poems which are obviously derivative, hardly Yeats at all; sometimes the voice was the voice of decaying Tennyson:

Gone the stars and gone the white moon, gone and puffed away and dead.
Never storm arose so swifdy; scarce the children were in bed,
Scarce the old and wizen houses had their doors and windows shut.
Ah! it dwelt within the twilight as the worm within the nut.

I have picked this grotesque example out of oblivion both because it is so untypical of Yeats and because it points the truth that a poet may be born but must also be made. Yeats was no exception to the rule that a man's early poetry is hampered by the poetry he has read. His first step forward was to abandon those vulgar rhythms 'as of a man running', in his own words, exemplified in the last quotation. With the exception of these suppressed poems, none of his work from now on lacked dignity — whatever else it may have lacked.

To the later Yeats, however, most of the early poems which he preserved seemed unsatisfactory; they had dignity but they lacked strength and precision. In revising them he tried to endow them with these qualities. Sometimes the result of this revision was a hybrid. He was anxious to purge his verse of poeticisms but his earlier self had used these poeticisms structurally just as A.E. Housman used his clichés structurally. Housman, without his clichés, might have written a higher kind of poetry, but it would have been fatal to revise *The Shropshire Lad* merely by removing them. Usually there is no harm done when Yeats merely makes minor changes to bring the language nearer to ordinary speech, when, for instance,

Ye waves, though ye dance 'fore my feet like children at play

is changed to

You waves, though you dance by my feet like children at play.

Sometimes, however, even these minor changes lose more than they gain. When the two lines —

While slowly answered he whose hand held hers —
'Often has passion worn our wandering hearts.'

68

become

> While slowly he whose hand held hers replied:
> 'Passion has often worn our wandering hearts.'

the first line loses in sound value and also in appropriateness ('replied' to my ear is too snappy a word at the end of the line and conflicts with 'slowly'; 'answer' is a richer and slower word) while in the second line the grammatical inversion, given the emotional premises of the poem, was perfectly in keeping; by removing the inversion Yeats does not bring the poem any nearer life because the sort of life that he was here treating is a life where grammatical inversions float in the air. Later he preferred to treat a different kind of life—in my opinion a more vital kind. But the old poems could not be successfully wrenched from their old allegiance.

When in revising Yeats merely omits, his omissions are usually justifiable. *The Indian to his Love* is a better poem since he dropped the inept verse of Keatsian allegory:

> There dreamy Time lets fall his sickle
>   And Life the sandals of her fleetness,
> And sleek young Joy is no more fickle,
>   And Love is kindly and deceitless,
>   And all is over save the murmur and the sweetness.

But this verse impaired the unity of the poem even according to his standards at the time of writing; he was then a sworn enemy of rhetoric and mistrusted allegory. When however he does not merely omit or make minor grammatical changes but tries to force a new attitude on to the old poem, the result is too often unsatisfactory. Some of these poems are practically re-written. I feel that he would have done better to have left the original poem alone and have written a new poem not on the same theme but on what he now thought was the same theme.

It is worth while taking an instance of his revision in detail. Here is the original version of *The Sorrow of Love*, a poem in the *Countess Cathleen* selection:

> The quarrel of the sparrows in the eaves,
>   The full round moon and the star-laden sky,
> And the loud song of the ever-singing leaves
>   Had hid away earth's old and weary cry.

And then you came with those red mournful lips,
   And with you came the whole of the world's tears,
And all the sorrows of her labouring ships,
   And all the burden of her myriad years.

And now the sparrows warring in the eaves,
   The crumbling moon, the white stars in the sky,
And the loud chanting of the unquiet leaves,
   Are shaken with earth's old and weary cry.

That is a very attractive poem of its kind, in the languid, self-pitying, late Victorian manner. The epithets are 'poetic'—'star-laden', 'ever-singing'. The mood is piled up with hyperboles (poetic clichés)—'the *whole* of the world's tears', 'all the sorrows', '*all* the burden', '*myriad* years'. The last verse is clinched with a fine Romantic piece of décor—' The crumbling moon, the white stars in the sky.' Finally, the poem is all of a piece. It is clear what it is about—Nature set over against the troubles of humanity. In the first verse the poet escapes to nature and forgets humanity; in the second verse he falls in love, the beloved, according to late Romantic precepts, being essentially a lady of sorrows; in the third verse this contact brings him violently back to humanity and human troubles infest that world of nature which just now had seemed immune from them.

The later Yeats came back to this poem with a different view of poetry, being now less fond of chiaroscuro, less opposed to rhetoric, less obsessed with self-pity, more interested in hard statement. And so he re-wrote it:

The brawling of a sparrow in the eaves,
The brilliant moon and all the milky sky,
And all that famous harmony of leaves,
Had blotted out man's image and his cry.

A girl arose that had red mournful lips
And seemed the greatness of the world in tears,
Doomed like Odysseus and the labouring ships
And proud as Priam murdered with his peers;

Arose, and on the instant clamorous eaves,
A climbing moon upon an empty sky,
And all that lamentation of the leaves,
Could but compose man's image and his cry.

The new version is certainly—even in the indentation—less 'poetic'. The epithets have been cut down from seventeen to nine. The verse has been stiffened, partly in respect of sheer sound, partly through a balanced alliteration—' brawling' and 'brilliant', 'clamorous' and 'climbing'. Every hint of sloppiness has been removed. The new lines are sonorous and bell-like. The new words accumulate strength and glitter—brawling, brilliant, harmony, doomed, murdered, clamorous, lamentation. The over-running into the last verse, 'Arose, and on the instant . . .', is in itself very effective. And the poem is no longer languid.

But perhaps this poem ought to be languid. There is no law which demands that all poems should be close-knit or vigorous or virile. The poem is no longer languid but it no longer rings true. Yeats, with a different poem in his mind's eye, has distorted it. It has become neither one thing nor the other. Mantegna may be a higher kind of painter than Giorgione but Mantegna must not tamper with Giorgione's canvases. The new version as a whole is both ill-digested and obscure. For example, in the last line the word 'compose' appears ambiguous; at first sight it might mean the exact opposite—i.e. might mean 'lay to rest'. The introduction of Odysseus and Priam is high falutin, disrupting the original simplicity. The substitution of 'A girl arose' for the second person, 'And then you came,' dissipates the lyrical feeling and introduces a pompous note which is here discordant. Considering the fate of this poem I agree with A.E. who wrote: 'I feel a little sad sometimes that the later selfconscious artist could not let the earlier halfconscious artist be.'

In the last chapter I discussed Yeats's Irish background. The Irish element, hardly stressed in his first book of lyrics, comes to preponderate in its successors. He tells us in *Autobiographies* that during the years 1887–91 he was keeping his mind on Ireland; during those same years he was writing articles 'from your Celt in London' for two American papers, the *Boston Pilot* and *the Providence Sunday Journal*. In these articles he made painstaking efforts to discover talent, if not genius, in contemporary Irish writers such as Ellen O'Leary and Rose Kavanagh. He could even bring himself to admire a poem by the former which ends—

> And oh, my darling, I am true
> To God—to Ireland—and to you.

Again he laments that T. W. Rolleston would not canalize his writing into national channels: 'He is a fine Greek scholar and quite the handsomest man in Ireland, but I wish he would devote his imagination to some national purpose. Cosmopolitan literature is, at best, but a poor bubble, though a big one. Creative work has always a fatherland.' In another article, written in 1888, he praises Allingham as being exempt from the 'bubble thoughts' typical of the nineteenth century: 'To the greater poets everything they see has its relation to the national life, and through that to the universal and divine life. . . . You can no more have the greater poetry without a nation than religion without symbols. One can only reach out to the universe with a gloved hand—that glove [sic] is one's nation, the only thing that one knows even a little of.' In Ireland it is a custom to write on walls 'Up So-and-So!' 'Down So-and-So!' 'To Hell with So-and-So!' Yeats shared this inclination. Down Huxley! Down Ibsen! Down French realism! Down internationalism of all sorts!

One of the most directly patriotic of his early poems is his dedication to a Book of Irish Tales. This poem he later re-wrote and the alterations are significant of a change in his attitude to Ireland. He is writing of the 'bell-branch' held by the reciting bardic poet to cast a spell upon his hearer. The last three verses of the early version run thus:

> I tore it from green boughs winds tossed and hurled,
>   Green boughs of tossing always, weary, weary,
>   I tore it from the green boughs of old Eri,
> The willow of the many-sorrowed world.
>
> Ah, Exiles, wandering over many lands,
>   My bell-branch murmurs: the gay bells bring laughter,
>   Leaping to shake rafter;
> The sad bells bow the forehead on the hands.
>
> A honied ringing, under the new skies
>   They bring you memories of old village faces,
>   Cabins gone now, old well-sides, old dear places,
> And men who loved the cause that never dies.

Here we find the traditional dirge for the Irish emigrant, the traditional sentimental conception of Mother Ireland, the traditional, almost fulsome, patriotism—' the cause that never dies'. The re-written version has a very different tone:

> I tore it from green boughs winds tore and tossed
> Until the sap of summer had grown weary!
> I tore it from the barren boughs of Eire,
> That country where a man can be so crossed;

Can be so battered, badgered, and destroyed
That he's a loveless man: gay bells bring laughter
That shakes a mouldering cobweb from the rafter;
And yet the saddest chimes are best enjoyed.

Gay bells or sad, they bring you memories
Of half-forgotten innocent old places:
We and our bitterness have left no traces
On Munster grass and Connemara skies.

It would be superfluous to note the changes here in detail.

More often in the early poems Yeats's nationalism was not expressed directly but indirectly through the new themes of Gaelic mythology. Later generations of Irish nationalists may have found this mixture too diluted; we might compare the *Idylls of the King* which were intended as an epic expression of English virtues but which will survive, if they do survive, for their elegance as tapestry and for the opportunities they give their reader of escaping to an unreal world. This comparison, however, is unfair to Yeats. He wrote to the *Boston Pilot* that it is necessary to 'really know the imaginative periods of Irish history'. Now these imaginative periods, to which the ordinary man had been introduced by Standish O'Grady, are not in fact separated from modern Ireland by the same great gulf that separates modern England from the Round Table. Ireland has remained a far more primitive country in which the primitive saga-virtues still awake echoes among the people at large. It is not a mere affectation that a statue of Cuchulain stands in the Dublin Post Office as a memorial to the 1916 rebels.

Yeats, however, failed to do justice to 'the imaginative periods of Irish history' because he emasculated them, just as Tennyson had emasculated Lancelot and Gawaine. The Irish sagas, though highly fantastic, have a hard matter-of-factness, which is also, as I have said, characteristic of the early Irish lyric. Even the fairy Midir gave a very earthy invitation to the hero whom she was trying to seduce. Yeats himself, in his old age, speaks in a poem of one of his early heroines as 'great bladdered Emer' and explains in a note that this conception (so very un-twilight) is derived 'from some early version of *The Courting of Emer*. Emer is chosen for the strength and volume of her bladder. This strength and volume were certainly considered signs of vigour. A woman of divine origin was murdered by jealous rivals because she made the deepest hole in the snow with her urine.'

This recognition of brute physical energy was alien to the early Yeats, the poet who 'remembers Forgotten Beauty'; he expurgated the Celtic world accordingly. The legends which he selected in his early days were those which presented escape from the ancient heroic world itself—

> Niamh calling, Away, come away:
> *Empty your heart of its mortal dream.*

Niamh, the heroine of *The Wanderings of Oisin*, was no flesh and blood virago like Maeve but a supernatural being with whom Oisin eloped into fairy countries—

> A pearl-pale, high-born lady, who rode
> On a horse with bridle of findrinny.

She has affinities with the Witch of Atlas and the Lady of Shalott, also with the fairy child in *The Land of Heart's Desire*. A similar figure is Fand—

> walking among flaming dew
> By a grey shore where the wind never blew.

The wife of the sea god Mannannan MacLir, she took Cuchulain for her lover in the country of the gods. These love affairs between human and superhuman always had a strong symbolic value for Yeats: in later life his favourite figure of the sort was Leda. Among the men the most typical *persona* perhaps in the early period is that of Fergus who sold his birth-right for a mist of dreams—

> I see my life go dripping like a stream
> From change to change; I have been many things—
> A green drop in the surge, a gleam of light
> Upon a sword, a fir-tree on a hill,
> An old slave grinding at a heavy quern,
> A king sitting upon a chair of gold,
> And all these things were wonderful and great;
> But now I have grown nothing, being all.

This nostalgia for another world, for a dream-world which is all know-ledge and no action, reached its culmination in *The Shadowy Waters*, published in 1900.

Why did Yeats take to these legends? It was partly because under the influence of the Romantic poets ('Shelley', he wrote in 1900, 'had reawakened in himself the age of faith') he craved for a mythology which would be for him what the Virgin Mary and Veronica with her napkin are for the Catholic Irish peasantry. It was partly because under the influence of the school of Pater he had a passionate desire to find a style and a style for him implied a mythology. It was partly because under the influence of John O'Leary he wished to emulate the passion of the Young Ireland poets while avoiding their pamphleteering vulgarity. It was partly because under the influence of A.E. he began to believe, or to wish to believe, that the pagan Irish pantheon was something still existing. (What its 'existence' meant to Yeats it is hard to decide; A.E. seems to have taken it almost literally.)

All these motives were fused together. Celtic legend became a panacea for the poet who could not face Kipling's world of Tommies or Henley's world of chloroform and hansoms; Henley had written in *London Voluntaries* 'The gas burns lank and jaded in its glass,' but for Yeats, as for some of his followers in Ireland to this day, the Industrial Revolution was something which must not be recognized; everything connected with it was lank and jaded and that which was lank and jaded had no place in poetry. He found in Celtic legend what Johnson and Dowson found in Catholic ritual; Celtic legend had the advantage of not having been recently exploited. I have already quoted Yeats on his own search for a religion—a highly ritualistic one. In pursuing this search he gave to Shelley's underground rivers the same sort of significance that the believing Christian finds in the star of the Magi. Being eclectic on principle, holding that all imaginative thinkers can tap the same sources of faith, he was able to equate the caves of Shelley's poetry with Plato's cave in the *Republic* and Porphyry's *Cave of the Nymphs*.

What seems curious to us to-day is that in building up this esoteric world Yeats thought he was approaching a 'popular poetry'—a disloyal thought for he still accepted the doctrine of the Aesthetes, still agreed with his father that 'poetry is the voice of the Solitary Spirit'. It must be remembered, however, that when Yeats says 'popular' here, he has a very special conception of 'the people', based on an idealized Irish peasantry. In an essay written in 1901 he once more pays a tribute to the poets of Young Ireland who had moved him more than Shelley or Spenser. *But*, he goes on, 'If they had something else to write about besides political opinions, if more of them would write about the beliefs of the people like Allingham, or about old legends like Ferguson, they would find it easier *to get a style*' (italics mine). He then admits that he himself began with the fallacy of spontaneity: 'I thought that one must write without care, for that was of the coteries, but with a gusty energy that would put all straight if it came out of the right heart.' This illusion soon disappeared for he found, like researchers in other spheres, that to be primitive does not mean to be art-less: 'I learned from the people themselves, before I learned it from any book, that they cannot separate the idea of an art or a craft from the idea of a cult with ancient technicalities and mystery.' So the wheel came full circle; the poet who tried going back to the people found himself back in the company of the Symbolists for whom beauty connotes an obscurity.

In his Introduction to the *Oxford Book of Modern* Verse Yeats mentions the efflorescence in the Nineties of something like folk-song and shows that he recognizes its dangers. He himself preferred as poets both Ferguson and Allingham to the poets of Young Ireland. He often praises Alling-ham's local feeling which is not, in any direct sense, patriotic. In his earliest books he shows a tendency to follow Allingham and treat directly the simple themes of the modern Irish countryside. Eventually it was Ferguson whom he followed into the sphere of Irish legend. Yeats's approximation to folk-song was, however, very significant and in this context it is interesting to compare him with the one poet of the time who followed—at least nominally—the folk road without falling, as the Georgians did later, into insipidity and ineptitude. I mean A. E. Hous-man.

Housman, in my opinion, was an excellent poet but his range was narrow, as narrow as that of the early Yeats. Much nonsense has been talked about his classicism. Housman is neither classicist or realist. His realism is mainly bluff, his Shropshire a mythological country, his folk characters disingenuous projections of his sophisticated self. He is the English Romantic masochistically practising heroics in the last ditch. If the early Yeats was escapist, the Housman of *A Shropshire Lad* is escapist too. The hyperboles of Yeats's love poems—

> You need but lift a pearl-pale hand,
> And bind up your long hair and sigh,
> And all men's hearts must burn and beat . . .

are no more false and no more true than Housman's gush about soldiers—

> Leave your home behind you,
> Your friends by field and town:
> Oh, town and field will mind you
> Till Ludlow tower is down.

Similarly, Housman's diction—

> Up, lad: thews that lie and cumber
> Sunlit pallets never thrive—

is certainly not in any sense more realistic than Yeats's

> I dreamed that one had died in a strange place
> Near no accustomed hand. . . .

The beat and glitter of Housman's verse, partly derived from Heine and the Border Ballads, partly, I suspect, inspired by Latin rhetoric, is no less artificial a product than the grey sheens and wavering rhythms of the early Yeats.

As for the content of the two poets, I cannot see that Housman's folk-spun world of romantic yokels, romantic boozers, romantic jail-birds, romantic redcoats, this world of hangman's nooses and nettles growing on graves and drums and golden lads, is, as some of his admirers would contend, any truer to life than Yeats's world of the Sidhe and curlews and dockleaves growing on graves. Neither Yeats nor Housman came very near to real folk-song but, to indicate the parallel and the difference between the two poets, I would recommend readers to compare *Down by the Salley Gardens* (which, it must be admitted, is a crib from folk-song proper) with Housman's poem beginning *When I was one-and-twenty.* Housman's poem is slicker, heavier, more rhetorical, more strumming in its rhythms, and—one might say—more English. It is successful but it lacks Yeats's delicacy. Housman, a highly sophisticated poet using a genre which relies on apparent naïveté, was often in danger from his own facility. Yeats was never facile but he too was sophisticated; he was wise, as he went on writing, to move away from folk-song.

Yeats set out from the beginning to write a *traditional* kind of poetry; the result, he admitted later, was not what he had intended. The traditional forms were to be the vehicle of passion. 'Poetry and sculpture', he used to say as a young man at the Art School in Dublin, 'exist to keep our passions alive.' It might be argued in return that for some of the Nineties poets passions existed in order to keep poetry alive. Yeats in his early twenties 'wanted the strongest passions, *passions that had nothing to do with observation* (italics mine), and metrical forms that seemed old enough to have been sung by men half asleep or riding upon a journey'. Passion, for him, was something incompatible with either rhetoric or modernity; hence he disliked Henley's vers libre. His poem, *Innisfree,* was inspired by the sight of a London shop-window where a little ball was dancing on a jet of water. A poet like W. H. Auden (and, maybe, Shakespeare too) would most probably have included the little ball in the first verse of the poem, which would not necessarily have been either better or worse for it but which would then have become a different poem. But Yeats's assumption that it would then have been a less passionate poem is incorrect. Neither observation nor cerebration is necessarily inimical to passion. Witness John Donne.

Yeats in after-life criticized *Innisfree*, but only on technical grounds. He says that it was 'my first lyric with anything in its rhythm of my own music. I had begun to loosen rhythm as an escape from rhetoric and from that emotion of the crowd that rhetoric brings, but I only understood vaguely and occasionally that I must for my special purpose use nothing but the common syntax. A couple of years later I would not have written that first line with its conventional archaism—"Arise and go"—nor the inversion in the last stanza.' Yeats for his special purpose, that is, meant to meet the man in the street halfway, to break the barrier between poetic and common syntax. There was perhaps no need for him, being who he was, to do more. He failed to recognize, however, that other poets might have equally good reasons for meeting the man in the street three-quarters way, for breaking the barrier between poetic and common *material*.

For the poets of the Nineties there was too much that was common and unclean; they drew in their robes so much from vulgar contacts that they walked around hobbled. 'Then in 1900,' Yeats wrote, 'everybody got down off his stilts,' It was not of course quite so sudden as that. He himself during the last decade had been making his earthy contacts—paradoxically under the influence of women whom he insisted on regarding as ethereal. Maud Gonne led him into Irish politics, Lady Gregory a little later propelled him into the theatre. Lady Gregory's influence to some extent cancelled Maud Gonne's but both came trailing clouds of anxiety and practical problems; from now on it was difficult for Yeats to be the Solitary Spirit incarnate. He had to have truck with humanity. In 1897 he took part with Maud Gonne and Connolly in the anti-Jubilee demonstrations in Dublin. Shortly afterwards he had become a social figure at Coole; on which Maud Gonne comments bitterly: 'But when these writers came back from Coole they seemed to me less passionately interested in the National struggle and more worried about their own lack of money.' But whether it was national problems or money problems, he was now having to grapple with the outside world. And this necessity, as we shall see, affected his poetry.

During the Nineties decade Maud Gonne was the dominating figure in his life. Fascinated by her beauty and her passion, he also found in her a rather crude mystical belief akin to his own (she, too, dabbled in psychical experiences). She writes in her *Autobiography*, after explaining why in 1897 she joined the Church of Rome: 'I believe every political movement on earth has its counterpart in the spirit world and the battles we fight here have perhaps been already fought out on another plane and great leaders draw their often unexplained power from this.' This shows clear affinities with Yeats's favourite doctrines, if not his direct influence. He himself could never quite attain to Maud Gonne's one-mindedness—any more than he could have turned Roman Catholic. There was always a sceptic in Yeats; even at the height of his enthusiasm for Young Ireland he confesses that 'one part of me looked on, mischievous and mocking'. He also, as against Maud Gonne, agreed with John O'Leary that 'There are things a man must not do to save a nation'. So while his devotion to Maud Gonne as a woman remained intense he was equivocal in his allegiance to her as a public figure. And she, in her turn, was impatient with the Celtic Twilight. I suspect that he had an unconscious revenge in throwing the twilight on her in his love poems. In his 'white woman with numberless dreams' it is a little difficult to recognize the notorious political agitator who thought that Parnell 'had failed when he repudiated acts of violence' and who plotted with a Belgian to blow up British troop ships during the Boer War.

Yet, as the woman could not be divorced from the political agitator, so Yeats could not sort out what he admired in her from what he deplored. He explained her to himself as a figure from another world, falling back once more on Pater's doctrine of the Body Beautiful: 'I was sedentary and thoughtful, but Maud Gonne was not sedentary, and I noticed that before some great event she did not think but became exceedingly superstitious. Are not such as she aware, at moments of great crisis, of some power beyond their own minds? . . . Her power over crowds was at its height, and some portion of the power came because she could still, even when pushing an abstract principle to what seemed to me an absurdity, keep her own mind free, and so when men and women did her bidding they did it not only because she was beautiful, but because that beauty suggested joy and freedom . . . she looked as though she lived in an ancient civilization where all superiorities whether of the body or the mind were part of a public ceremonial . . . her face, like the face of some Greek statue, showed little thought, her whole body seemed a master work of long labouring thought. . . .' The anomaly of his relations with Maud Gonne created a bitter loyalty in him. The mere fact that she was unattainable put her on a plane with the old masters but, as the years went on, his loyalty — at least to her ideals — fell away and his bitterness increased in proportion. He wrote long afterwards in *Dramatis Personae*: 'My devotion might as well have been offered to an image in a milliner's window, or to a statue in a museum, but romantic doctrine had reached its extreme development.' The truth probably was that in the Nineties Yeats admired statues in museums.

Lady Gregory, catching him when he was ill, swept him away from the world of political chimeras and shrill voices, restored his interest in the solid traditions of peasantry and aristocracy, and encouraged him to take to the theatre. The creation of an Irish theatre canalized his ambitions anew. Some years later Synge, an Irishman without politics, came as a powerful reinforcement to Lady Gregory's non-political creed; he made explicit and concrete those elements in John O'Leary's nationalism which had especially appealed to Yeats. Yeats writes of O'Leary that he 'cared nothing for his country's glory, its individuality alone seemed important in his eyes' and quotes him as saying 'No gentleman can be a socialist . . . he might be an anarchist'. Coole Park strengthened Yeats's faith in the gentleman; Synge enforced the lesson of an individuality which sometimes verged on anarchism.

By 1909, after much intimacy with Synge, we find Yeats turning his back on platform glory and comparing Thomas Davis unfavourably with Allingham because Davis was concerned 'with conscious patriotism. His Ireland [like Maud Gonne's?] was artificial, an idea built up in a couple of generations by a few commonplace men. This artificial idea has done me as much harm as the other [i.e. Allingham's *genius loci*] has helped me. . . . One cannot sum up a nation intellectually, and when the summing up is made by half-educated men the idea fills me with alarm.'

This chapter, it will have been noticed, gathers up the threads indicated in Chapters II and III: Aestheticism and Ireland. During the whole of this decade Pater's influence is very perceptible in Yeats, both in his doctrine and his manner. Thus in a fantastic story, *Rosa Alchemica*, published in 1896, Yeats, through a puppet figure, Michael Robartes, speaks of 'beings who were, I understood, in some way more certain than thought, each wrapped in his eternal moment, in the perfect lifting of an arm, in a little circlet of rhythmical words, in dreaming with dim eyes and half-closed eyelids'. Marius is still among us. In the same story he mentions writers 'who were a little weary of life as indeed the greatest have been everywhere'. I have already quoted Joyce's Pateresque essay on Mangan, written in 1902, which must, I think, have also been influenced by Yeats: for instance, Joyce writes: 'in that great memory which is greater and more generous than our memory, no life, no moment of exaltation is lost.' Joyce broke away from Pater's closed circle of exalted moments and wrote *Dubliners*. Yeats also broke away, though less blatandy. In the next chapter we can watch the break beginning.

CHAPTER V

Transition

Thus have I had thee, as a dream doth flatter,
In sleep a king, but waking no such matter.

SHAKESPEARE

I have already quoted Yeats's 1906 preface to a collection of his poems in which he attributes his recent preoccupation with drama to 'the search for more of manful energy, more of cheerful acceptance of whatever arises out of the logic of events, and for clear outline, instead of those outlines of lyric poetry that are blurred with desire and vague regret'. His experience of drama, in its turn, affected his writing of lyrics and the false assumption that the outlines of a lyric must be blurred was gradually disproved by his practice. He was tiring of Pateresque femininity, wished his work to be athletic. Thus in 1904 he wrote to A.E., renouncing his early play, *The Land of Heart's Desire*: 'We possess nothing but the will and we must never let the children of vague desires breathe upon it nor the waters of sentiment rust the terrible mirror of its blade. . . . Let us have no emotions, however abstract, in which there is not an athletic joy.'

His new interest both in the will and in clear outline was enhanced by his friendship with Lady Gregory. He found in the aristocracy the great exponents both of will and ceremonial; they had forced their way on top and they maintained themselves there in an elegant routine. It was a relief from the vulgarities of nationalist committee rooms and the travesty of will displayed by politicians.

In paying homage to the Big House, Yeats was accepting the values of his father, who wrote of a 'mediaeval' country house in Co. Wicklow that it 'stirred the historical sense and made you think of some golden age when no one was in a hurry and so all had time to enjoy themselves, and for the sake of enjoyment to be courteous and witty and pleasant. . . .' This snob idyllicism Yeats and his followers chose to refer to Ireland's mediaevalism. Thus he writes that Lady Gregory's 'point of view was founded, not on narrow modern habit, but upon her sense of great literature, upon her own strange feudal, almost mediaeval youth'. Stephen MacKenna agrees, though less enthusiastically, that 'Ireland is still mediaeval, beautifully and dismally mediaeval'. Present-day Irish poets, disciples of Yeats, argue that Ireland has greater capacity for poetry than England because she never felt the Renaissance, much less the Industrial Revolution. It was on this double assumption: that Ireland is mediaeval and mediaevalism is good, that Yeats worked when he began writing plays. He jettisoned the whole Elizabethan legacy of character study.

During the first decade of the twentieth century Yeats appears dis-illusioned and dissatisfied. He was equally ready to take refuge in Coole Park and in the more prosaic business of managing the Abbey; there is no spiritual narcotic like a balance sheet. His plays themselves were naturally an escape from the world which harassed him—the world of political agitation and intrigue, the world where people hurry and get nowhere. But the fact that his chief motive was escape made his plays un-dramatic. In reaction from contemporary conflicts and moral problems, he elimin-ated, so far as possible, morality and conflict from the Heroic world of his drama. Aristode would not have considered them plays at all.[1] They are pieces of tapestry. Yeats's blank verse is not dramatic verse. The diction is simple but it lacks suppleness and life. The movement is almost that of the *Idylls of the King* or the narrative poems of Morris—the slow circulation behind glass of elegant fairy story fishes. Yet, for all that, Yeats's exercises in drama had a purifying and strengthening effect upon his poetry.

His doctrine of tragedy was founded on an admitted hatred for 'the real world'. Tragedy, he said, was like love; in both 'we try to exclude character' (a view which throws some light on Yeats as a love-poet). Consequently he refused to admit Ibsen a true tragedian for Ibsen's themes are contemporary and his characters characters. Tragedy had no room for psychology. Even Shakespeare was only a writer of tragi-comedy, for 'tragedy must always be a drowning and breaking of the dykes that separate man from man, and . . . it is upon these dykes comedy keeps house'. Here he has fastened upon a half truth. Nietzsche in *The Birth of Tragedy* argued that Greek tragedy is a blend of what he calls the Apollon-ian and Dionysian elements, Appolo tending to stress distinctions, Dionysus to obliterate them. This is not the place to criticize Nietzsche's topsy-turvy application of this doctrine; what is pertinent is his recognition of Apollo—of the rational genius. At the apex of a tragic story there

---

[1] The only one of the early plays which is really a play is *Catbleen ni Houliban* (1902), a fine piece of Irish propaganda. But it is in prose.

is perhaps a moment when distinctions are submerged and we are left in the high air with nothing but *lacrimae rerum*. No tragedy, however, is merely an apex; it must be the whole pyramid. Yeats mistakenly wished to dispense with the base.

Shakespeare took themes from Plutarch but translated them into Elizabethan, so that ordinary people could believe in them. Yeats, taking his themes from Celtic legend, deliberately kept them caviare to the general. There was an interesting controversy on this subject in the *Dublin Daily Express* as early as 1899, when the Irish theatre was still in its infancy. John Eglinton, a lonely rationalist, wrote attacking Yeats's view of the 'poet as passive to elect influences and endowing old material with new form'. He saw in this doctrine a bias 'toward theory, diffuseness, insincerity'. 'The poet', he argued, 'looks too much away from himself and from his age, does not feel the facts of life enough, but seeks in art an escape from them.'

Yeats answered that art is not for the crowd and praises Wagner for having gone back to the world of legend. Wagner, he admits, became popular, but it is not his popularity that matters but his influence on 'the best intellects of our day'; as for instance Villiers de l'Isle Adam. I will quote once more the rest of this passage.[1] 'I believe', he writes, 'that the renewal of belief which is the great movement of our time [where had he discovered it?], will more and more liberate the arts from "their age", and from life, and leave them more and more free to lose themselves [notice the word *lose*] in beauty, and to busy themselves, like all the great poetry of the past and like religions of all times [he seems to ignore most evangelical religion as well as poets like Euripides, Villon, Chaucer, Wordsworth], with "old faiths, myths, dreams", the accumulated beauty of the age. I believe that all men will more and more reject the opinion that poetry is a "criticism of life", and be more and more convinced that it is a revelation of a hidden life, and that they may even come to think "painting, poetry, and music" "the only means of conversing with eternity left to man on earth."' There are two amusing inconsistencies here. First, having just declared himself an enemy of *popular* literature, he seems oddly interested in the opinions which 'all men' are going to accept or reject. Secondly, while implicitly attacking Matthew Arnold, he is at the same time accepting Arnold's view of the arts as man's only means of communication with eternity. When Arnold used the term 'criticism of life' he meant not surface comment but the demonstration of the Universals which lie beneath the particular. Yeats on the contrary writes here as if the

[1] See page 40.

Universals were cut off from us in some transcendent world of their own, like the gods of Epicurus.

Eglinton, in replying to this, fastened once more on Yeats's subject matter, arguing, to use the terms of the Romantic Revival, that it belonged to Fancy rather than to Imagination. A poem like Milton's *Samson*, he claims, is not divorced from life, whereas a work like Morris's *Sigurd* or Ferguson's *Congal* is 'not in the same way an original poem or the utterance of the author's age, as the highest poetry always is'. He goes on to exalt Wordsworth as the type of the great poet: 'The poetry of thought in this century—the poetry of Wordsworth, Tennyson, Browning [we might object that Tennyson, at least, is at his best when not thinking]—is more important than the poetry of art and artifice—the poetry of Coleridge, Rossetti, Swinburne—because of its higher seriousness and more universal appeal. . . .' Eglinton then criticizes the idols of the Aesthetes, Verlaine and Villiers de l'Isle Adam, and concludes his Arnold-like discourse by asserting the primary importance of the 'normal human consciousness'.

At this point A.E. entered the controversy as a peacemaker, blandly explaining that Yeats is not really divorcing art from life but only from that less real life which the man in the street wrongly calls life or reality. It is, A.E. argues, mainly a question of words: 'To liberate art from life is simply to absolve it from the duty laid upon it by academic critics of representing only what is seen, what is heard, what is felt, what is thought by man in his normal—that is, his less exalted, less *spiritual* moments, when he is least truly himself.' This argument ignores the possibility that certain things seen or felt in normal moments can serve—as has often been proved—as symbols for spiritual truths; it also, in its generalized form, does not answer the opposition's probable contention that Yeats's cat-headed figures or hounds with one red ear are no more spiritual than the everyday figures or objects met with in the Greek Anthology or in Burns or Wordsworth. A.E., however, follows Yeats loyally in bringing out God in a machine. 'To sum it all up,' he concludes, 'Mr Yeats, in common with other literary men, is trying to ennoble literature by making it religious rather than secular, by using his art for the revelation of another world rather than to depict this one.' In answer to this it might be argued that much of the highest art (witness Shakespeare) has been a kind of bluff—presenting God by writing about men, paying homage to the spirit under the guise of created objects. The later Yeats seems to have realized this in his admiration for Balzac.

The next article in the series is by the poet, William Larminie, who sheds some common sense on 'Legends as Material for Literature'. Criticizing the *Idylls of the King*, he also criticizes the aestheticism of Morris, Swinburne, and Rossetti. Poetry, he contends (it would have been safer to say *great* poetry), 'is seldom written with success if there are no great animating ideas stimulating the whole community. There are no such ideas now.' (Larminie evidently did not believe in Yeats's 'great renewal of belief'.) Poets nowadays, as a result of this, 'naturally attribute extravagant importance to form.' Larminie regrets the influence of the French poets and expresses a dislike for Symons's translations from Mallarmé. He would agree with A.E. that poetry is in a sense a spiritual activity but adds the qualification: 'When, however, we have agreed that transcendental faith or sentiment is a necessary condition for the health of the soul, we have by no means settled that the substance of art should be transcendentalism, pure and simple. We are living on the physical plane; we are embodied spirits, and we must accept the conditions.' If and when, he infers, the barriers between visible and invisible are broken down, art will probably cease to be necessary.

Yeats began the next article, entitled *The Autumn of the Flesh*, not with an argument but, as was often his way, with a grandiose flourish: 'Our thoughts and emotions are often but spray flung up from hidden tides that follow a moon no eye can see.' When he wrote first, he explains, he wanted 'to describe outward things as vividly as possible. . . . And then, quite suddenly, I lost the desire of describing outward things, and found that I took little pleasure in a book unless it was spiritual and unemphatic'. (Notice the odd conjunction of epithets.) He is struggling, he says, against 'that "externality" which a time of scientific and political thought has brought into literature'. But he fails to distinguish the 'externality' of the scientist or politician from that of the ordinary man who sees and feels. Often in his criticism he suffers in this way from the use of facile and exclusive categories.

In the same article, which is written throughout with typical arrogance and which some four years later, to judge from a letter to A.E., he regretted, he once more tries to overpower his readers with a bible, instancing de l'Isle Adam and Maeterlinck.[1] In England too, he maintains, 'a new poetry, which is always contracting its limits [and rightly, it is implied] has grown up under the shadow of the old.' First introduced by Rossetti, it is now being tended by Robert Bridges who 'elaborated a rhythm too

[1] See the passage already quoted, page 42.

86

delicate for any but an almost bodiless emotion, and repeated over and over the most ancient notes of poetry, and none but these'. Bridges, in fact, was a more thorough-going adherent of the Aesthetes than Yeats himself. It was not till long afterwards that he compromised his poetry by writing *The Testament of Beauty*, a work which by aesthetic standards is impure because it is didactic.

The new poets, says Yeats, putting aside Kipling, who is not serious, and conveniently forgetting Housman and Hardy, 'speak out of some personal or spiritual passion in words and types and metaphors that draw one's imagination as far as possible from the complexities of modern life and thought.' He then gives that astonishing résumé of the history of the world's poetry from which I have already quoted his aspersion on Goethe, Wordsworth, and Browning. But it is not only they who are culpable; Homer, Virgil, Dante, and Shakespeare were successively descending the stair, betraying the golden age, the purity of the primitive priest-poet. He then turns upon Larminie to defend Symons and Mallarmé—Mallarmé who wanted 'the horror of the forest or the silent thunder in the leaves, not the intrinsic dense wood of the trees'. We may sympathize with Mallarmé's preference but it does not prove Yeats's point. The horror of the forest may be more spiritual than the intrinsic dense wood of the trees but it is also more physical; that is, *our* physical, as well as our spiritual, reaction to it is stronger than our physical reaction to the intrinsic dense wood. Yeats at this period habitually assumed a false separation between spiritual and physical; he did not see that in that between-world, which is the world both of poetry and normal life, they are as closely related as convex to concave. In later years he escaped from this fallacy of *chorismos*, to use the Greek word for the rigid separation of two spheres.

This arid newspaper controversy took place, as I said, in 1899. My generation to-day would probably take sides with Eglinton, the orthodox follower of Arnold. But even if we think that Eglinton's theory is on the whole truer of poetry in general, that does not prove that *at that date* Yeats was in the wrong and Eglinton in the right—always supposing that both parties meant what they said or said what they meant. What is good generally, as Aristotle said, may not be good *for us*. A comparatively false theory of art may in certain circumstances be more stimulating to creation than a comparatively true one. 'By their works ye shall know them.' Arnold, who took his standards from the Greeks and desired normality and 'high seriousness', wrote poetry which was morbid and sentimental. More morbid, I would say, than the poetry of Baudelaire who took his cues from vice and disease. More sentimental than the poetry of the Symbolists who did not believe in 'high seriousness' and whose last wish was to be normal. One might argue that in the Nineties abnormality was the norm; it was a phase which had to be worked through. Eglinton in that case was wrong to try to tamper with history. There is no absolute recipe for poetry. One recipe may give a richer or higher kind of poetry than another but recipes are useless unless you have the ingredients. The recipes of fifth-century Athens were useless to Alexandria.

The year 1899 saw the first performance in Dublin of *The Heather Field* by Edward Martyn and *The Countess Cathleen* by Yeats. Yeats was now embarked on that extraordinary adventure described—maliciously, of course—by George Moore in *Ave*, and was trying to collaborate with people most unlike himself. His partnership with Moore is significant of the period. They were temperamentally antipathetic to each other but they were united in many of their dislikes and in some of their likes. Both of them, for instance, regarded *Marius the Epicurean* as the greatest English prose. Moore, again, who held that 'The philanthropist is the Nero of modern times' was at one with Yeats who in an essay on Ireland and the Arts, written in 1901, uttered another warning against the 'Englishman with his belief in progress'. They were alike in despising the middle classes and in preaching the all-importance of style (though Moore, in Yeats's eyes, had neither style nor 'class'.) In answer to Moore's malice in *Ave* Yeats long afterwards retaliated in *Dramatis Personae*, the wittiest of his prose writings. His picture of Moore throws a good deal of light on himself: 'He had gone to Paris straight from his father's racing stables, from a house where there was no culture, as Symons and I understood the word, acquired copius inaccurate French, sat among art students, young writers about to become famous, in some café; a man carved out of a turnip, looking out of astonished eyes. . . . He spoke badly and much in a foreign tongue, read nothing, and was never to attain the discipline of style. . . . A revolutionary in revolt against the ignorant Catholicism of Mayo, he chose for master Zola as another might have chosen Karl Marx.' Yeats also at this period objected to his amours. 'A romantic, when romanticism was in its final extravagance,' he wrote, long after he had abandoned this opinion, 'I thought one woman, whether wife, mistress or incitement to platonic love enough for a lifetime. . . .' It would require a professional psychologist to assess the effect on Yeats's theory and practice of his unusually long virginity, which, according to his friends, lasted until he was forty. In any case it is a fact that after he was forty (and it is the reverse with many poets) his poetry became stronger and more decided.

For Yeats's antipathy to Moore there was also, I suspect, a deeper, if less conscious, reason. Moore, for all the realism of his early novels, was essentially a child of the Aesthetic movement. Following its tenets more logically than Yeats he was a walking example of its ultimate sterility. Plumping for 'beauty' without regard to other criteria he was, quite logically, an eclectic dilettante, a flaneur, a proof of the paradox that those who follow beauty alone shall miss her; D. H. Lawrence, cumbered with theory and message, and hit-or-miss in his methods, achieved far more of beauty—and even of style—by the way. Moore was—what was to Yeats anathema though it was the logical outcome of aestheticism—a man without roots. In so far as he had any consistent outlook, it was dictated by snobbery and by dislikes, for example dislike of Christianity. The paganism he exalted against Christianity was as chimerical as the paganism of Swinburne. Witness in his very early *Confessions of a Young Man* the attack on the 'pale socialist of Galilee' and the panegyric to 'injustice': 'Man would not be man but for injustice. . . . What care I that some millions of wretched Israelites died under Pharaoh's lash or Egypt's sun? It was well that they died that I might have the pyramids to look on, or to fill a musing hour with wonderment. What care I that the virtue of some sixteen-year-old maiden was the price paid for Ingres's *La Source*? That the model died of drink and disease in the hospital, is nothing when compared with the essential that I should have *La Source*, that exquisite dream of innocence, to think of till my soul is sick with delight of the painter's holy vision.' Moore of course is writing like a naughty boy *pour épater les bourgeois* ; his thesis is an affectation. But the fact was that Moore had no creed which was not affectation and Yeats perceived this. Being in danger from affectation, himself, he disliked having the lesson of it pointed to him so obviously.

In Yeats's life Moore can be regarded as a foil to Synge (of whom, incidentally, Moore was jealous). Synge had the virtues which Moore conspicuously lacked; if Moore is an example of what Yeats might have become, Synge is an example of what he would have liked to become. But Yeats was too much set upon his own strange path to become either. And it must be remembered that Synge, in a sense, was his own creation. Yeats had found him in Paris losing himself in the quicksands of French Symbolism and brought him back to Ireland—which had very different results from bringing Moore back to Ireland. Moore returned to his native country not to re-discover a lost continuity but to try to impose the

Parisian salon upon Dublin. Irish material for him was copy—and nothing more. He professed to turn his back on abstractions but in approaching the concrete world he approached it as a theorist—a theorist of the concrete. He is comparable to those poets of the Nineties who cultivated 'passionate experience' for the sake of a theory—doctrinaires of the 'pure gem-like flame'. Whereas Synge was no doctrinaire or theorist. He returned to the concrete world not as a mere collector of specimens. He returned to it and stayed in it because it 'came natural' to him; he found himself, in the full sense of the phrase, in places like the Aran Islands.

Yeats showed a flash of intuition in sending Synge to Aran; Synge discovered there what Yeats could not discover himself—something whose existence he had divined but could not lay hands on. When Synge had brought it to light, Yeats tried to make use of it; he lacked the peculiar sensibility ever to be its master but it affected his work—and usually to the good—for the future. *The Playboy of the Western World* is unlike anything Yeats ever wrote or could write but it fulfilled a need in him. He wrote in *Reveries*: 'It is so many years before one can believe enough in what one feels even to know what the feeling is.' The writings of Synge helped him to discover his own feelings. The tributes which he paid to Synge are unusual, for Yeats, both in their wholeheartedness and their insight.

Synge's writing was essentially Irish but unsullied by the vulgarities of the Young Irelanders. The unfavourable reception of the *Playboy* increased Yeats's contempt for the Ireland of the press and the public platform while it enhanced his admiration for the Ireland of his mind's eye; at the same time, I suggest, it altered that mental Ireland in shape and texture. Synge—at least until he wrote *Deirdre*—was as little interested in the Heroic Age as he was in politics.[1] He wrote in 1907 'The artistic value of any work of art is measured by its *uniqueness*. . . . No personal originality is enough to make a rich work unique, unless it has also the characteristic of a particular life and locality and the life that is in it. For this reason all historical plays and novels and poems . . . are relatively worthless. Every healthy mind is more interested in *Titbits* than in *Idylls of the King*. . . . The most that one can claim for work of this kind—such as Keats's *Isabella*—when it is beautiful, is that it is made for a Utopia of art.' In 1908 he put it more fairly, distinguishing two kinds of poetry—that of real life and that of a world of fancy. But fancy alone will never

[1] Stephen MacKenna recalls that he was repelled by the activities of Maud Gonne.

reach the heights. 'What is highest in poetry', he writes, 'is always reached where the dreamer is leaning out to reality, or where the man of real life is lifted out of it, and in all the poets the greatest have both these elements, that is they are supremely engrossed with life, and yet with the wildness of their fancy they are always passing out of what is simple and plain.' Some of Yeats's later poetry shows the combination of these elements—a combination never, I think, achieved for example by A.E.

By 1906 Yeats had already moved towards this new point of Synge's and was forgetting the Autumn of the Flesh. Thus he writes at this time in *Discoveries*: 'What moves natural men in the arts is what moves them in life,' and instances Villon as against Shelley. Speaking of Villon's 'feeling for his own personality' he confesses that he himself at one time would not have appreciated this: 'Without knowing it, I had come to care for nothing but impersonal beauty. I had set out on life with the thought of putting my very self into poetry and had understood this as a representation of my own visions and an attempt to cut away the non-essential, but as I imagined the visions outside myself my imagination became full of decorative landscapes of still life.' That is, the Aesthetic fallacy had made a half man of him. He goes on,[1] conceding points unconsciously to Eglinton: 'we should ascend out of common interests, the thoughts of the newspapers, of the market-place, of men of science, but only so far as we can carry the normal, passionate, reasoning self, the personality as a whole.' He is beginning to realize that abstractions arise not only from science and politics, that Nineties aestheticism also in a sense suffered from them: 'Art bids us touch and taste and hear and see the world, and shrink from what Blake calls mathematic form, from every abstract thing, from all that is of the brain only, from all that is not a fountain jetting from the entire hopes, memories, and sensations of the body.' This new recognition of the body I would attribute largely to the influence of Synge. Yeats's old text 'Then nowise worship dusty deeds' is becoming obsolete, the 'thought-woven sails' of the Rose of Battle are falling limp. And he inevitably begins to write a different kind of poetry.

The change however was not clear-cut; the old self persisted beside the new. In 1906 he published a verse-play, *The Shadowy Waters*, which is an extreme example of old-fashioned Romantic escapism, full of the murmur of Keats's 'perilous seas'. The properties are 'poetic' in the narrowest sense:

[1] I have already quoted this passage, page 45.

Edain came out of Midhir's hill, and lay
Beside young Aengus in his tower of glass,
Where time is drowned in odour-laden winds
And Druid moons, a murmuring of boughs,
And sleepy boughs, and boughs whose apples made
Of opal and ruby and pale chrysolite
Awake unsleeping fires. . . .

The whole poem to which these lines are a prelude, is concerned with the drowning of time. Notice the Ninetyish enumeration of precious stones, elsewhere often repeated—'chrysoberyl, or beryl, or chrysolite'—and the too easy epithets; even Fiona MacLeod objected to Yeats's use, or abuse, of the word 'druid'. I find the echoes of this manner – turned rococo and socially smart—in Miss Edith Sitwell's long poem *The Sleeping Beauty*.

The hero of this poem, Forgael, is a man sailing through faerie seas haunted by man-headed birds, and pursuing a dream against the wishes of his crew who are ordinary men with a normal endowment of common sense and sensuality—

You will have all you have wished for when you have earned
Land for your children or money in a pot.

Whereas Forgael is looking for love,—

But of a beautiful, unheard of kind
That is not in the world.

He wants in fact, to use Yeats's own terminology, a love within the Great Memory—a love on the astral plane. But there is an irony in the fact that his lady, when he finds her, is 'one that casts a shadow'. It is most probable that, in writing this poem, he was still thinking of Maud Gonne.

To turn now to his new lyrics. The immediate effect upon his lyrics of the influences I have been discussing was that their poetry became not richer but barer. The late Victorian beauty is evaporated and what we might call the neo-classical beauty has not yet been built up. Where the same moods persist, especially that of frustrated love, he no longer wraps them, like Rossetti, in a sumptuous aura of melancholy; he *states* his feelings, with a cold and exact bitterness. He wrote few lyrics between 1899 and 1910, being preoccupied with drama. In 1903 he also published two narrative poems, *The Old Age of Queen Maeve and Baile and Aillinn*. Both are flat, faded, two-dimensional pieces. The rather insipid *Baile and Aillinn*, written in four-stress rhyming couplets, is chiefly interesting for its personal interpolations on the old theme that history repeats itself in love; Yeats's own passion is thus drawn up into mythology. *The Old Age of Queen Maeve* is written in the blank verse of the plays, a verse actually more suited to narrative than to drama, and here again the poet's private life intrudes on the world of legend—

> O unquiet heart,
> Why do you praise another, praising her,
> As if there were no tale but your own tale
> Worth knitting to a measure of sweet sound?

Among the shorter poems the same theme is treated directly, but with a very different movement from that of his earlier love-poems. Thus, in one of the poems from *In the Seven Woods*, published in 1903, he writes:

> There's no man may look upon her, no man,
> As when newly grown to be a woman,
> Tall and noble but with face and bosom
> Delicate in colour as apple blossom.
> This beauty's kinder, yet for a reason
> I could weep that the old is out of season.

Notice here the minor innovations in technique, especially the use of the off-rhyme, later a favourite trick of Yeats and especially useful for suggesting disillusionment or weariness. In this volume we also find him beginning to write poems which in their manner and content are casual or occasional; for instance, *Adam's Curse*. As for the world of legend, it appears only to be renounced—

> I have no happiness in dreaming of Brycelinde.

His next lyrics appeared in 1910 bound in one volume with the satirical play, *The Green Helmet*. The process has now gone further. There is one poem here that might have come out of Rossetti—

> I swayed upon the gaudy stern
> The butt end of a steering oar—

but on the whole the sheen and mystery are gone; statement preponderates over suggestion. The mood is consistenly depressed, his hopes both of love and of Ireland having reached a low ebb. He is working out a manner which is flat but at the same time distinguished; either through lack of vitality or lack of skill he has not yet developed his peculiar gift of making something memorable and even sensuous out of ordinary words, austere rhythms and statements bleakly direct. For the moment he gives us an almost Wordsworthian simplicity —

> I had this thought a while ago,
> My darling cannot understand
> What I have done, or what would do
> In this blind, bitter land —

or, following another line, he compromises with his old arch-enemy rhetoric and, in an era of insipid versifying, makes the English language sound as if it meant business. *No Second Troy* is his first fine poem in this manner; the love which had inspired the old wavering rhythms and twilight atmosphere, now, in the stage of resignation, expresses itself through straightforward diction, a powerful traditional metric, and the controlled rhetoric of the classicists —

> Why should I blame her that she filled my days
> With misery, or that she would of late
> Have taught to ignorant men most violent ways,
> Or hurled the little streets upon the great,
> Had they but courage equal to desire?

Ireland, as well as Maud Gonne, has disappointed him. His 1909 diary shows how depressed he was by contemporary Ireland's soullessness. 'Ireland is ruined by abstractions,' he writes, and he complains of the 'ill-breeding of the mind' prevalent among Irishmen — 'every thought made in some manufactory and with the mark upon it of its wholesale origin'. In 1909 he met Thomas MacDonagh but expected little of him. The revolutionary movement had turned sour in his mouth. He renounces Young Ireland and his own earlier attitude, attributing his escape from them, as I have attributed it above, to the influence of Synge: 'I did not see, until Synge began to write, that we must renounce the deliberate creation of a kind of Holy City in the imagination, and express the individual.'

The poems about Ireland in *The Green Helmet* are consistently disillusioned. He complains in a poem to Douglas Hyde, thinking no doubt of the Abbey Theatre audience, that the populace is wilful, fickle, and ignorant:

> Is there a bridle for this Proteus
> That turns and changes like his draughty seas?
> Or is there none, most popular of men,
> But when they mock us, that we mock again?

In another poem he portrays the decline of Irish nationalism:

> These are the clouds about the fallen sun,
> The majesty that shuts his burning eye:
> The weak lay hand on what the strong has done,
> Till that be tumbled that was lifted high
> And discord follow upon unison,
> And all things at one common level lie. . . .

In another poem he deplores the fall of the big houses (wearied by the Land Agitation he can see nothing but loss in it):

> Although
> Mean roof trees were the sturdier for its fall,
> How should their luck run high enough to reach
> The gifts that govern men, and after these
> To gradual Time's last gift, a written speech
> Wrought of high laughter, loveliness and ease?

Notice the typical implication that literature is man's most valuable possession.

Yeats's cult of the Big House is to be correlated with his dislike for democracy, liberalism, the facile concept of progress. This dislike was by no means peculiar to him among twentieth-century poets. T. S. Eliot, complaining that the world is 'worm-eaten with liberalism', appears to hanker for a hierarchial régime where Church and State are above the individual's questionings. D. H. Lawrence, while hating the soullessness of capitalism, found an equally barren prospect in democracy, socialism, communism. He fell back upon 'the mystery of lordship. The mystery of innate, natural, sacred priority. The other mystic relationship between men, which democracy and equality try to deny and obliterate. Not any arbitrary caste or birth aristocracy [here he is more elastic than Yeats]. But the mystic recognition of difference and innate priority, the joy of obedience and the sacred responsibility of authority.' (*Kangaroo*, published in 1923.) Roy Campbell again, a poet devoted to vigour and individuality, drew the inference that these qualities are inseparable from a system of social inequality and therefore appeared in the Spanish Civil War as a rabid reactionary, regarding General Franco as the saviour of human dignity because he was the saviour of the land-owners.

In Yeats also the love of tradition merged into support of reaction. Following his father, who had stressed the *conservativeness* of the Irish peasantry—'as conservative as the people behind the barriers of privilege' —he wanted to maintain with the barriers of privilege around the aristocracy those other barriers (of illiteracy and penury?) around the peasant. In 1907 he wrote, in an essay on Poetry and Ireland: 'Three types of men have made all beautiful things. Aristocracies have made beautiful manners, because their place in the world puts them above the fear of life, and the countrymen have made beautiful stories and beliefs, because they have nothing to lose and so do not fear, and the artists have made all the rest, because Providence has filled them with recklessness.' The corollary is that artists must remain reckless, must not accept any discipline from without (see page 99), that the aristocrats must be kept on their pedestals ('Leisure, wealth, privilege', Yeats wrote in 1909, 'were created to be a soil for the most living'), that the peasants, finally, must remain where they have nothing to lose.

Yeats, like Eliot, assumes that a world built upon communist principles would imply a mechanical equality, a drab uniformity. It is to be hoped that this is a wrong assumption, though it is supported by many examples so far given of communist *intellectual* dictatorship, of the wholesale issue of machine-made and trade-marked opinions. Yeats and Eliot again assumed that a democratic world implies a low standard of thinking and taste, implies jerry-building, barren competitiveness, a waste of energy and words; for this assumption too they can easily find plenty of evidence. These assumptions may be wrong, but granted that they believed them, Yeats and Eliot have acted upon them honestly. No doubt they were also influenced by ulterior, that is personal, motives; each wanted a world in which he, as an intellectual, could live. The left wing intellectual, before he throws a stone at them, should consider whether his own motives for advocating 'the classless society' are disinterested. I have a suspicion that many intellectuals of the Left fancy this society with a special niche for themselves in it, that they take it the writer will be honoured when the banker and the aristocrat have gone—looking at the circulation of novels and even poetry in the U.S.S.R.

What horrified Yeats in politics was the disregard of human individuality. He wrote in the last year of his life: 'If ever Ireland again seems molten wax, do not try to pour Ireland into any political system. Think first how many able men with public minds the country has, how many it can hope to have in the near future, and mould your system upon those men. It does not matter how you get them, but get them.' By that date, though still clinging to the idea of dynasties, he was prepared to admit that a new dynasty can always be begun, and expressed the hope that the descendants of the present generation of Irish bureaucrats, '*if they grow rich enough for the travel and leisure that make a finished man* [italics mine], will constitute our ruling class, and date their origin from the Post Office as American families date theirs from the *Mayflower*.' In pre-War years, however, before the Irish burnings, he was still pinning his faith to the Big House,[1] and preferring to ignore the fact that in most cases these houses maintained no culture worth speaking of—nothing but an obsolete bravado, an insidious bonhomie and a way with horses. These qualities themselves, it must be admitted, came to fascinate him—an intellectual jumping his hedges by proxy. So, in this 1910 collection of poems, he expresses a nostalgic yearning for 'horsemen for companions,

> Before the merchant and the clerk
> Breathed on the world with timid breath . . .'.

For in his contempt for the merchant and the clerk, if in nothing else, Yeats joins hands with the Communists. His remedy, however—like William Morris's before him—was to put the clock back, not forward.

A contemporary reviewing *In the Seven Woods* and *The Green Helmet* might justifiably have inferred a loss of vitality and inspiration. The chief impression received from these volumes is one of weariness. In succeeding books of verse Yeats rallied most remarkably, displaying a vigour which is no longer adolescent but mature. The whole man is at last represented; he ceases to suppress his own hardheadedness (he was an excellent business man), his wit, his talents for gossip and generalization, his anger or sensuality or love of speculation.

Technically, his later verse owed much to his experiments in drama. In *Dramatis Personae* he recounts how he used to argue with Moore about words: In later years, through much knowledge of the stage, through the exfoliation of my own style, I learnt that occasional prosaic words gave the

---

[1] Contrast Stephen MacKenna who wrote in 1924: 'I don't know anything about the MacKennas, and frankly I care less: one of the very few things in the Ireland of to-day that really pleases me is that cobblers and ploughers are at the top and that no one talks, as far as I know, of any social glory or birth-ban.'

effect of an active man speaking. In dream-poetry, in *Kubla Khan*, in *The Stream's Secret*, every line, every word, can carry its unanalysable, rich associations; but if we dramatize some possible singer or speaker we remember that he is moved by one thing at a time, certain words must be dull and numb. Here and there in correcting my early poems I have introduced such numbness and dullness, turned, for instance, "the curd-pale moon" into the "brilliant moon", that all might seem, as it were, remembered with indifference, except some one vivid image. When I began to rehearse a play I had the defects of my early poetry; I insisted upon obvious all-pervading rhythm. Later on I found myself saying that only in those lines or words where the beauty of the passage came to its climax, must rhythm be obvious.' This new principle became characteristic of the later Yeats and of much other modern poetry, which fails to please those critics who demand highlights in every line.

Synge wrote in 1908: 'In these days poetry is usually a flower of evil or good [he himself, it should be remembered, had had his term with the Symbolists]; but it is the timber of poetry that wears most surely, and there is no timber that has not strong roots among the clay and worms. . . . Even if we grant that exalted poetry can be kept successful by itself, the strong things of life are needed in poetry also, to show that what is exalted or tender is not made by feeble blood. It may almost be said that before verse can be human again it must learn to be brutal.' These prophetic words could serve as a comment on the subsequent development of Yeats and of modern English poetry in general. A more rapid and violent parallel to Yeats's development—though perhaps a less genuine one—is found in Mr Ezra Pound. Pound, in the same year that Synge wrote the above words, published his early *Personæ*, a book which shows clearly the influence of the earlier Yeats—

> There are there many rooms and all of gold,
> Of woven walls deep patterned, of email,
> Of beaten work; and through the claret stone,
> Set to some weaving, comes the aureate light.

I would instance particularly the whole of the short poem, *The Tree*. But Pound soon abandoned this manner which was sometimes decorative on the Victorian pattern, sometimes atmospheric on the Symbolist pattern, but which was certainly lacking in 'timber'. Too deliberately, perhaps, he set out to learn to be brutal; it was the same impulse that drove Mr W. J. Turner to leave the prettiness of *Chimborazo, Cotopaxi for The Seven Days of the Sun.* In Eliot we find from the start elegance and sentiment and Symbolist impressionism subsisting side by side with hard facts brutally stated.

During the period discussed in this chapter Yeats was becoming more and more speculative, was developing the philosophy implicit in his later work. Like most philosophies this was largely conditioned by his dislikes. Added to his old dislike of the mere 'literature of logic' which 'conquering all in the service of one metallic premise, is for those who have forgotten everything but books and yet have only just learnt to read', there is his new distrust of political enthusiasm and even of the 'religious genius'. His dominating conception now is wholeness—the whole man, the whole of life. He has decided that the logician, on the one hand, makes distinctions in the wrong places, and the religious man, on the other, obliterates distinctions which are necessary. On this ground he criticizes A.E.: 'His poetical genius does not affect his mind as a whole, and probably he puts aside as unworthy every suggestion of his poetical genius which would separate man from man. The most fundamental of divisions is that between the intellect, which can only do its work by saying continually "thou fool", and the religious genius which makes all equal.' From now on Yeats began to give the reins to his intellect, was no longer content to write in a half-sleep where distinctions are lost in a perpetual chiaroscuro.

Going closely with this new concept of the human world as a whole of parts in which the parts must neither usurp the whole nor be merely merged in it, is Yeats's favourite doctrine of the Mask. The adolescent Yeats had been a dreamer and proud of it. Now having come to admire men of action he rationalized his admiration by the theory that the man of action is a dreamer who embraces his opposite, who dramatizes his dream in action; he finds this true of the heroes of Plutarch's Lives. This theory absolves the man of action from the vulgar motivation of mere animal spirits or a merely mechanical necessity. Julius Caesar or Napoleon is playing a part; he is in fact what Nero wanted to be—an artist. Yeats might have instanced the hero of Synge's *Playboy* who begins by pretending to be a violent character and ends by becoming one.

'There is a relation', Yeats wrote in his diary of 1909, 'between discipline and the theatrical sense. If we cannot imagine ourselves as different from what we are, and assume that second self, we cannot impose a discipline upon ourselves, though we may accept one from others.' It is implied that the latter kind of discipline is antipathetic to art; Yeats could never admit that a poet, for instance, who turned Communist, was not deceiving himself. 'Active virtue', he continues, 'as distinguished from the passive acceptance of a current code, is therefore theatrical, consciously dramatic, the wearing of a mask. It is the condition of arduous full life. One constantly notices in very active natures a tendency to pose. . . .' He goes on to criticize Wordsworth 'because his moral sense has no theatrical element'. As usual with Yeats's theories, his theory is too simple; it is the rationalization of his own theatricality. Many great men may have been, in a sense, poseurs, but that does not mean that pose—at any rate conscious pose, for he uses the phrase 'consciously dramatic'—is a prerequisite of greatness. Again the alternative disciplines are too rigorously separated. Does a man who accepts a current code—as so many of the Greeks did, for instance—only accept it *passively*? And is it possible to discipline oneself without coming to terms with external circumstances and society?

This insistence on pose might suggest that he was relapsing into Ninetyism; it is suspiciously reminiscent of Lionel Johnson's 'life as a ritual'. Yeats however had left the fold of the Aesthetes in as much as he had admitted that the 'theatrical sense' can display itself in almost any walk of life. He no longer accepted Art for Art's Sake in the narrower sense in which art is opposed to life or, at least, to life in a community. Logically the Aesthetes were anarchists as regards the community. Whereas Yeats now tends to think, like Aristotle, that the community can be a work of art; so can the life of an individual—and not merely of an individual 'artist'. The material for such forms of art (in the wider sense) is men in relation to each other; the differences, therefore, between one man and another must be maintained and recognized. This meant readmitting the importance of both character and morality. Thus in the 1909 diary we find a very significant recantation: 'I now see that the literary element in painting, the moral element in poetry, are the means whereby the two arts are accepted into the social order and become a part of life and not things of the study and the exhibition.' He here as good as admits that the Aesthetes' divorce of art from life, and a *fortiori* from any social order, was founded on a fallacy. Later, in 1936, in his Introduction to the *Oxford Book of Modern Verse*, he repudiates very soundly his earlier purism: 'When my generation denounced scientific humanitarian preoccupation, psychological curiosity, rhetoric, we had not found what ailed Victorian literature. The Elizabethans had all these things, especially rhetoric. . . . The mischief began at the end of the seventeenth century when man became passive before a mechanized nature. . . .' Being W. B. Yeats, he could not be expected to add that the isolationism of the Nineties poets, intended as a cure for the Victorian disease, was really a symptom of it. The Victorian poets had lost their place in the community; to argue that a poet belongs outside the community was merely an (unconscious) attempt to gloze over the sense of loss.

CHAPTER VI

Responsibilities

Adieu, sweet Aengus, Maeve and Fand,
Ye plumed yet skinny Shee.

J. M. SYNGE

'In dreams begins responsibility.' This quotation, put at the beginning of Yeats's next book of poems, *Responsibilities*, published in 1914, is significant of his change of outlook. The bulk of his early poetry belonged to the dream-world; but that world was essentially irresponsible, implied a reversal or abnegation of the values of the physical world we live in; *The Shadowy Waters* was his last great acclamation of that dream-world. Now the wheel has moved round; the dream-world is taken as a sanction of the world we live in, which latter for Yeats as for Plato is governed by eternal patterns outside itself. Yeats is now shaking free of the concept of transcendence; the relationship between the two worlds is not to be a one-sided one. 'Eternity', he quoted from Blake, 'is in love with the pro-ductions of time,' or, in the words of an Irish peasant which he was fond of repeating, 'God possesses the heavens—but he covets the earth.' Our earthly dignity has been vindicated; Yeats is no longer ashamed of our world of conflicting people, of oratory and flesh; he is even beginning to be proud of it as something which may be the disguise of the eternal verities but is also their necessary embodiment. In fighting for a political creed one is following a mythical archetype; in sexual love one is tuning to the music of the spheres.

He was nearly fifty when he published *Responsibilities* and, in the same year, another short narrative poem, *The Two Kings*. The latter is of little interest except that, while it is on the old theme of a woman who is wooed by a supernatural lover, this time the woman is allowed to refuse the lover and make a good case for doing so—

> Never will I believe there is any change
> Can blot out of my memory this life
> Sweetened by death, but if I could believe,

That were a double hunger in my lips
For what is doubly brief.

The blank verse of this poem shows little development. It is Victorian blank verse with a fondness for the Swinburnian final anapaest—'More hands in height than any stag in the world.' (For the historian of English blank verse Swinburne would be a significant figure. Since Milton blank verse had been steadily flagging, becoming less alive, more literary. In Tennyson, with his marvellous technical accomplishment, it still retains the aura of a museum. Swinburne, the virtuoso, attempted to galvanize it, applying alliteration and sensual rhythm. *Atalanta in Calydon is a tour de force* but the verse fails to be dramatic and its vitality is something factitious.)

Responsibilities, on the other hand, is full of novelties. It is a versatile collection. There are a number of direct personal or occasional poems and some satirical ones. There are examples of a new kind of fable-poetry which avoids becoming allegory. There are a couple of those poems in a ballad form with a refrain which he later was to use so often (see Chapter VIII); these 'ballads' are examples of sleight-of-hand; appearing carefree and frivolous they convey a simple serious statement of a particular mood or idea. Lastly, there are the two poems on *The Magi and The Dolls*, forerunners of his later philosophical poetry.

The fable-poems—*The Grey Rock, The Three Beggars, The Three Hermits, The Hour before Dawn*—are dry, unromantic pieces; an everyday, sometimes colloquial, diction is blended with turns of speech which, though unostentatious, come out of the poetic tradition. *The Grey Rock* is less interesting for its story rather than for the moral which it points, namely, that a man must keep faith with the eternal powers (the archetypes of art) rather than with any political forces of here and now—'the loud host before the sea'. In an aside Yeats pays a nostalgic tribute to Dowson and Johnson for their single-minded devotion to Art. The story once again presents a supernatural being in love with a man and, in this case, embittered by that man's treachery (a treachery which from another angle is, as in *The Two Kings*, the man's loyalty to his own world)—

Why must the lasting love what passes,
Why are the gods by men betrayed?

The poem implies Yeats's peculiar dialectic—eternity in love with the reductions of time, the antagonism between gods and men who are divided by a gulf which demands to be bridged so that upon that bridge they can fight or love each other. In different poems Yeats appears to take different sides, an ambiguous partisan because he believes in the final resolution of the rivalry.

The Three Beggars is a satirical comment upon everyday avarice; the hero is a crane who, like the fool or the saint elsewhere in his poetry, shows no competitive spirit (the heron for Yeats represents solitude, contemplation). The moral seems to be that quiescence pays in the end—

> 'Maybe I shall be lucky yet,
> Now they are silent,' said the crane.
> 'Though to my feathers in the wet
> I've stood as I were made of stone
> And seen the rubbish run about,
> It's certain there are trout somewhere
> And maybe I shall take a trout
> If but I do not seem to care.'

The Hour before Dawn points a different moral; it is a defence of the waking life against the man who intends to sleep till the Day of Judgement—'For all life longs for the Last Day.' Yeats had in his time expressed this longing himself and was to continue to express it on occasions, his allegiance being divided. Now, however, he is on the whole an accepter of life instead of a rejecter of it; one can see the influence of Synge—

> The beggar in a rage began
> Upon his hunkers in the hole,
> 'It's plain that you are no right man
> To mock at everything I love
> As if it were not worth the doing.
> I'd have a merry life enough
> If a good Easter wind were blowing,
> And though the winter wind is bad
> I should not be too down in the mouth
> For anything you did or said
> If but this wind were in the south.'

Compare Synge's Tramp in *The Shadow of the Glen*: 'We'll be going now, I'm telling you, and the time you'll be feeling the cold, and the frost, and the great rain, and the sun again, and the south wind blowing in the glens, you'll not be sitting up in a wet ditch, the way you're after sitting in this place, making yourself old with looking on each day, and it passing you by. You'll be saying one time, "It's a good evening, by the grace of God," and another time "It's a wild night, God help us; but it'll pass surely."'

The same individualist bravado comes out in the magnificent little poem, *The Peacock*, which begins:

> What's riches to him
> That has made a great peacock
> With the pride of his eye?

and in another poem here that pays homage to a squirrel:

> Nor the tame will, nor timid brain,
> Nor heavy knitting of the brow
> Bred that fierce tooth and cleanly limb
> And threw him up to laugh on the bough;
> No government appointed him.

Technically, the poems in *Responsibilities* are, for the most part, very accomplished. Yeats, who composed with extraordinary difficulty, is outstanding among modern poets for his mastery of the short-line poem with three or four stresses to a line. Any one who has tried to write such a poem, when it is not broken into short stanzas, knows how hard it is so to arrange the sentences as to avoid breaking the run of the whole, and so to control the rhythms that the poem does not get into a skid. Yeats, as Mr Oliver St John Gogarty has put it, keeps his poem balanced in the middle of the page; it does not run off into the margins. His sentence-construction and rhythmical variation are structurally functional. Witness the opening lines of a poem from *Responsibilities* called *Friends*:

> Now must I these three praise —
> Three women that have wrought
> What joy is in my days:
> One because no thought,
> Nor those unpassing cares,
> No, not in these fifteen
> Many-times-troubled years,
> Could ever come between
> Mind and delighted mind. . . .

It will be noticed here that, though the rhyme scheme is in quatrains, the chief syntactical stops do not coincide with the ends of the quatrains. This is a simple mechanical principle, as is the splitting between one line and the next of epithet and noun or preposition and noun, but Yeats's craftsmanship is something more than mechanical. He uses many tricks without overdoing any of them. Some intuition guided his half-rhymes, repetitions, counterpointing,[1] his omission or interpolation of syllables.

The best poems in *Responsibilities* are two short, very direct ones addressed to Maude Gonne's daughter, which have a Greek and sinewy spareness. There are more poems for her in his next book and she ranks among the few persons who could evoke from Yeats this personal directness. It is incorrect to say, as some have done, that directness is *the* characteristic of Yeats's later poetry or to think that his best poems are necessarily the direct ones. Much of his later poetry, and some of his finest at that, was oblique, complicated, even obscure. What we can say is that his later poetry showed a marked increase in strength and concentration. This strength is sometimes achieved by directness, sometimes by the powerful girders of ideas, sometimes by the old enemy rhetoric. Yeats had an epigrammatist in him who hardly shows himself in his early poetry. As the Celtic mists rolled away, he was able to look after him and build up his poems more economically. His material is carefully selected, though he uses the same properties again and again—the same real life figures, the same particular events and places, the same stock *persoæ* and more or less rigid symbols, the same quasi-philosophical concepts and generalizations. The charge of repetition is a favourite weapon of the book-reviewer, a weapon which is often employed stupidly. Provided a concept or a symbol or an image still rings true to a poet, why should he be forbidden to repeat it? It might be pointed out that T. S. Eliot, who has written much less verse, repeats himself frequently both in phrase and image; witness his use of the symbolic figure Coriolanus.

Responsibilities contains two remarkable 'philosophical' poems—*The Magi* and *The Dolls*—which foreshadow much that is to come in later volumes. Yeats wrote them, as he explains in a note, after having 'noticed once again how all thought among us is frozen into something other than human life'. The dolls, who represent intellectual Being in opposition to physical or physiological Becoming, make an indignant uproar because

---

[1] *Counterpointing*: I use Gerard Manley Hopkins's term for the inversion of the normal metrical stresses; 'Of Man's first disobedience . . .' is counterpointed, U——U—U instead of U—U—U—U

the doll-maker's wife has had a baby. She, vacillating—like Yeats himself—between the values of life and thought, apologizes to her husband that it was an accident. The Magi in the other poem, 'complementary forms of those enraged dolls,' are perceived in the sky with

> all their eyes still fixed, hoping to find once more,
> Being by Calvary's turbulence unsatisfied,
> The uncontrollable mystery on the bestial floor.

As I understand this, it is another view of the dialectic between Being and Becoming. The dolls merely objected to the fact of a human birth. The Magi, being attendants on a birth which is both human and divine, represent that Eternity which is in love with the productions of time but which is repeatedly disappointed by them. Calvary for the Magi is merely a frustration.

Yeats believed—or tried hard to believe—in historical cycles. The birth of Christ therefore, not being a unique phenomenon, was something which must recur. (See his later poem, *The Second Coming*.) The eternal Powers can only find satisfaction in the dramas played under their own influence or inspiration on the stage of history—as if Plato's Forms could only find themselves in their *mimesis* by particulars. No one point or episode or agent in the drama is satisfying to them; they must have the whole, *the whole of parts*. The defeat of the hero in the play is their defeat because he is their hero but the play as a whole is their triumph because it is their play. So Yeats wrote later in the chorus in *The Resurrection*:

> Odour of blood when Christ was slain
> Made all Platonic tolerance vain
> And vain all Doric Discipline.

The Magi, in so far as they are thought frozen into something other than itself, into Platonized or Doricized transcendentals, were thereby defeated. But, Yeats seems to admit, the Magi themselves are our misrepresentation —ours or Plato's or Lycurgus'—of the supreme spiritual powers. Thought at its highest merges into spirit, Yeats being an idealist who assumes that spirit is the primary and ultimate reality. The descent into time means a splitting of this primary reality into those secondary half-realities opposed to each other whose mutual antagonism implies their mutual dependence. This metaphysical dialectic underlies much of Yeats's later poetry and is involved with his doctrine of reincarnation as well as with that of historical cycles. Neither of these two subsidiary doctrines follows necessarily from the dialectic but Yeats prefers to find them in its manifestations because they enforce the pattern so emphatically.

The discovery that real life is a play and that legend is always in the making encouraged Yeats to jettison his romantic bric-à-brac, to 'hurl helmets, crowns, and swords into the pit'. In *Responsibilities* he abdicates the throne of the twilight:

> I made my song a coat
> Covered with embroideries
> Out of old mythologies
> From heel to throat;
> But the fools caught it,
> Wore it in the world's eyes
> As though they'd wrought it.
> Song, let them take it,
> For there's more enterprise
> In walking naked.

He did not forgo embroideries altogether but from now on they are applied more sparingly and to better advantage.

His next book of lyrics, *The Wild Swans at Coole*, was published in 1919. In the meantime two very important things had happened to him—the Easter Rising in 1916 and his own marriage in 1917. Marriage for almost any artist must be something of a descent to earth, a renunciation of the fantasy-life; Yeats, who had indulged his fantasies more than most men, must have found, marrying when past fifty, the renunciation a great one. But what his wife took away with one hand she gave back with the other. Being a spiritualist medium it was she who introduced him to the extraordinary system he has described in *A Vision*, a system which at least provided a scaffolding for his poetry.

The Easter rising, as I wrote in the third chapter, gave Yeats a shock at once enlivening and horrifying. He had built an Ireland out of words and now he saw them translated into action. Many people had come to think, like the German engineer in Denis Johnston's *The Moon in the Yellow River*, that Ireland was a country 'where nothing ever happens'. The rising, when it happened, contradicted not only this belief but common sense. Its final result was still more unexpected, and proved—what Yeats always wished to have proved—that merely quantitative values are untrue and that a gesture, even if absurd, can conquer the machinery of logic. And yet this gesture frightened him, contrasting oddly no doubt with the gestures of the heroes of his dreams.

The Wild Swans at Coole is a similar assortment to *Responsibilities* but in each genre Yeats seems to have gained in power. Most noticeable are the direct poems about his own experiences—the people he really knew, the swans he really saw. According to the criteria of the Aesthetes such poetry has no advantage over the poetry which is purely fantastic or merely decorative. If however we admit that poetry cannot be assesse 1 in terms of itself, we have to grant that the poetry of direct experience, though not necessarily better than the other kind, has at least this advantage from the reader's point of view that it saves him certain preliminary adjustments and allows him to stand on the *facts* implied in the poem while he reacts to the poetry. It is a human weakness to look for facts but, when we are given them, they may cease to distract us. Humanly also each apparent remove from life tends to weaken our interest; in Homer we are less interested in what happens on the shield of Achilles than in what Achilles does with his shield. The model of the Parnassian poets is too static for most of us. A poet's life—whatever his model—overflows into his poetry but the reader also likes to feel the current. Thus Rilke wrote many poems about works of art because they were as real to him as people or physical experiences; the reader however prefers a work of art which is not 'about' a work of art because the double remove obscures the current from life. In Yeats's treatment of ancient Irish legend the current flowed often underground.

His poems about, or for, the friends whom he admired were something unusual in what he himself called the age of the satirists. T. S. Eliot's *Prufrock*, published in 1917, heralded the cynicism of a whole post-war decade. The title poem in that volume was a most delicate piece of self-analysis, self-satire, the portrait of an intellectual who finds nothing worth while, who makes not the great but the complete refusal (there is no greatness in it for he does not believe in what he refuses)—

'I am no prophet—and here's no great matter.'

The Portrait of a Lady, again, throws a cold, cruel light on the sort of woman whom Yeats regarded as a masterpiece of civilization. Eliot presents these characters in the manner of a modern novelist, showing up their makebelieve worlds and leaving them puppets. It is strange to turn to Yeats and find him admiring individual human beings, not questioning their individuality, not stressing their subservience to circumstance—

And that inquiring man John Synge comes next,
That dying chose the living world for text
And never could have rested in the tomb
But that, long travelling, he had come
Towards nightfall upon certain set apart
In a most desolate stony place,
Towards nightfall upon a race
Passionate and simple like his heart.

Yeats in his poems treated Synge or Major Robert Gregory in the same way that Shakespeare treated his tragic heroes and heroines; the hero is conceded full individuality, his Marxist conditioning is ignored. This means simplification, means—in Shakespeare and in Yeats—the elimination from the tragic figure of all psychology except some simple trends, it means the explanation of a man not by his daily life but by one or two great moments; thus we get the paradox that in Shakespeare death is so often the great moment of life and Cleopatra's suicide an assertion of the joy of life. This is what Yeats meant when he wrote in his old age that 'Hamlet and Lear are gay'. The characters are simplified into bold symbolical figures; all Synge's significance is for Yeats summed up in the line—'dying chose the living world for text'.

In keeping with this simplified world of more than life-size figures, of trends which are never merely approximate, is Yeats's peculiar grand manner. This is not, like that of Shakespeare or Milton, florid and re-dundant. It appears often to be governed by the principles of prose (it is significant that in his later years Yeats would often first write a poem in prose and then versify it). His language is not Wordsworth's 'language of ordinary men' but it has an insidious relation to it; Yeats, unlike Bridges, for instance, who also writes simply and directly but with a patent poeticality, bluffs the reader into giving him his attention. What he is say-ing is still often very peculiar, sometimes esoteric, but he says it with an air as if it were the whole man speaking; consequently the reader, who thinks of himself as a whole man too, approaches the poem with more sympathy than if he suspected it of being written merely with the fingertips (a suspicion easily aroused by much of Yeats's early work). In his rôle of the poet as whole man Yeats now uses all the tricks, combining them cunningly, not overdoing any one; reconciled to rhetoric he does not abandon the romantic picture; using mainly the words of prose he is always prepared—unlike the theoretical Wordsworthian—to slash in colour, to heighten. His most consistent weapon is rhythm. Rhythm and rhetoric in wedlock produce a poetry unique in his time and which is essentially, in his own word, athletic—

> Some burn damp faggots, others may consume
> The entire combustible world in one small room
> As though dried straw, and if we turn about
> The bare chimney is gone black out
> Because the work had finished in that flare.

This quotation is from his formal memorial poem for Lady Gregory's son, such formality being an infringement of his early creed. On the same subject he wrote a much shorter, much simpler poem, of equal excellence, *An Irish Airman Foresees his Death*. The moral of these pæans to Major Gregory seems to be the moral of Synge—

> Nor law, nor duty bade me fight,
> Nor public men, nor cheering crowds,
> A lonely impulse of delight
> Drove to this tumult in the clouds . . . .

The 'lonely impulse of delight' had been for the early Yeats the differentia of the artist; now he sees it in the world of instinctive creatures, especially in men of action, and is at times inclined to admit that in the artist this impulse is handicapped for the artist knows too much, thinks too much. Every so often now Yeats attacks knowledge—'I would be ignorant as the dawn'. Witness the poem in this book about Catullus, a type of the poet who lived fully and did not let his art destroy the integrity of his instincts. At the same time inevitably, the instinctive man, the sensual man, the sportsman, the adventurer, are turned by Yeats into myths. The Fisherman, in the poem of that name, is a product of wishful thinking, an intellectual's projection, a non-intellectual hero.

> The freckled man who goes
> To a grey place on a hill
> In grey Connemara clothes
> At dawn to cast his flies

is not to be found on any stream in Ireland—

> A man who does not exist,
> A man who is but a dream.

Yeats was too shrewd and too truculent not to know the nature of real-life anglers. The physical man is properly gregarious; the physical man of Yeats's dreams is, like his impulse of delight, essentially lonely. Thus the 'man of action' in the political sphere who came nearest his ideal was Parnell.

Yeats no longer held that 'Words alone are certain good,' nor yet that dreams alone are certain good; he had come to recognize the immanence of the dream in physical fact while maintaining that it is the dream which gives the fact its value. The sensualist proper abandons himself to flux whereas Yeats wanted pattern, continuity, every moment's experience referred to the Great Memory. Even in those later poems of his which show a franker and starker sensuality, lust is elevated into something other than itself, fulfilling the same function as the troubadourish affections of his youth. To admire an unattainable lady can give a poet a nucleus for his chance sensations and thoughts. To sleep with a woman can do the same, especially if, as in Yeats's case, the act of copulation is thought of not as a fleeting episode—a hailstone that falls and melts, but as one more link in a chain which stretches through history and binds the world together. In his introduction to the *Mandukya Upanishad* (1935) he praises the belief of certain Indians who seek the divine self in sexual union. A similar idea appears in D. H. Lawrence, for instance in his poem *Don Juan*—

> It is Isis the mystery
> Must be in love with me.

The Wild Swans at Coole contains several poems which are obscure because they imply an esoteric world system. This system Yeats was working out from 1917 on, partly through 'spirit messages' obtained by his wife when she was in a state of trance, partly through the folk-beliefs, the Indian and cabbalistic philosophy, which he had been exploring since his youth. Some of his new poems he wrote, according to himself, 'as a text for exposition'. The exposition is to be found in *A Vision*, first published in 1925. This book is the most ingenious, the most elaborate, and the most arid of his writings. He attached vast importance to it. Although from one angle a romantic individualist, even an anarchist, he had always had a desire to docket the universe. He did not fancy himself beating his wings in a void. He could say 'An aimless joy is a pure joy,' thinking of the tramps in Synge, but would then go further back and argue that there is a *point* in being aimless; fool, libertine, vagrant, are following the path of the stars. Being unable to accept the established religions or to understand the professional philosophers, he had begun with a vague predilection for psychic experiences which he could not co-ordinate and ended by producing a system which professed to be a blue print for reality but was actually a sop to his own conscience; hating scientists and rationalists he set out to be scientifically irrational. He succeeded in writing a book more unreadable than most orthodox philosophy. Here and there in the book are statements which give him away. He recounts that when his wife began transmitting the messages from the spirits, he made them an offer that he would spend the rest of his life 'explaining and piecing together those scattered sentences'. 'No,' was the answer, 'we have come to give you metaphors for poetry.' The spirits had taken the place of Standish O'Grady.

A.E.' s comment on *A Vision* was: 'It is of much more importance to us to have experience than to have philosophies.' But Yeats, although he paid lipservice to experience, was never one of those who write as the bird sings. Both his themes and his images were selected rather than spontaneous. His life was not a series of unexpected illuminations punctuating the irrelevant darkness of every day; it was rather a sustained and conscious effort to illuminate that darkness and make it relevant. He was no Rimbaud or Blake. His writing was not, in the narrower sense, 'inspired'; Inspiration for him was a sort of First Cause which had set him on a road where he had to look after himself. Hence his longing for rigid symbols. The French Symbolists wanted their symbols fluid because for them each experience was unique, the component parts of a complex of sensation and thought must not be separable from the whole and in a poem representing such a complex the individual words must only exist in and for the poem. To write by these standards a poet must have unusual physical sensitivity or a habit of genuinely mystical experience. Yeats, I think, had neither. As a poet he was as deliberate as Virgil. He wanted to dig out from history, or from what he called the Great Memory, a set of properties which would serve him as Virgil was served by the leavings of the Greeks. His desire for a creed and for poetry whose imagery, as well as ideas, is based on that creed, is in tune with his desire for schools of poetry. In spite of his Romantic genealogy he had a Roman liking for the poet in a formal niche; poets were to be members of a priesthood, handing down their mysteries to their successors, and conferring with one another when they wished to develop or modify their ritual.

The world of *A Vision* is determinist. Where D. H. Lawrence said 'Not I, not I, but the wind that blows through me,' Yeats would have said 'Not I but the stars,' meaning an inexorable cycle which binds the individual. It is not however the stars themselves which govern the individual, for Yeats writes approvingly in *A Vision*: 'Ptolemy must have added new weight to the conviction of Plotinus that the stars did not themselves affect human destiny but were pointers which enabled us to calculate the condition of the universe at any particular moment and therefore its effect on the individual life.' This concession does not mitigate his determinism. Freedom for Yeats, as for Engels, was a recognition of necessity—but not of economic necessity, which he considered a vulgarism. Yeats's necessity is even more rigorous than the Communist's. The Communist can die for his cause in the belief that he is part of an inevitable forward process. For Yeats the inevitable process is not forwards but round and round, like his favourite Indian symbol of eternity, a serpent with its tail in its mouth. Hence A.E.' s complaint about *A Vision*: 'I feel to follow in the wake of Yeats's mind is to surrender oneself to the idea of Fate and to part from the idea of Free Will. . . . Yeats would have me believe that a great wheel turns ceaselessly, and that I and all others drop into inevitable groove after groove.' Yeats however continued to blend into his system a sort of Berkeleian idealism, founded on the principle that things only exist in and for a perceiving mind. This mind, for Yeats, is not so much the mind of God as the super-mind of humanity of which all individual human minds are partial manifestations. Thus he wrote in his old age in *On the Boiler*: 'Vico was the first modern philosopher to discover in his own mind, and in the European past, all human destiny. "We can know nothing", he said, "that we have not made."' This conception is prevalent in his later poetry; for instance—

> Whatever flares upon the night
> Man's own resinous heart has fed

or, putting an extreme case,

> Man has created death.

This view is essentially monist and refuses to recognize any pure objectivity because such objectivity implies too great a separateness in the objects concerned. Thus Yeats will not admit that spiritualism is merely a means of obtaining information about a certain sphere of outside experience; spiritualism is an art, not a science: 'I consider it certain that every voice that speaks, every form that appears, whether to the medium's eyes and ears alone or to some one or two others or to all present . . . is first of all a secondary personality or dramatization created by, in, or through the medium' (from his introduction to *The Words upon the Windowpane*).

A large section of *A Vision* consists of a classification of human types. Yeats disregards psychology as much as he disregards economics. According to his friends he was a poor judge of men, could be deceived by charlatans. Lacking intuitive knowledge of people he declined also to accept the explanations offered by professional psychologists. As in the other sections of *A Vision* he wants the vigour of an *a priori* philosophy but he wants vigour without logic. He would have thought it an indignity that a man's life should be conditioned by a word of his nurse's overheard when he was in a pram. If life is to be conditioned by accidents, the accidents must be supernatural.[1]

Where he most nearly approaches psychology is in his basic principle that a man desires his opposite; he had observed this in himself—the contemplative man envying the life of action. This being so, a man's poetry, which is the expression of his desires, tends to be in a sense the contradiction of his life. He had written earlier, in *Per Amica Silentia Lunae*: 'When I think of any great poetical writer of the past . . . I comprehend, if I know the lineaments of his life, that the work is the man's flight from his entire horoscope, his blind struggle in the network of the stars.' In a sense then the poet as poet can escape up to a point from determinism. There is a curious parallel in Schopenhauer who makes art the only escape from the wheel of will-work (will, for Schopenhauer, implying necessity). Yeats goes on: 'We make out of the quarrel with others, rhetoric, out of the quarrel with ourselves, poetry.' This principle, of a man desiring his opposite, is worked out in detail in *A Vision*. For example, the man of *Phase III*, which is almost without intellect, . . . a phase of perfect bodily sanity, becomes a *persona* for poets of the opposite phase, *Phase XVII*, which Yeats calls the phase of the *Daimonic* man, exemplified by Shelley and Landor; such poets, themselves confused and violent persons harassed by their own intellects and desires, look to the man of *Phase III* for patterns of idyllic innocence.

This idea of the quarrel with ourselves, of the artist's search for his

---

[1] In a very late poem, however, *The Circus Animals' Desertion*, he seems to admit the Freudian conditionings of Art—

> Those masterful images because complete
> Grew in pure mind but out of what began?
> A mound of refuse or the sweepings of the street,
> Old kettles, old bottles, and a broken can . . .

opposite, appears in *The Wild Swans at Cook* in the poem *Ego Dominus Tuus*—

> By the help of an image
> I call to my own opposite, summon all
> That I have handled least, least looked upon.

The examples given here are Dante who, being himself lecherous and irresponsible, 'set his chisel to the hardest stone' and built a world upon Beatrice; and Keats whose 'art is happy, but who knows his mind?' The pursuit of one's opposite is also connected by Yeats with reincarnation. In a poem some ten years later he wrote:

> Old lovers yet may have
> All that time denied—
> Grave is heaped on grave
> That they be satisfied—
> Over the blackened earth
> The old troops parade,
> Birth is heaped on birth
> That such cannonade
> May thunder time away,
> Birth-hour and death-hour meet,
> Or, as great sages say,
> Men dance on deathless feet.

The poet is always quarrelling with himself, perhaps because he half remembers himself in a past life as having been some one different. The quarrel is partly, but only partly, resolved in his poetry. He knows, however, that, to put it vulgarly, there is still time for everything; this is not his only day.

How far he really believed these doctrines it is, as I have said already, difficult to say, but they make a good vehicle for that cosmic pride which is common among artists. The artist is proud to be of the world but it enrages him to know himself such a small part of it. This latter fact can be glozed over in various ways—for instance, by an idealist philosophy which makes man the centre of things and any one man the standard of the whole, or by a mysticism which allows the individual to overflow himself. Yeats, who liked a processional order and hierarchies, preferred neither to be all things at once, like the mystic, nor to be all things by proxy, like the philosopher. He preferred to think of history as an enormous kaleidoscope where each man in the changing but recurring patterns can play all the different rôles: only there must be no fusion, the pattern is always the pattern. *A Vision* with its seemingly arbitrary complexities is to be regarded as a diagram for something which Yeats knew to be unknowable; that he knew how any such diagram must be unjust to its concrete subject is proved by those poems which are professedly on the same theme; here what was static becomes dynamic, what was abstract concrete. That the diagram is merely ancillary to the poetry is admitted at the end of his introduction to *A Vision* (1928): 'Some will ask whether I believe in the actual existence of my circuits of sun and moon. . . . To such a question I can but answer that if sometimes, overwhelmed by miracle as all men must be when in the midst of it, I have taken such periods literally, my reason has soon recovered; and now that the system stands out clearly in my imagination I regard them as stylistic arrangements of experience comparable to the cubes in the drawing of Wyndham Lewis and the ovoids in the sculpture of Brancusi. They have helped me to hold in a single thought reality and justice.'

The Wild Swans at Coole was followed by *Michael Robartes and the Dancer* in 1921. *The Tower*, where his new poetry reached considerable greatness, did not follow till 1928 but some of the poems in it were written much earlier, some as early as 1919 and 1920. This was the period of the Troubles in Ireland; Yeats himself was troubled spiritually and physically.

His reaction to the Irish rebellion was, as I said, equivocal. The little poem, *Michael Robartes and the Dancer*, reasserts his old doctrine that the job of a beautiful woman is to be beautiful; he finds a paradox proving this in the art of Michelangelo who demonstrated

> How sinew that has been pulled tight,
> Or it may be loosened in repose,
> Can rule by supernatural right
> Yet be but sinew.

His cult of the body, so evident in the later books, always has this qualification—that the body rules by supernatural right. Going with this is his belief that opinions, especially political opinions, destroy a woman's integrity, involving the sale of her birthright. Thus in a poem here he pictures Constance Markievicz as a political prisoner playing in her cell with a seagull—

> Did she in touching that lone wing
> Recall the years before her mind

117

Became a bitter, an abstract thing,
Her thought some popular enmity:
Blind and leader of the blind
Drinking the foul ditch where they lie?

He writes similarly about Maud Gonne in the poem, *A prayer for my Daughter*:

An intellectual hatred is the worst,
So let her think opinions are accursed.
Have I not seen the loveliest woman born
Out of the mouth of Plenty's horn,
Because of her opinionated mind,
Barter that horn and every good
By quiet natures understood
For an old bellows full of angry wind?

The year before he wrote this both Maud Gonne and Constance Markie-vicz had been imprisoned in Holloway, but he had long before, when under the inspiration of Synge, expressed the same antipathy; he had written in 1909: 'Women, because the main event of their lives has been a giving themselves and giving birth, give all to an opinion as if it were some terrible stone doll.'

He could not deny, however, that every opinion, however deadening, implies an ideal and ideals are admitted to give life. This book contains three poems of homage to the martyrs of the 1916 rising. They are typical products of one who was not a man of action (Connolly had written popular propaganda poetry on the same principles which govern much working-class poetry in England to-day). The man of action must not qualify, must not have any doubts. Yeats qualifies continually. Even in the patriotic memorial poem, *Easter 1916*, he suggests:

Was it needless death after all?
For England may keep faith
For all that is done and said.
We know their dream; enough
To know they dreamed and are dead;
And what if excess of love
Bewildered them till they died? . . .

His attitude is still slightly patronizing and at the same time envious. He represents the rebels as ordinary enough men transformed by an ideal.

In 1909, when he met Thomas MacDonagh, he had described him as 'a man with some literary faculty which will probably come to nothing through lack of culture and encouragement. . . . In England this man would have become remarkable in some way, here he is being crushed by the mechanical logic and commonplace eloquence which give power to the most empty mind, because, being "something other than human life", they have no use for distinguished feeling or individual thought. I mean that within his own mind this mechanical thought is crushing as with an iron roller all that is organic' In the same year he lamented the lack of a poetic 'model of the nation' in the mind of the people and suggested that a higher nationalism could find such a model in the work of Lady Gregory, Synge, Lionel Johnson, and himself. In fact the nationalists dispensed almost entirely with these writers. It was men like the Gaelic enthusiast, Pearse, and the dockhand balladist, Connolly, who made the rising and Yeats admits—admiringly—that they were transformed by it. But their hearts, he goes on, were thereby turned to stone. It is the stone doll again; one suspects that he is admiring the ritual of idolaters whose sacrifices he thinks are perhaps unnecessary.

The same book contains a great prophetic poem, *The Second Coming*, which is based upon his cyclic philosophy of gyres and reincarnation but which, allowance being made for this parable convention, can be taken as a direct prophecy of imminent disaster. There have been many such poems since the Great War, by such different poets as D. H. Lawrence and W. H. Auden, but Yeats differs from the others in that he implies that even the coming anarchy has its place in a pattern; the strong movement of the verse is appropriate to a poet who does not really expect the triumph of flux—

> Turning and turning in the widening gyre
> The falcon cannot hear the falconer;
> Things fall apart; the centre cannot hold;
> Mere anarchy is loosed upon the world,
> The blood-dimmed tide is loosed, and everywhere
> The ceremony of innocence is drowned;
> The best lack all conviction, while the worst
> Are full of passionate intensity.

This has been taken by Mr Stephen Spender (in *The Destructive Element*) to refer to the coming of fascism. It is doubtful whether Yeats meant his prophecy so precisely, but 'the blood-dimmed tide' does represent that upsurge of instinctive violence which, other outlets being barred, finds a natural outlet in fascist mob-mania. That the rise of this tide is heralded with a certain relish is attributable to the fact that Yeats had a budding fascist inside himself. With a fatalism parallel to that of the Marxists he felt that the world was ripe for the rule of 'the worst'. Paradoxically, perhaps, he felt that this would give the individual freedom as prison has been known to give it to prisoners and the Roman Catholic Church to Catholics; he never made the idea of freedom contingent on democracy. In his introduction to *The Words upon the Windowpane* (1931) he justifies his own (perhaps sadistic, perhaps masochistic) determinism: 'though history is too short to change either the idea of progress or the eternal circuit into scientific fact, the eternal circuit may best suit our preoccupation with the soul's salvation, our individualism, our solitude.' Yet he himself—or the larger part of him—looked back longingly to an earlier 'phase of the moon', to 'the ceremony of innocence'. It is this ceremony which governs his *Prayer for my Daughter*.

It is interesting to compare *The Second Coming* with T. S. Eliot's crying in *The Waste Land*. Eliot, anti-Bolshevik like Yeats, is obsessed, as he admits in a note, with 'the present decay of eastern Europe', with the enervation of the general European tradition. But the passionate intensity of the worst holds no compensation for him. For him this is not merely a necessary turn of the wheel; it is the end, sheer dissolution—

> What is that sound high in the air
> Murmur of maternal lamentation
> Who are those hooded hordes swarming
> Over endless plains, stumbling in cracked earth
> Ringed by the flat horizon only
> What is the city over the mountains
> Cracks and reforms and bursts in the violet air
> Falling towers
> Jerusalem Athens Alexandria
> Vienna London. . . .

The mere difference in versification between Eliot and Yeats represents here an essential difference in attitude; for Eliot both hope and heroism have vanished with regular metric, with punctuation. When the Auden school appeared, who were nominally affiliated to Communism, they showed much superficial resemblance to Eliot but, below the surface, they were actually nearer to Yeats; their early poetry was most often gloomy but it was more the gloom of tragedy than of defeatism, of nihilism. Like Yeats they opposed to the contemporary chaos a code of values, a belief in system, and—behind their utterances of warning—a belief in life, in the dignity, courage, and stamina of the human animal. Falling towers— yes. But, they suggest (their Marxist premises leading in the same direction as Yeats's) when a tower falls something comes up in its place.

CHAPTER VII

The Ash of Poetry

Cela commençait par toute la rustrerie, voici que cela finit par des
anges de flamme et de glace.   RIMBAUD

The Tower, published in 1928, and The Winding Stair, published in
1933, can be taken together as the highest achievement of Yeats's genius.
When I first looked at The Tower soon after its publication I found it
frigid, unsympathetic. Being then dominated by the poetry of T. S. Eliot
I thought that the poets of the time should suit their manner to their world
—'These fragments I have shored against my ruins.' Yeats by these
standards was too mannered; like a figure from a fancy-dress party he
looked wrong in the daylight. A few years later I felt differently towards
him, perhaps because I had realized the Eliot's poetry itself is largely both
mannerism and fantasy and that the daylight of 'realism' is itself largely a
fiction.

Yeats, as I have mentioned, claimed that his poetry grew younger as he
grew older. His verse is now full of sinew and less dependent on facile
associations or facile mystery. In mind and body it is compact. The
thought taken from its context is esoteric and, indeed, unsound, but that
does not matter for it is perfectly fused into the poetry. Diction and rhythm
are happily wedded to their subject. Yeats was always a great trickster
with words, but now there is something more solid beneath the gilding.
Some of his old admirers lamented the passing of the Twilight, finding it
cold in this night of frozen stars. Many people demand from poetry nothing but dreams and music; the later Yeats, long tired of 'dreaming of
Brycelinde', outraged his readers with judgements, rhetoric, critical or
presumptuous statements.

A.E. says fittingly of The Winding Stair that it is 'the justification of the
poet's intellectual adventures into philosophy, mysticism, and symbolism,
into magic and spiritualism, and many ways of thought which most
people regard as by-ways which lead nowhither. . . . It is his habit of
continual intellectual adventure which has kept his poetry fresh. It is

possible the Muse will forsake us unless we keep the intellect athletic,[1] and she will reward us even if we forsake her and go mountain-climbing, if we return to her more athletic than when we left. . . .' Yeats's efflorescence in old age is perhaps unique in recent English poetry. We might compare Euripides who after a long life spent in struggling with and digesting new ideas, in gradually formulating a sceptical, rationalist attitude, had in his old age the elasticity to admit that there was a case for Dionysus; and we might perhaps contrast Wordsworth and Tennyson, both of whom were intellectually more gifted than Yeats, but who starting, like him, as poets of sentiment, failed in their old age to pass beyond their outgrown sentimental attitude.

When Yeats was an old man he was not, according to his friends, in the least tortured by fear of death and even welcomed jokes about his own. Being a vain man he was well pleased with himself and with his latter-day fame and even with the publicity of the Senate House. He also drew strength from two new kinds of adventuring—into the world of sense and sensuality on the one hand, and into the magical philosophical world of *A Vision* on the other. His poetry kept pace with these adventures and his poetic energy accumulated. It is generally admitted that in his last ten years he became more 'human'. He could now allow himself to be human for in theory he no longer divorced spirit from matter, soul from body, and in practice he was well enough established to go his own way—to be malicious or sensual or a Senator without having to apologize for his unpoetic behaviour. No longer thinking of himself, like Morris, as 'the idle singer of an empty day', he found with relish his days growing fuller and busier. Some ten years earlier he had written:

> But I grow old among dreams,
> A weather-worn, marble triton
> Among the streams.[2]

Now he is older but both braver and more active; he recognizes his age but he mocks and browbeats it.

Some of the poems in *The Tower* and *The Winding Stair* are rendered obscure by private symbols. Such symbolism is a common cause of

[1] 'Athletic': Yeats himself had used this word—see page 82—when renouncing *The Land of Heart's Desire*.

[2] Mr Eliot, who mildly deplores the triton, himself wrote when considerably younger:

> Why should the aged eagle stretch its wings?

obscurity in modern poetry; it is only necessary to mention Rilke. With the growing recognition of the Unconscious poets have ceased to censor images which seem to them significant but whose significance they cannot define. Thus T. S. Eliot[1] explains that an author's imagery 'comes from the whole of his sensitive life since early childhood. Why for all of us, out of all that we have heard, seen, felt, in a lifetime, do certain images recur, charged with emotion, rather than others? The song of one bird, the leap of one fish, at a particular place and time, the scent of one flower, an old woman on a German mountain path, six ruffians seen through an open window playing cards at night at a small French railway junction where there was a water mill: such memories may have symbolic value, but of what we cannot tell, for they come to represent the depths of feeling into which we cannot peer'. But though Eliot cannot tell their symbolic value, he uses the symbols; the six ruffians and the water mill appear in his poem *Journey of the Magi*. The extreme example of this kind of writing is Rimbaud who, by his systematic 'derangement of the senses', enabled himself to tap all the sources of the paradoxical world of forgotten memories. Yeats however used this kind of symbolism comparatively little; his symbols are mostly deliberate, sanctioned by literature or by his own peculiar philosophy, more comparable to Eliot's use of the figure 'Corio-lanus'. It is likely of course that such symbols also had a latent reference of which he was unaware; his sympathy with Shelley's caves (see page 75) could be otherwise explained by psychologists.[2]

Consciously, however, Yeats attempted a rigid symbolic algebra, thus distressing many readers such as Mr L. A. G. Strong, who wrote in 1932: 'You are a magical poet in that you have by ceaseless diligence and labour found a way of arranging concrete symbols that shall awake in us huge shadows of our wonder. . . . No one since Blake has made a few words signify so much.' But, he goes on, 'the belief in permanent symbols has been dangerous to you as an artist . . . it is difficult to handle precisely any universal symbol.' And it must be admitted that, whatever Yeats intended, he did not always handle his symbols precisely; not that this is necessarily to the bad if it is conceded that a poet may not himself know exactly what he is driving at (Coleridge held that a poem gives most

[1] T. S. Eliot: *The Use of Poetry and the Use of Criticism*, 1933.
[2] It would be tempting to regard Cathleen ni Houlihan, the Poor Old Woman, as a mother-image and so to refer much of Irish nationalism to a mother-fixation, even to an Oedipus complex, England representing the father. Any such study should also weigh the effect of the Virgin Mary upon Ireland.

pleasure when it is 'not perfectly understood' by the reader; it is at least possible that some poems are more effective because they were not perfectly understood by the poet himself). Yeats, who in *A Vision* had arranged the universe in pigeon holes, wished to treat his poetry similarly. But his poetry resisted him. The symbols, which were meant to retain their identity like the separate pieces of a mosaic, are always melting, fusing, becoming equivocal. The moon for example, as he himself had found in examining Shelley, can stand for so many different things. For Yeats indeed the moon, being the mistress of the world's dialectic, not only contains all opposites but can identify herself now with one set of opposites, now with another.

Let us examine the first poem in *The Tower, Sailing to Byzantium*. The first verse is a fine example of Yeats's maturest manner:

> That is no country for old men. The young
> In one anothers' arms, birds in the trees,
> —Those dying generations—at their song,
> The salmon-falls, the mackerel-crowded seas,
> Fish, flesh, or fowl, commend all summer long
> Whatever is begotten, born, and dies.
> Caught in that sensual music all neglect
> Monuments of unageing intellect.

He is expressing a wish, confirmed in the tide poem of *The Tower*—

> Now shall I make my soul,
> Compelling it to study
> In a learned school. . . .

—but denied in other poems of this period, to renounce 'that sensual music' for Byzantium which represents a world of Platonic Forms free of the flux of Becoming (a world which, being the world of the contemplative artist, is truly more Schopenhauer's than Plato's). Eternity means 'the *artifice* of eternity' [italics mine]. Yeats is still, though reluctantly, asserting the supremacy of art, art, as always for him, having a supernatural sanction. It is his old creed; as he puts it in another poem here,

> The abstract joy,
> The half-read wisdom of daemonic images,
> Suffice the ageing man as once the growing boy.

He   seems here to use the epithet 'abstract' in a mystical sense, to represent not any quick shorthand formula but something like what a mystic might mean when speaking of Absolute Blue. Byzantium is a world where Blue is always blue, unlike the physical world where a blue object changes with every change in the light.

In *Sailing to Byzantium* it is the soul that is allowed to have its say, the soul, which contemplates Being, being opposed to the self embroiled in Becoming. In a poem in *The Winding Stair* the dialectic is adjusted; in a dialogue between the two Self has the last word, choosing to forgo both Byzantium and the Oneness of religion and to face the sensual music—

> I am content to live it all again
> And yet again, if it be life to pitch
> Into the frog-spawn of a blind man's ditch,
> A blind man battering blind men. . . .

We cannot pin Yeats down on either side of this fence. His philosophy has become a philosophy of antinomies, a dialogue where himself does all the talking. Or perhaps, as A.E. suggests, it should not be called a philosophy: 'there is no definite philosophy, the units of the thought arising from the peculiar temperament or imagination of the poet rather than from any logical system he has thought out, and into which all must fit or be outcast. It is much better as it is, for the intuitions of a poetical nature are more exciting and profound than any logical philosophy of literature could be. We find what seem to be contradictions, but these are the natural reactions we find in ourselves from all our moods. . . . We have always to strike a balance between our own opposites and the wisest thinker is he who is conscious that our nature is made up of opposing elements, all necessary, and who will not be afraid of speaking now from one pole of his being and now from another.' We might add that the opposites are not always vocal in alternation, they may both be present at one and the same time; in some of Yeats's earlier poems, whether about Maud Gonne or about Ireland, there is apparent the tug between attraction and repulsion.

In *Sailing to Byzantium* the poet expressed a wish to go on singing but as a golden bird, that is, to be himself a work of art producing works of art, and so immortal. In later poems it is implied that this immortality may be a fallacy; there is a parallel in Hans Andersen's story of the Emperor and the Nightingale. In a poem in *The Winding Stair, Byzantium,* the same antithesis recurs; 'The unpurged images of day recede' and give place to the eternal (presumably purged) images of the night. The world of Becoming, of human beings, is a world of 'mire and blood', of impermanent and unsatisfying movement. Byzantium also has its movements but they are, to use Aristotle's terminology, *energeia* instead of *kinesis*; that is, movement for its own sake, self-contained, self-governing, absolute, eternal, instead of movement originated from without, a means to an end outside itself, contingent, relative, and doomed to cessation. Yeats admits that it is possible to cross from one world to the other; the 'blood-begotten spirits' can join the dance of the 'flames begotten of flame'. It may not be irrelevant here to mention a personal experience: in 1936, visiting the Prado several times, whenever I looked at a certain picture by El Greco, I remembered this phrase 'flames begotten of flame'; I am half inclined to agree with Mr Somerset Maugham that Greco was not so much a religious artist in the Christian sense, that is, genuinely inspired by his themes, as a mystic who translated his experiences into very peculiar relationships of forms.

In *Byzantium* the poet is once again to be a metal cock. Mr L. H. Daiken, editor of a book of Irish revolutionary verse, *Goodbye, Twilight*, must have been thinking of Yeats when he wrote: 'Bourgeois poets in Ireland have always heralded doomsday or kingdom come like the crowing of a clairvoyant cock.' But Yeats was doing something still more bourgeois than Mr Daiken suggests; he was crowing for a kingdom which, in defiance of all Marxist doctrines of progress, had come already, was, and ever shall be. A parallel to his conception of Being and Becoming can be found in another poet with an aristocratic bias, Rilke. For Rilke, Death, which corresponds to Plato's world of Forms, is the mainspring of Life, Yeats's world of 'blood and mire'. And Rilke, like Yeats, when his dialectic is considered as a whole, emphasizes the possibility, indeed the necessity, of *Verwandlung*, 'transformation'; that is, the process by which the finite can surmount itself. This process is extolled in the Ninth of the *Duino Elegies* —

> Hier ist des Säglichen Zeit, hier seine Heimat.

Man's gift of seeing is, paradoxically, for Rilke a bridge to the inner invisible world. Sense experience can surmount the senses. Articulation in speech instead of pinning things down can release them from the slavery of the moment. And the descent into time, which Rilke found so painful, can be justified as time's salvation. As he wrote in the *First Elegy* (Leishman and Spender's translation):

> Yes, the Springs had need of you. Many a star
> was waiting for you to espy it. Many a wave

would rise in the past towards you; or else, perhaps,
as you went by an open window, a violin
would be giving itself to some one. All this was a trust

Das   alles war Auftrag. Yeats expressed himself differently but he too was
ready to vindicate Here and Now as means of canalizing eternal truth.

For, in spite of his homage to Byzantium, he is by this time prepared to
flout the Magi, its proper inhabitants. In the dialogue between Self and
Soul, Self remains defiant, unabashed. In *Blood and the Moon* he blesses the
'bloody, arrogant power' of men of action and envies the shedders of
blood. The world of Becoming is a world of mire and stains whereas the
moon cannot suffer stain, but his allegiance to the moon is no longer
wholehearted; he has recognized the necessity of the descent into time, of
what later in *A Full Moon in March* he called 'desecration and the lover'
night'. 'Wisdom', he writes in *Blood and the Moon*

> is the property of the dead,
> A something incompatible with life; and power,
> Like everything that has the stain of blood,
> A property of the living. . . .

With this can be correlated certain more direct poems about himself—

> The intellect of man is forced to choose
> Perfection of the life or of the work. . . .

He himself had chosen the latter but he continued to envy those who
gambled on life. At other times, inconsistently, he appears not to oppose
the two but refer the poet to the world of action as his proper subject of
context, thus vindicating Self against Soul. 'I am content to live it all
again'—because, if I did not live it, I could not write about it So in
Vacillation there is another but shorter dialogue, this time between Soul
and Heart—

> *The Soul* Seek out reality, leave things that seem.
> *The Heart* What, be a singer born and lack a theme?
> *The Soul* Isaiah's coal, what more can man desire?
> *The Heart* Struck dumb in the simplicity of fire!
> *The Soul* Look on that fire, salvation walks within,
> *The Heart* What theme had Homer but original sin?

In an earlier section of *Vacillation* he gives an image, typically borrowed

from the *Mabinogion,* of his metaphysical wedding of opposites—a tree
that

> Is half all glittering flame and half all green
> Abounding foliage moistened with the dew;
> And half is half and yet is all the scene;
> And half and half consume what they renew. . . .

Similarly we find that among the *personae* of his later poems the sage who,
cutting himself off from life, has clambered to the high Platonic planes,
is complemented by the man or woman whose eyes are on the ground or
on the bed. Yeats's obsession during this period with the myth of Leda
also signifies his belief that, in defiance of Aristotle, history has its roots
in philosophy, that the eternal (Zeus) requires the temporal (Leda),
further (for the myth is complex) that the human being (Leda) requires
the animal (the swan), that God and Nature in fact require each other
and that the world will only make sense in terms of an incarnation.

One of the richest but more ambiguous of his symbols is the Tower
itself. This was, first, an actual tower near Coole in County Galway which
he had bought and repaired, partly in order to be near the home of the
Gregorys round which he had already built a mythology, partly because
he liked to translate his intellectual symbols into outward and visible signs
(compare the ancient sword given him by a Japanese friend which often
appears in these poems). He had, as he put it in an earlier poem in *The
Wild Swans at Coole* —

> chosen this place to live in
> Because, it may be, of the candle-light
> In the far tower where Milton's Platonist
> Sat late, or Shelley's visionary prince. . . .

Shelley's visionary prince was Prince Athanase whose

> soul had wedded Wisdom, and her dower
> Is love and justice, clothed in which he sate
> Apart from men, as in a lonely tower. . . .

but Yeats was also thinking of other passages in Shelley. On the paradise-
island in Epipsychidion there is a tower representing blissful escape from the
world. In *Julian and Maddalo* (a poem which in a sense looks forward to
Axël) the soul is compared to a madhouse belfry (an actual belfry on an
island at Venice pointed out to Shelley by Byron)—

> And like that black and dreary bell, the soul
> Hung in a heaven-illumined tower. . . .

Lastly there was the phrase from *Laon and Cythna* which especially haunted Yeats—'towers of thought's crowned powers'.

At the same time, as shown in the quotation above, Yeats was now fancying himself a kind of 'Platonist'—

> It seems that I must bid the Muse go pack,
> Choose Plato and Plotinus for a friend,
> Until imagination, ear and eye,
> Can be content with argument and deal
> In abstract things. . . .

At other moments, as in the title poem of *The Tower*, he attacks Plato and Plotinus. There is a commentary on this in *A Vision*: 'Aristotle and Plato end creative system—to die into the truth is still to die—and formula begins. Yet even the truth into which Plato dies is a form of death, for when he separates the Eternal Ideas from Nature and shows them self-sustained he prepared the Christian desert and the Stoic suicide.' The coming of system and the development of system into formula, were in Yeats's philosophy inevitable but he does not think of this process as progress; he regrets the 'passionate fragmentary man' of Homer. In his own system he wanted to avoid the split, the *chorismos*, in Plato's between the worlds of Being and Becoming, to vindicate passionate fragmentary men who do not see beyond their own horizon but are nevertheless the vehicle of dynamic eternal principles; they need those principles to motivate their actions *but the principles also need them* as a means to realization. Yeats naturally reacted against Plato's extreme intellectualism and therefore, as he explains in the introduction to *The Words upon the Window pane*, preferred Plotinus who was 'the first to establish as sole source the timeless individuality or daimon instead of the Platonic idea, to prefer Socrates to his thought. This timeless individuality contains archetypes of all possible existences whether of man or brute, and as it traverses its circle of allotted lives, now one, now another, prevails'.

The Tower therefore sometimes represents the heaven-aspirations of the solitary intellect, but these tend to merge with the different heaven-aspirations of the soul. The intellect articulates, dealing in 'abstract things', but the soul aims directly at the mystic One which swallows up and cancels speech and thought itself. Thus in *A Dialogue of Self and Soul* the

Soul summons to 'the winding ancient stair',[1] commanding:

> Fix every wandering thought upon
> That quarter where all thought is done:
> Who can distinguish darkness from the soul?

The tower here is 'emblematical of the night', as in another poem, *Symbols*,—

> A storm-beaten old watch-tower,
> A blind hermit rings the hour.

The Self counters with 'emblems of the day'—Sato's sword, representing war, and the embroidery in which it is wrapped, representing love; or, as *Symbols* repeats it more epigrammatically—

> Gold-sewn silk on the sword-blade,
> Beauty and fool together laid.

So far the Tower has been a symbol of retreat, of intellectual or spiritual asceticism. In *Blood and the Moon* on the other hand it becomes a symbol of the Self's assertiveness, of physical egotism, of the urges of earth and blood—

> A bloody, arrogant power
> Rose out of the race
> Uttering, mastering it,
> Rose like these walls from these
> Storm-beaten cottages. . . .

Yet almost immediately it turns into a parody of the modern nation—'half dead at the top'—while in the next section its winding stair becomes the pilgrim's progress of four typical eighteenth-century thinkers, whom Yeats now classes as typical Irishmen, Swift, Goldsmith, Berkeley, and Burke.

In some of his writings Yeats expresses envy of the believing Roman Catholic (he probably grudged Maud Gonne the ease of her conversion). His visible, localized symbols—the tower, the stream flowing underground from Ballylee to Coole, the swans in Coole Park—are to take the place of the crucifix standing by the crossroads. Wherever possible he equates these localized symbols with the images of other poets; the underground river has many precedents in Shelley, while the Swan, according

---

[1] Tower, stair, and sword have, of course, a different, but almost a classic significance for psychologists.

to Yeats himself, was unconsciously borrowed from Mr Sturge Moore. (In a note on *Calvary* he explains that certain birds, 'especially such lonely birds as the heron, hawk, eagle, and swan, are the natural symbols of subjectivity.' Hence his own use of 'the moon-crazed heron' in *Calvary* and of the earlier heron in *Responsibilities*. These bird-symbols however are, like the tower-symbol, ambiguous; thus the hawk is often equated with the hero Cuchulain who at first sight is a typical extravert — a view however which must be modified if we remember Yeats's view that the man of action is an artist, and his ideal of the *lonely* hero, Parnell.)

From 1924 to 1928 Yeats's chief reading was philosophy; he admits that he had read no philosophy before. He began with Berkeley, probably because he was an Irishman, and opposed him to the typical utilitarian Englishman, Locke, who in some way in Yeats's eyes was responsible for the Industrial Revolution —

> Locke sank into a swoon;
> The Garden died;
> God took the spinning-jenny
> Out of his side.

He objected to Locke's theory that there is 'Nothing in mind that has not come from sense,' preferring Henry More's doctrine that bees and birds learn from *Anima Mundi* how to make their combs and nests. Locke, according to him, had betrayed the flesh and blood of the world on the one hand and its spirituality on the other by denying 'innate ideas' and supposing that space was a thing existing in itself independently of its content. Then came Berkeley (I quote Yeats's own phrases) with his 'anarchy and scepticism', with his 'Irish hatred of abstraction', and 'fought the Salamis of the Irish intellect'.

Some of Yeats's poems at this time suggest, at first sight, that he had forgotten 'the mind of God' and was crediting Berkeley with solipsism —

> I mock Plotinus' thought
> And cry in Plato's teeth,
> Death and life were not
> Till man made up the whole,
> Made lock, stock and barrel
> Out of his bitter soul . . .

But it must be remembered that 'man' here does not mean any individual man inside the circle of time. Individual men are merely the recurring expressions of the *Anima Mundi*, a non-temporal, spiritual principle which is self-begetting. Individual men beget each other. Man-in-Himself (that is, as the *Anima Mundi* incarnate) is self-begotten. Bishop Berkeley no doubt would have considered this adaptation of his theory a blasphemy for it ignores the *chorismos* between Man and God; yet it is perhaps no more un-Christian than his own system where, when every one else is asleep, God is brought in in a machine to save the house of cards from collapsing.

Yeats did not approach any philosopher with an open mind (I have heard him argue with a professor of Greek that the Ionian physicists were really spiritualists). He wanted to find in Berkeley an anarchist—that is, an anarchist from the point of view of Dr Johnson who kicked the stone to refute him—who would make *percipi*, or rather *perdpere*, supreme over *esse*. Naturally he found what he was looking for—

God-appointed Berkeley, that proved all things a dream,
That this pragmatical preposterous pig of a world, its farrow that so solid seem,
Must vanish on the instant if the mind but change its theme.

Whose mind? we might ask. Yeats's answer, I suspect, would be equivocal. Berkeley, by bringing in God at the eleventh hour, preserved the *status quo*. Yeats, who was using the Berkeleian system to bolster up the supremacy of the contemplating artist, would have liked to identify creation with the artist's contemplative processes. When he writes 'Man has created death,' what he means in his heart of hearts, I suspect, is: 'I, W. B. Yeats, am old and soon shall die. But only because I choose to. Death is one of my inventions and I choose to try it out.'

During this period he once more found what he was looking for in conversations with an Indian monk, Shri Purohit Swami, in whom he discovered a typically Indian 'care for the spontaneity of the soul' as opposed to merely utilitarian virtues. The courtesy of the East which, according to Yeats, is substituted for the moral indignation of the West, is founded on 'the conviction that there are many lives'. (*See Mohini Chatterjee*, a poem in *The Winding Stair*.) A young Indian writer, who knew Swami, told me that, first, Swami is not typical of the spirituality of the East, and, secondly, that the East is not essentially spiritual; he seemed to think that Indian spirituality was a myth built up by retired, sentimental Anglo-Indians. Whether he was correct or not, his account would have horrified Yeats. An inner necessity made Yeats think of Indians as essentially spiritual, just as an inner necessity made him think of the Irish peasantry as in touch with the Ancient Gods. The two conceptions were related to each other; Irish country people, he writes in the introduction to *The Cat and the Moon*, had 'lived in Asia until the battle of the Boyne'.

It may seem paradoxical that, while engaged with the real or supposed mysticism of the East and the new spiritualism of the West, Yeats became at the same time a champion of the Eighteenth Century—'that one Irish century', in his own words, 'that escaped from darkness and confusion.' In maintaining this he was moving against the current of traditional Irish nationalism and of his own earlier principles. In defiance of the Gaelic League he found pre-eminent Irish heroes in Berkeley, an Anglican bishop, Goldsmith whose poetry was typically English and his *Vicar of Wakefield* more English still, Swift who detested the Irish, and Burke who had maintained that Ireland can never be politically independent because 'it is a struggle against nature'. In Yeats's eye, just as Berkeley was attacking smug English empiricism and Locke and the Industrial Revolution, so Burke was showing his Irish sense of spiritual values 'in his attack on mathematical democracy'. Burke, and the people he stood for, were, according to Yeats, generous but not from any equalitarian promptings—

> The people of Burke and of Grattan
> That gave, though free to refuse.

As for Swift, who had learned 'to hate his neighbour as himself', his generosity too was found to be undemocratic. And in all his four favourites Yeats found the gift of style; clarity and strength seem now more important than political integrity or enthusiasm. Even Mr Bernard Shaw takes the same nationalistic attitude towards Swift. 'When I say that I am an Irishman I mean that I was born in Ireland, and that my native language is the English of Swift and not the unspeakable jargon of the mid-nineteenth-century London newspapers.'

Living in the Irish Free State Yeats had come to realize more vividly the drawbacks of Catholic Ireland, such as the censorship, and his opinion of the old Protestant Ascendancy rose accordingly. He wrote in 1938: 'Berkeley, Swift, Burke, Grattan, Parnell, Augusta Gregory, Synge, Kevin O'Higgins, are the true Irish people and there is nothing too hard for such as these.' Though he had the grace to add: 'If the Catholic names are few history will soon fill the gap.' But his nostalgia for the eighteenth century was, in fact, coupled with a scepticism about the present; he thought there would be many gaps in Ireland for some time.

Thus he explains in *The Tragic Generation* that in the present historical phase a nation *qua* nation cannot arise out of heterogeneous circumstances: 'the dream of my early manhood, that a modern nation can return to Unity of Culture, is false; though it may be we can achieve it for some small circle of men and women, and there leave it till the moon bring round its century.'

His nostalgic poem *In Memory of Eva Gore-Booth and Con Markievicz*, reveals his feeling that the recent Irish revolutionaries had prostituted their own personalities. In general his political attitude now appears Machiavellian, as is shown in his poem *The Three Monuments*:

> And all the popular statesmen say
> That purity built up the State
> And after kept it from decay;
> Admonish us to cling to that
> And let all base ambition be,
> For intellect would make us proud
> And pride bring in impurity:
> The three old rascals laugh aloud.

His great political hero, as I have said, was Parnell, a proud and lonely, almost an inhuman figure, whose one notorious human error only added a tragic irony to his history—

> Through Jonathan Swift's dark grove he passed, and there
> Plucked bitter wisdom that enriched his blood.

It was Yeats's predilection for oligarchy, his belief that in politics vigour is more important than honesty and order than justice, that led him into his misguided support of that vulgar crusader, General O'Duffy, and allowed him to write, like any fascist suffering from mob-frenzy, 'a good strong cause and blows are delight.'

Of the more political poems of this period, *Meditations in Times of Civil War* was written in 1923. It begins with his customary homage to the Big House, with the regret that the society which founded such houses is vanishing. (As an old lady in Ireland put it to me sadly, 'Now there are no *neighbourhoods*.') Then he once more conceives a man looking for, and evolving his own opposite—

> Some violent bitter man, some powerful man,
> Called architect and artist, that they,

> Bitter and violent men, might rear in stone
> The sweetness that all longed for night and day,
> The gentleness none there had ever known . . .

He passes on to his own house, the Tower, and to the symbol of Sato's sword, then falls to thinking of his descendants (as has been said before, he was one of those Irishmen who take great pride in family). The next section presents a Republican soldier who had come to Thoor Ballylee during the Civil War and blown up a bridge, and this leads on to brooding on the Civil War itself—

> We had fed the heart on fantasies,
> The heart's grown brutal from the fare;
> More substance in our enmities
> Than in our love; O honey-bees,
> Come build in the empty house of the stare.

In the last section, written in old, nostalgic alexandrines, he moralizes on the sterility of hatred, symbolized by phantoms of cloud brawling in the air, and of merely logical or mechanical thinking, symbolized by brazen hawks—

> The innumerable clanging wings that have put out the moon.

Yet even here he does not seem happy in his own aloofness from the men of logic on the one hand and the fanatical men of action on the other—

> I turn away and shut the door, and on the stair
> Wonder how many times I could have proved my worth
> In something that all others understand arid share.

Still greater bitterness towards politics and towards political wars is shown in *Nineteen Hundred and Nineteen,* a poem written four years earlier, which also begins with a lament—'Many ingenious lovely things are gone'—and also ends with a vision representing futile violence. His description here of the Black and Tan terror is almost Shakespearean in tone—

> Now days are dragon-ridden, the nightmare
> Rides upon sleep: a drunken soldiery
> Can leave the mother, murdered at her door,
> To crawl in her own blood, and go scot-free;

The night can sweat with terror as before
We pieced our thoughts into philosophy,
And planned to bring the world under a rule,
Who are but weasels fighting in a hole.

Once more he extols the solitary soul, symbolized by a swan,—'The swan has leaped into the desolate heaven'—while he recognizes that such a soul deceives itself when it risks an entrance into the world of politics and action. Once more again he verges on cynicism in the section beginning *Come let us mock at the great*, but the section ends:

Mock mockers after that
That would not lift a hand maybe
To help good, wise or great
To bar that foul storm out, for we
Traffic in mockery.

This seems to be in keeping with his general dialectical system. Action and politics are degrading and belong to the multitude; lofty ideas and ideals belong to solitary souls; as, however, it is only such souls—as Parnell, for instance—who can fertilize the world of politics, it is their duty and their tragedy—but perhaps also their necessary fulfilment—to enter this brutalizing world. In so doing they are acting on a cosmic principle, for 'Eternity is in love with the productions of Time,' or, as *A Full Moon in March* puts it, to the question—

Why must those holy, haughty feet descend
From emblematic niches . .?

we must answer:

For desecration and the lover's night.

His attitude to politics must be correlated with his reactions to his old age. It is common for men who have been crusaders in their youth to turn comfort-loving cynics when they are old. But within Yeats, just as there was a grain of salt in his early enthusiasms—'Part of me looked on mischievous and mocking,'—so his latter-day bitterness, cynicism, disgust, weariness, are qualified, never final. He speaks, for instance, of 'the crime of death and birth' but recognizes that they are crimes that have to be committed and can at least be committed with an air. This qualification is more stressed in *The Winding Stair* than in *The Tower* where he was more obsessed by the 'absurdity' of 'decrepit age'. In those poems that are still later than *The Winding Stair* he actually seems to revel in his own old age, in the exercise of 'an old man's eagle mind'. This is borne out by what his friends say of his last years.

His title poem *Death in The Winding Stair* is typical. Having contrasted man, full of dread and hope, with the animals who are free from both, he builds up from his own pride in man and his belief in (literal or symbolical) reincarnation the astonishing statement:

> A great man in his pride
> Confronting murderous men
> Casts derision upon
> Supersession of breath;
> He knows death to the bone—
> Man has created death.

He may have fancied that he had a sanction for this in Berkeley. We can compare—and contrast—Rilke who made death not only a higher reality than Here and Now but the guiding principle of Here and Now; man therefore in dying is fulfilling himself. But Rilke is closer to Yeats when he writes: 'So many concepts of motion have had to be re-thought, that it will also come to be recognized, gradually, that what we call destiny comes out of people, not into them from outside. . . . The future is stationary . . . but we are living in infinite space.'

It is interesting to compare Yeats's poems about death with D. H. Lawrence's. The difference in form, Lawrence's being written in a free verse full of naive repetitions, is significant of a difference in outlook. Lawrence, though much younger, is more genuinely tired than Yeats. Where Yeats looks forward—or for the purpose of his poetry looks forward—without terror to a clearer existence where the wheel of time can be seen, so to speak, from above, Lawrence, who could not disentangle the purposes of poetry and life, looks forward to oblivion—and is terrified of the passage. Yet even Lawrence envisages some kind of immortality—

> the long and painful death
> that lies between the old self and the new.

Oblivion is the first necessity:

> if there were not an absolute, utter forgetting
> and a ceasing to know, a perfect ceasing to know
> and a silent, sheer cessation of all awareness
> how terrible life would be!

But after that—

> I am in the hands of the unknown God,
> he is breaking me down to his own oblivion
> to send me forth on a new morning, a new man.

Lawrence, like Yeats, was an advocate of the Unity of Being, but how differently he interprets that unity. For Lawrence it is the return of the drop to the ocean—

> I have always wanted to be as the flowers are
> so unhampered in their living and dying . . .

Yeats   did not feel this invalid's envy of flowers, perhaps because he lacked Lawrence's extraordinary physical sensitivity; he had an inhuman Greek admiration for humanity and even enjoyed seeing human beings *hamper* each other. This hampering was assumed to be part of the pattern of the play; for Yeats, as for Hegel, apparent frustration and failure are part of the eternal process and, if seen from outside—from some eternal auditorium—purposive. (Pope had maintained this long before in *An Essay on Man*.) The pity of it, of course, is that the frustrated and the men who fail cannot themselves see the logic—or the harmony—of their own misfortunes. But neither Yeats nor Hegel was much worried by pity.

CHAPTER VIII

Crazy Jane

If you were as old you would find it easy to get excited
W. B. YEATS

Yeats went on writing till his death in January 1939. The poems of his old age, in atonement for the *Weltschmerz* of his youth, all display one quality—zest. Many of these poems belong to a peculiar genre—something between epigram and nursery rhyme. Some of them look superficially like light verse, even like nonsense verse; on examination they will be found to carry in a concentrated form the same passion and the same ideas that he uttered elsewhere *ex cathedra*.

Lighter verse forms had of course been used before—habitually, for example, by Emily Dickinson—to carry a content which is primarily religious or moral or philosophic; A. E. Housman used his tripping measures to express the profoundest pessimism. In these poems of Yeats, however, the doctrine is disguised and all but lost in the concrete unity of the poem; whereas Emily Dickinson was primarily interested in her message, Yeats would have agreed with I. A. Richards that 'It is never what a poem says which matters, but what it *is*'. He treats his lyrics in the same way that he treated his plays—

> Heart mysteries there, and yet when all is said
> It was the dream itself enchanted me:
> Character isolated by a deed
> To engross the present and dominate memory.
> Players and painted stage took all my love
> And not those things that they were emblems of.

Similarly, in the Introduction to *The Cat and the Moon* he wrote: 'I had to bear in mind that I was among dreams and proverbs, that though I might discover what had been and might be again an abstract idea, no abstract idea must be present.' Long before in 1902 he had written about Spenser: 'though I love symbolism . . . I am for the most part bored by allegory.'

So, in these late little poems we can recognize the symbols and the *personae*, but it would be a mistake to labour their allegorical significance.

An Irish poet said to me lately 'Do poets of your school never *sing*?' His assumption was that a poet should sing rather than think. Yeats, who began as a lyric poet of the Victorian kind, passed through a period of hard, if perverse, thinking and then, returning to the lyric, produced something hard and crazy which has few parallels among the Victorians but has affinities with Shakespeare's songs and with Blake's *Songs of Innocence* and *Songs of Experience*. Yeats is nearer to Blake than Housman who quoted him as one of his models; Housman is hard too, but he suffers from a Latin varnish. In Blake we find an easy music, an apparent naïveté, and—inside his pictures—a kernel of intense thought or feeling. When the thought is ironic, the irony is enhanced by the simplicity of the form—

> Soon my Angel came again;
> I was armed, he came in vain;
> For the time of youth was fled,
> And grey hairs were on my head.

Blake's moral or metaphysical or political ideas can only express themselves in pictures—

> How the chimney-sweeper's cry
> Every blackening church appals;
> And the hapless soldier's sigh
> Runs in blood down palace walls.

He too verged upon allegory without losing grip of the concrete. *The Clod and the Pebble* and *A Poison Tree* are not poems 'with a moral' but they have a moral fused into them.

Yeats, according to himself, began writing his 'little mechanical songs' when he was in ill-health. They appeared in *The Tower* and *The Winding Stair* in the sections entitled *A Man Young and Old*, *A Woman Young and Old*, and—the best of them—in *Words for Music Perhaps*. Other little poems on the same model followed in *New Poems* and *Last Poems*, together with a number of ballads, a form in which his interest was now revived. All these poems, whether they are 'mechanical' or not, are characterized by their subtle music and their nervous imagery; they hardly ever have that pat, ready-made appearance so common in poems of this shape. This may be the place to comment on Yeats's 'ear'. One of his friends tells me that Yeats's extraordinary effective rhythmical variations were not intended, that he counted the syllables in the line and would, if he could, have preferred the stresses to fall *tum-ti-tum*. I find this hard to believe, but whatever Yeats's intention was, the result is far superior to *tum-ti-tum* versification. Possibly he was helped by his own lack of facility (the birth-pangs of his work were notorious). The poet who writes 'as the bird sings' is liable to write slackly and vulgarly; paradoxically it is Yeats, picking his way so painfully among words, who achieves the effect of bird-song. It is also possible that his verse is so musical because music proper was foreign to him. Thus Mr F. R. Higgins writes of him: 'That very lack of a honied musical ear may have offered verbal compensation. It saves him, at worst, from an easy jingle of softly flowing sounds; from the monotonous regularity of well-timed stresses. Indeed, his innocent offences against the laws of musical grammarians, his unconscious flaws in conventional melody, are responsible maybe for his curiously haunting harmonics in rhythm. These unexpected gaps staying his music, these hesitations in verbal sureness, dramatize his cadence. His carefully poised verse is tuned, as it were, slightly off the note.'

Yeats's role in these poems is that of the singing fool of his plays, whose philosophy can now be referred back to Synge's belief in natural vigour, to Yeats's own latterday sensuality, and to the dialectic of *A Vision* which recognizes brutality as a complement to beauty. The same moral appears again and again—

> Love has pitched his mansion in
> The place of excrement;
> For nothing can be sole or whole
> That has not been rent.

The hero of *A Full Moon in March* is a swineherd, harping on 'the dung of swine'; the moral, which I have quoted before, is the necessity of 'desecration'. The woman in *A Woman Young and Old* and Crazy Jane in *Words for Music Perhaps* have both experienced this desecration and both are proud of it. The light woman is being endowed by Yeats with some of the divinity that used to halo the virgin:

> If I make the lashes dark
> And the eyes more bright
> And the lips more scarlet,
> Or ask if all be right

From mirror after mirror,
No vanity's displayed:
I'm looking for the face I had
Before the world was made.

(italics mine.)

The singing fool affirms the spirituality of blood. Yeats, who now prefers to speak through the mouths of lunatics, lovers, and dancers, speaks thus through a figure called Tom the Lunatic:

Whatever stands in field or flood
Bird, beast, fish or man,
Mare or stallion, cock or hen,
Stands in God's unchanging eye
In all the vigour of its blood;
In that faith I live and die.

The pure intellect is distrusted as a liar because it relies upon diagrams; the simple-minded fool and the natural physical man remain in touch with the truth because their world remains concrete. Many years earlier Yeats had written in *Stories of Red Hanrahan*: 'a voice out of the Rose had told him how men would turn from the light of their own hearts, and bow down before outer order and outer fixity, and that then the light would cease, and none escape the curse except the foolish good man who could not think, and the passionate wicked man who would not.' The light of a man's own heart has now become for Yeats also the light of his sex. See his *Prayer for Old Age*:

God guard me from those thoughts men think
In the mind alone;
He that sings a lasting song
Thinks in a marrow-bone;

I pray—for fashion's word is out
And prayer comes round again—
That I may seem, though I die old,
A foolish, passionate man.

The natural man is now enthusiastically accepted—but with a super-natural reference. Love comes from outside time. Yeats's favourite myth of Leda is a key to his thought—the union of god and man but the god, it must be noticed, disguised as a creature with less than human intelligence. In *A Vision* Yeats puts this myth at the beginning of European history, making the annunciation to Leda parallel to the annunciation to Mary. Sexual union, like time itself, is a paradox; appearing to be contingent and relative it is really the vehicle of an Absolute—

> Eternity is passion, girl or boy
> Cry at the onset of their sexual joy
> 'For ever and for ever'; then awake
> *Ignorant what Dramatis Personae spake* . . .
>
> (italics mine.)

This idea that we know not what we do because it is not we who do it, can be paralleled in W. H. Auden—

> We are lived by powers we pretend to understand:
> They arrange our loves; it is they who direct at the end
> The enemy bullet, the sickness, or even our hand.

So much for Crazy Jane's philosophy. It is worth discussing the manner of its expression. Yeats's most obvious weapon is music but his left hand is also ready with rhetoric. The metaphorical aphorism which he had often employed in prose, is now slipped in to stiffen what had seemed a carefree, inconsequent jingle—

> The stallion Eternity
> Mounted the mare of Time.

We may again compare Blake, with his blending of epigram and symbolism; it is a great mistake to think of Blake, as Housman did, as a poet whose *meaning* is unimportant. Blake can be as incisive as Swift—

> The prince's robes and beggar's rags
> Are toadstools on the miser's bags.

Yeats's use of epigram, like Blake's, is a properly *poetic* one, giving one a shock of surprise which is physical even when the thought is abstract; for example—

> Out of Ireland have we come.
> Great hatred, little room,
> Maimed us at the start.

Or—

Bodily decrepitude is wisdom; young
We loved each other and were ignorant.

Or the whole of the epigrammatic poem entitled *The Four Ages of Man* which begins—

He with body waged a fight,
But body won, it walks upright,

and ends—

Now his wars on God begin;
At stroke of midnight God shall win.

Many of the poems of the Crazy Jane type have refrains. It is worth considering the principle of refrain at some length because refrain in the twentieth century was in many circles for a long time under taboo. We suspected it, firstly, as an easy form of conventional decoration (we could point to Morris and Rossetti) and, secondly, as a well-known prop for sentimentality (we could point to Alfred Noyes) or for any poetry where it is risky to examine the content critically (we could point to the patriotic poems of Kipling and Newbolt). Housman had used it very effectively, but even his effects we found suspiciously pat. The twentieth century suspected most poetic repetition-devices on the ground that repetition saves thinking or excuses the lack of thought, that by sheer hypnotic force it can persuade the reader to buy his twopence coloured when he would certainly reject the penny plain. If we are honest, however, we must admit that all poetry involves this danger of hypnosis. (We must remember too that hypnosis can be illuminating.) My generation was afraid of other forms of repetition as well as of refrain—of regular rhyme, for example, or of the 'red, red rose'. It is, however, something which, if expelled in one form, reappears in another; witness Whitman or Eliot or Pound or the free verse of D. H. Lawrence.

The truer objection to the *rigid* refrain is that it is facile. We can accept it without demur in border ballads, in folk songs and the songs of the Elizabethans, but it is argued that in the modern world it must seem an affectation like morris-dancing, and that, as the refrain holds up the thought, bringing you back always to where you started, it is only to be used by a poet of the folk-musician type whose thoughts and emotions— whose world, in fact—are essentially simple, even naïve. This argument is based on the assumption that a complex, unmusical world demands— in all cases—complex, unmusical poetry—an assumption which Yeats never made. In some of his early poems he had, with his eye on traditional folk-song, aimed at a simplicity which became an affectation, but in his later years, as we have seen, he ceased writing on *negative* principles, ceased expurgating himself. Much of his later verse is as complex as Eliot's, combining speculation and topicality. It is hard to see why, as a relief from this verse, he should have been forbidden to write his 'little mechanical songs'. The critic is apt to be more of a Procrustes towards the lyric than towards the drama; this is wrong. No one complains that Desdemona's willow song is a piece of affected pseudo-simplicity because Shakespeare himself was capable of more sophisticated thought and was not one of the folk.

It may be objected that this is a false analogy because a dramatist speaks in many different voices whereas the lyric poet must speak only as himself, his whole self, and nothing but himself. I would reply to such an objector: 'That is just where you are crazy. You are suffering from the bug-bear of the puritanical book reviewer who demands that any one poet should be all the time a specialist, confined to his own sphere (the reviewer allocates the sphere), and all the time self-consistent. If a poet has been labelled serious, he must never be frivolous. If the poet has been labelled "love-poet", he is taken to be declining if he shows the Latin quality of "salt". If on the other hand a satirist starts writing from the heart, he is guilty of sentimentality. But the poet should not bother with this Procrustes who has to live by his bed. "So I am to speak only as myself," the poet might say, "my whole self, and nothing but myself?" If you know what my whole self and my only self is, you know a lot more than I do. As far as I can make out, I not only have many different selves but I am often, as they say, not myself at all. Maybe it is just when I am not myself—when I am thrown out of gear by circumstances or emotion—that I feel like writing poetry. I suggest that you read what Keats wrote in a letter about the poet's personality. I suggest even that you should study your own personality and consider whether from day to day you have consistently the same moods or even the same ideas—that is, the same self; and that, even if you have, you should consider, firstly, whether it would be possible to convey *all* those moods and ideas in any one poem, and, secondly, whether any one mood or idea can valuably be expressed more than once with exactly the same emphasis.' My poet's arguments are, of course, sheer truisms, but are worth repeating because critics are such fools.

If Yeats had written nothing but his refrain poems he would not be the great poet he is; this would prove to the typical book-reviewer that he is less great for having written them. Crazy Jane's songs are admittedly slight when seen against *The Second Coming or Byzantium*. They are not however, so slight as they appear superficially—certainly not if we relate them to Yeats's work as a whole. (I am not of those who hold that each one poem in the world must be isolated and appreciated in a vacuum.)

We must distinguish between a poet's reasons for adopting a device and the use he makes of it. Yeats, I suspect, had a quite child-like liking for simple poetry of the folk type; in *The Oxford Book of Modern Verse* his selections from this kind of poetry are much better than his selections from more intellectual work. He still liked to think of poetry as coming from the people (a rural people, it is assumed) or at least being in form and content sympathetic to them. Though much of his own work was highly sophisticated, he found most contemporary sophisticated verse repugnant —though he tried hard to take an interest in it. The sort of poetry he instinctively liked was more easily found in Ireland, which is why some critics had occasion to complain that his *Oxford Book* was primarily an Irish anthology. Yeats, I think, genuinely envied Douglas Hyde his primitive gift of spontaneous creation.

Irish folk songs and street ballads are very often refrained, and it was these models most probably which excited Yeats's emulation. But his use of the refrain is peculiar. With him it is not merely a stock tag like Henley's 'Over the hills and far away,' nor is it a slogan as in the patriotic songs of Thomas Davis, nor is it merely a bar or two of music in between the verses. Some poets again use the refrain as a rhythmical norm for the whole; this is often so in popular narrative poetry where, the verses being allowed to sprawl in order to accommodate the story, the refrain is used to pull the procession back on to the road. A refrain again, when it means anything, tends to be simpler in meaning than the rest of the poem; it gives the reader or hearer relief. Yeats's use of it, therefore, is often in two respects unusual. First the music of his refrain is often less obvious or smooth than that of the verses themselves, being sometimes flat, sometimes halting, sometimes strongly counterpointed. Secondly, his refrains tend to have either an intellectual meaning which is subtle and concentrated, or a symbolist or nonsense meaning which hits the reader below the belt.

In his earliest poems he used the refrain traditionally and sentimentally and usually within the rhyme scheme, thus making its effect more pat— 'When I was a boy with never a crack in my heart'; a later example is in *The Withering of the Boughs*. A new type of refrain appeared in *Responsibilities*, for example 'Beggar to beggar cried, being frenzy-struck,' a line which is not in the least glib in meaning or sound and which, by its position in the stanza as the third line of four (but unrhyming), is structural The first good examples, however, of his refrains which are memorable because of three things combined—pertinence of statement, effect of surprise, and subtlety of rhythm—come from the little verse play *Calvary* (1920). Here the opening song, in four-stress lines, has as refrain (spoken by another voice) the line 'God has not died for the white heron', and the song at the end has the refrain 'God has not appeared to the birds'. It is unnecessary to labour the functional significance of this.

In *Words for Music Perhaps* Yeats employs the refrain frequently. The first poem, with two refrains in each verse, is a good example—

> The Bishop has a skin, God knows,
> Wrinkled like the foot of a goose,
> (*All find safety in the tomb.*)
> Nor can he hide in holy black
> The heron's hunch upon his back,
> But a birch-tree stood my Jack:
> *The solid man and the coxcomb.*

Notice the rhythmical contrast between the two refrains, the vowel music, the lingering close.

Often his refrains are statements—'Love is like the lion's tooth' or 'All things remain in God' or

> Like a long-legged fly upon the stream
> His mind moves upon silence.

In these three examples the refrain, far from being a mere decoration, is practically the focal point of the poem. Others are more traditional, especially when he is using the ballad form—

> The Colonel went out sailing

or

> Day-break and a candle-end

or

> The ghost of Roger Casement
> Is beating on the door.

Occasionally, as in the very early anthology piece, *The Stolen Child*, he uses as a refrain a little self contained stanza. The most surprising examples of this are in his three Marching Songs (professedly to the tune of O'*Don-nell Abu*), for exampl—

> 'Drown all the dogs,' said the fierce young woman,
> 'They killed my goose and a cat.
> Drown, drown in the water-butt,
> Drown all the dogs,' said the fierce young woman.

It was a pity that in a later version he changed this to:

> Be still, be still, what can be said?
> My father sang that song,
> But time amends old wrong,
> All that's finished, let it fade.

Yeats's latter-day trend towards ballad finds a parallel in W. H. Auden and implies a recognition of the fact that 'light' verse is not the logical contrary of serious verse. Thus Auden's poem about 'the six beggared cripples', which has affinities with Yeats and which on the face of it is merely high-spirited nonsense, carries both genuine feeling and serious 'criticism of life'. But in both Yeats and Auden there is a compromise; they do not go more than halfway towards the genuine ballad or street-song; the poet achieves some of the simplicity or the directness or the swing of the primitive form but he does not pretend away (as the early Yeats tried to) his own sophisticated self.

One or two of Yeats's quasi-ballads are excellent, in particular *The Three Bushes, Colonel Martin,* and *John Kinsella's Lament for Mary Moore.* Though these are deeply stamped with his own personality, they have the story-telling virtues of the ballad proper, not appearing forced or affected but getting the proper effect of carefree matter-of-factness—

> What remains to sing about
> But of the death he met
> Stretched under a doorway
> Somewhere off Henry Street,
> They that found him found upon
> The door above his head
> 'Here died the O'Rahilly
> R.I.P.' writ in blood.
> *How goes the weather?*

Yeats's later poetry contains an element that is very like humour. When he attempted humour in his plays he usually failed, but in private life he had not only wit and an Irish joy in hyperbole but a fine supply of animal spirits which made him relish blasphemy, indecency, and malicious personal gossip. His mastery of gossip is shown in those pages of *Dramatis Personae* where he gives back to George Moore more than he got from him in *Ave*. He also had a vein of nonsense satire which flowed, though not very successfully, into *The Player Queen* and *The Herne's Egg*.

The humour in his later poems seems to be a blend of whimsicality, bravado, canniness, and sadism; he had already shown signs of it in the hermits and beggars of *Responsibilities*. Sometimes it is directed against his habitual enemies—

> John Bull has stood for Parliament,
> A dog must have his day,
> The country thinks no end of him
> For he knows how to say
> At a beanfeast or a banquet,
> That all must hang their trust
> Upon the British Empire,
> Upon the Church of Christ.

This may remind us what fun Yeats had in the controversy over the bequest of the Lane pictures. The bad rhyme in the last line is worth noticing, a device which elsewhere has the effect of beautiful sombreness but which here is used to secure a palpable bathos.

At other times the humour comes out in cynical epigrams as in the couplet on Parnell:

> Parnell came down the road, he said to a cheering man:
> 'Ireland shall get her freedom and you still break stone.'

Sometimes it bubbles up with the extravagance of an Irish broadsheet—

> All know that all the dead in the world about that place are stuck
> And that should mother seek her son she'd have but little luck
> Because the fires of Purgatory have ate their shapes away;
> I swear to God I questioned them and all they had to say
> Was fol de rol de rolly O.

More often it takes the form of an impudent defiance of popularly accepted values or an impudent proclamation of anarchic individualism—

CRAZY JANE

A statesman is an easy man
He tells his lies by rote;
A journalist makes up his lies
And takes you by the throat;
So stay at home and drink your beer
And let the neighbours vote . . .

Or else there is a frank avowal of domineering sexuality—

Could Crazy Jane put off old age
And ranting time renew,
Could that old god rise up again
We'd drink a can or two,
And out and lay our leadership
On country and on town,
Throw likely couples into bed
And knock the others down.

It is typical of Yeats that, anxious for his dignity, he balances the vulgarity
of the last poem with a hieratic refrain: 'From mountain to mountain ride
the fierce horsemen.'

Sometimes he turns this mocking and impudent humour upon himself (he is known to have relished Dr Gogarty's jokes at his expense) or
upon things which he reveres. Thus in *High Talk* he burlesques the
intellectual, the man with lofty pretensions, the great man who, as he had
so often explained, has taken to the Mask—

Because piebald ponies, led bears, caged lions, make but poor shows,
Because children demand Daddy-long-legs upon his timber toes,
Because women in the upper stories demand a face at the pane,
That patching old heels they may shriek, I take to chisel and plane.
Malachi Stilt-Jack am I, whatever I learned has run wild
From collar to collar, from stilt to stilt, from father to child.

In the same spirit he speaks in another poem of his favourite mythological
philosophers and sages as 'all the golden codgers' and ends the poem,
like a small boy putting out his tongue at a schoolmaster, with nymphs
and satyrs who 'copulate in the foam'. Compare the song in *A Full Moon
in March*:

Should old Pythagoras fall in love
Little may he boast thereof.
What cares love for this or that?

Crazy Jane, I think, was dominant in the later Yeats, but he continued also to produce both philosophical poems in the grand manner and more direct poems on topical subjects. As an example of the latter one can take *Beautiful Lofty Things*, an assortment of memories about the 'Olympians' whom he has known—O'Leary, his father, Lady Gregory, and—

> Maud Gonne at Howth station waiting a train,
> Pallas Athene in that straight back and arrogant head.

The fifth 'Olympian' is Standish O'Grady—

> Standish O'Grady supporting himself between the tables
> Speaking to a drunken audience high nonsensical words.

There are two things to notice here; first, that Yeats, whose deepest feelings are involved in the subject, has now reached a stage where he can cast it into rough-riding alexandrines and mention trains; secondly, that he is now able to take trains and banal dinner-parties and exalt them into mythology. The second point can be borne out by a comparison with George Moore, who describes the same dinner with typical malice in *Ave*, patronizing the Dublin notabilities—'not an opera-hat among them'; Moore mentions the presence of O'Grady—'a grey, round-headed man' —but says nothing about his speech. Yeats also described it in prose: 'Towards the end of the evening, when everybody was more or less drunk, O'Grady spoke. He was very drunk, but neither his voice nor his manner showed it. I had never heard him speak, and at first he reminded me of Cardinal Manning. There was the same simplicity, the same gentleness. He stood between two tables, touching one or the other for support, and said in a low penetrating voice: "We have now a literary movement, it is not very important; it will be followed by a political movement, that will not be very important; then must come a military movement, that will be important indeed."' The contrast here between Moore and Yeats is typical. That public dinner may have been all Moore said it was but it was Yeats who after years could extract from it a 'beautiful lofty thing'.

Mr F. R. Higgins writes of Yeats: 'There were for him only two commingling states of verse. One, simple, bucolic, or rabelaisian, the other, intellectual, exotic, or visionary.' His intellectual or visionary poetry continued to appear till the end. There are, for example, the pontifical utterances of the hermit Ribh, a new *persona* added to the gallery which includes Michael Robartes and Owen Aherne, and who, as Yeats explains, 'is an imaginary critic of St Patrick. His Christianity, come perhaps from Egypt like much earlier Irish Christianity, echoes pre-Christian thought.' Ribh, who objects to the orthodox *'masculine* Trinity', is certainly pagan enough to agree with the later Yeats and expresses in one of his poems a kind of dialectic of hatred—

> Why should I seek for love or study it?
> It is of God and passes human wit;
> I study hatred with great diligence,
> For that's a passion in my own control,
> A sort of besom that can clear the soul
> Of everything that is not mind or sense.

This is a far cry from the belief of the early Yeats that the poetic intellect 'neither loves nor hates because it has done with Time'. It seems possible that the later Yeats, the man who nearly became a fascist, tended at times to think of hatred as creative, if not an end in itself. Compare Aherne's remark in *The Tables of the Law*: 'Jonathan Swift made a soul for the gentlemen of this city by hating his neighbour as himself.'

The doctrines implicit in these philosophical poems are the same that were summarized in the last chapter. *A Vision* is still the book of reference. The same philosophy of history that produced *The Second Coming* produced the verse play, *A Full Moon in March*, and the prose play, *The Resurrection* (1931). The beginning of the Christian era meant for Yeats the defeat of the Greek doctrine of measure and the flooding of the world by what a neo-Platonist philosopher called 'that fabulous, formless darkness'. This darkness, in Yeats's eyes, belonged to Asia where miracle is substituted for reason; Christ overthrew Phidias. Nearly two thousand years having passed since Christ, the world, as was suggested in *The Second Coming*, is ripe for some equally significant and violent revolution. In his last prose-writing, *On the Boiler*, he wrote: 'There are moments when I am certain that art must once again accept those Greek proportions which carry into plastic art the Pythagorean numbers, those faces which are divine because all there is empty and measured. Europe was not born when Greek galleys defeated the Persian hordes at Salamis, but when the Doric studios sent out those broad-backed marble statues against the multiform, vague, expressive Asiatic sea, they gave to the sexual instinct of Europe its goal, its fixed type.' These ideas are reflected in his poem *The Statues* which represents Pythagoras and Phidias as having defeated 'All Asiatic vague immensities,' and which suggests that, although our modern world is orderless, there are still certain living conceptions from the past—conceptions of ordered beauty or clearly motivated vigour—which can, as if they were incarnate persons, inspire even members of our present world to action:

> When Pearse summoned Cuchulain to his side
> What stalked through the Post Office?

His cyclical philosophy also appears in a late poem called *The Gyres*, which contains the puzzling line 'Empedocles has thrown all things about'. I suspect that what he most liked about Empedocles was the name (he was delighted to find it in a poem by Lady Dorothy Wellesley) but Empedocles' significance can be discovered from *A Vision* where he is coupled with Heraclitus as having thought 'that the universe had first one form and then its opposite in perpetual alternation'; the Heraclitean doctrine of creative conflict had always appealed to Yeats. The gyres reappear in *Under Ben Bulben*, Yeats's poetic last will and testament: 'Measurement began our might' with the Egyptians and Greeks; Michelangelo proved that the artist's ideal is *'profane* perfection of mankind' (italics mine); in the nineteenth century, however, 'confusion fell upon our thought.' The moral seems to be that, though this is a period of confusion, what Yeats calls elsewhere a *heterogeneous* period, the artist at least must not surrender to it, must still essay measurement and order.

He continued to mythologize his own experiences. In *The Municipal Gallery Revisited* he reviews his dead friends; in *The Circus Animals' Desertion* (the title has humour in it) he reviews his own past as a playwright. In *Hound Voice* he reverts to the old ideal of *The Fisherman, Galway Races*, and the poems about Major Robert Gregory. And the grand manner still rings true, as in the magnificent ending of *To a Friend*—

> What climbs the stair?
> Nothing that common women ponder on
> If you are worth my hope! Neither content
> Nor satisfied Conscience, but that great family
> Some ancient famous authors misrepresent,
> The Proud Furies each with her torch on high.

A study both of the rhythms and vocabulary of his writing in this kind will show how far behind he has left his Romantic mists.

His later poems, as I have said, all show a zest, and this zest is something distinct from Romatic enthusiasm, something more virile and less contaminated with self-pity. There is plenty of self in it but it takes the form not of a young man's escapism who hankers for the wings of a dove, but of an old man's self-confidence who thinks he has the wings of an eagle. His confession of faith is found in brief in *An Acre of Grass*, of which I quote the last two verses:

> Grant me an old man's frenzy.
> Myself must I remake
> Till I am Timon and Lear
> Or that William Blake
> Who beat upon the wall
> Till truth obeyed his call;
>
> A mind Michael Angelo knew
> That can pierce the clouds
> Or inspired by frenzy
> Shake the dead in their shrouds,
> Forgotten else by mankind
> An old man's eagle mind.

The key-word here is frenzy. Yeats has often mentioned Michelangelo as an artist who lifted bodily form to a supernatural plane. Of the other three Timon and Lear are chosen because in both of them passion was stronger than reason and in both of them disillusionment, anger, and hatred, which would seem to lead to nihilism, lead actually to a most articulate assertion of human vitality and individuality; Yeats's paradox still holds good, that tragedy implies the joy of life. As for Blake, who had written 'Everything that lives is holy', he remains what he had always been for Yeats, the champion of the soul, or rather of the humanly embodied soul, against mere abstract reason. In his contempt for those 'thoughts men think in the mind alone' Yeats at the age of seventy was still more ready than in his youth to approve Blake's vindication of both God and the natural man and his attack on the rationalists—

> Mock on, mock on, Voltaire, Rousseau,
> Mock on, mock on; 'tis all in vain;
> You throw the sand against the wind,
> And the wind blows it back again.

Colonel Lawrence wrote admiringly of Yeats's later work as 'the ash of poetry'. The metaphor is misleading but it suggests why this work made such an impression on the younger English poets of the time, who had been brought up on *The Waste Land*. The earlier Yeats had been too remote from them, subsisting on *fin de siècle* fantasies. But now he had broken into the twentieth century; *he had been through the fire*.

It must be admitted that there was a certain snobbery in our new admiration, a snobbery paralleled in Yeats's own remark: 'I too have tried to be modern.' The word 'modern' is always relative. What did Yeats's modernity—a quality which in his youth he had violently repudiated—consist in? As far as content goes (though it is always unsatisfactory to divorce content from form) Yeats was 'modern' in the following respects. He had widened his range; the poet of Niamh and Fand was now prepared to write a poem about a visit to a school kept by nuns. He was now dealing fairly directly with contemporary experience, some of it historical, some of it casual and personal. As well as admitting contemporary matter into his poetry, he was also admitting moral or philosophical problems. And he was expressing many more moods, not only the 'poetic' ones. He was writing at one moment as a cynic, at another as an orator, at another as a sensualist, at another as a speculative thinker. His poetry was sometimes critical, sometimes near to nonsense. The critical poetry pleased us because we demanded that a poet who had meddled with the world should admit it. The nonsense elements (to be discussed further in the next chapter) pleased us too, for nonsense poetry was the one nineteenth-century Romantic self-indulgence that had escaped stigmatization.[1] But on the whole it was Yeats's *dryness* and *hardness* that excited us. T. E. Hulme, in an essay on Romanticism and Classicism written some time before the Great War, prophesied an era of dry hard verse in reaction against the Romantic habit of 'flying up into the eternal gases'. Yeats, who had flown up there himself, had managed—on occasions, at least—to come down again. Therefore, we admired him.

We admired him too for his form. Eliot in 1921 had argued that, as the modern world is so complex, the poet must become 'more allusive, more indirect, in order to force, to dislocate if necessary, language into his meaning'. A chaotic world, that is, could only be dealt with by the methods of *The Waste Land*. Yeats went back to an earlier tradition and suggested by his example that, given a chaotic world, the poet is entitled, if he wishes,

---

[1] A.E. Housman, another spiritually lonely figure, enjoyed writing nonsense poetry in the narrow sense. Mr Edmund Wilson, in an article in *The Triple Thinkers*, groups Housman significantly with, among other English monastics, Lewis Carroll.

to eliminate some of the chaos, to select and systematize. Treatment of form and subject here went hand in hand. Yeats's formalizing activity began when he *thought* about the world; as he thought it into a regular pattern, he naturally cast his verse in regular patterns also. A parallel process can be observed in W. H. Auden, in whose system something like Groddeck's 'It' takes the place of Yeats's Anima Mundi.

In diction—and in syntax also—Yeats offered us a compromise with the Wordsworthian 'real language of men'. Wordsworth set out to use the words of common speech, though, as Coleridge pointed out, in theory he meant to exclude the common speech of the educated classes. Yeats took the words of common speech, including those of the educated, but he put a twist on them; as A.E. says, he *made them aristocratic*. A.E. writes elsewhere in a review of *The Winding Stair*: 'How can one convey any impression of that arrogant yet persuasive mentality, of that style where simplicity and bareness are suddenly varied by some image rich as a jewel and we are as delighted by the contrast as if we saw some lovely gem-bedight[1] queen walking along an undecorated corridor, noble only because of its proportion.'

Lastly, we found that Yeats appealed to the ear. It is absurd to think, as is often thought, that poets of my generation do not consider the ear. We had found music in *The Waste Land*, but we found music more to our purpose on the whole, in the later Yeats. His versification was traditional but at the same time fresh and adaptable. His few comparative innovations, such as the half rhyme, were good both because they were fresh and because sometimes—when giving effects of solemnity or melancholy—they were functional. And his very subtle rhythmical 'counterpointing', as Gerard Manley Hopkins would have called it, was more congenial to us than Hopkins's own 'sprung rhythm' (Hopkins in my opinion, was a 'special case', a very peculiar person, and so his versification is a special case too).

The direct influence of Yeats on the younger poets can best be shown by examples; it will be noticed that he affected not only their diction and metric but the stylization of their thoughts. Thus Auden wrote in an early poem:

[1] Yeats would have repudiated the epithet 'gem-bedight'; he himself wrote of A.E. as a prose-writer that he 'seems convinced that spiritual truth requires a dead language'. Yeats would not have agreed with the Preface to the Lyrical Ballads, but he himself is remarkable for avoidance of 'poetic diction' in the narrow sense; there is far more of it in A. E. Housman.

CRAZY JANE

> to-day
> I, crouching behind a sheep-pen, heard
> Travel across a sudden bird,
> Cry out against the storm, and found
> The year's arc a completed round
> And love's worn circuit re-begun.

Much   of Day Lewis's earlier work was similarly derivative. More recently a young American poet, Delmore Schwartz, can cast his philosophical ideas into almost pure Yeats:

> The ape and great Achilles,
> Heavy with their fate,
> Batter doors down, strike
> Small children at the gate,
> Driven by love to this,
> As knock-kneed Hegel said,
> To seek with a sword their peace,
> That the child may be taken away
> From the hurly-burly and fed.

Such writing was often too derivative but it proved that Yeats had developed an instrument suitable to his age.

It is still more interesting to notice the parallels with the later Yeats among older poets who had developed quite independently, for instance T. S. Eliot. Yeats's remarks about Eliot, in his Introduction to the *Oxford Book of Modern Verse* and elsewhere, show that he was deaf to Eliot's music and blind to his pictures (his comparison of Eliot with Manet shows that he was blind also to the colour of Manet). Yet Eliot has much in common with Yeats; both dislike intensely the flux of the modern world, both insist on the importance of tradition, both are anti-liberal. Eliot speaks in *After Strange Gods* of a world 'worm-eaten with liberalism' and in *The Rock* reviles his secular contemporaries—

> Turning from your vacancy to fevered enthusiasm
> For nation or race or what you call humanity;
> Though you forget the way to the Temple . . .

But he is perhaps more comparable to Yeats in his beautiful *Burnt Norton*, a melancholy metaphysical poem built upon the paradox of Time. Here too the anti-liberal tends towards determinism—

CRAZY JANE

The dance along the artery
The circulation of the lymph
Are figured in the drift of stars . . .

Eliot, like Yeats, refuses to conceive of time as mere succession. 'At the still point of the turning world' history can be concentrated, made intelligible, or, rather, intuitively apprehensible —

concentration
Without elimination, both a new world
And the old made explicit, understood
In the completion of its partial ecstasy,
The resolution of its partial horror.

I   do not suggest that the *thought in Burnt Norton* (not   that a thought in its purity ought to be abstracted from any poem) is very like the thought in the later poems of Yeats, but the impulse thus rationalized by Eliot in metaphysical terms is comparable to the impulse formulated by Yeats in his professed doctrines of Unity of Being, re-incarnation, and the rest. (I shall make a further comparison of Eliot and Yeats in Chapter X.)

Another poet of our time who seems independently to have moved along paths similar to Yeats's was Rilke, whose poetry, like Yeats's, continued to develop, to become steadily stronger, more complex, and more delicate. He too moved away from prettiness and sentimentality, from poetry inspired by other art, towards a more metaphysical and more personal utterance. Rilke, as compared with Yeats, had the profounder mind and the greater experience of suffering. Beside the plasticity of Rilke's   maturer thought, Yeats's would be dogmas and stock symbols look gimcrack. And where Rilke was what might be called a natural aesthete, Yeats was an aesthete by the book. Rilke again had had genuine mystical experiences where Yeats, in all probability, had only wished to have them. Consequently Rilke, who had had a precise and not fully translatable experience, purposely kept his language plastic when he tried to express it; Yeats, who only knew the original by hearsay or by what Plato called 'divination', produced a professed translation in which his own uncertainty was disguised by comparatively rigid symbols and *personae*. Compare Rilke's 'Angels' with Yeat's 'Magi'.

So much for their obvious differences; in what lies their affinity? Firstly, they both look inwards, both are primarily interested in their own relationships to a world which seems extraordinarily *other* to them. (Both of them were, according to ordinary standards, remote from ordinary humanity.) Thus Rilke wrote in a note: 'Art cannot be helpful through our trying to help and specially concerning ourselves with the distresses of others, but in so far as we can bear our own distresses more passionately, give, now and then, a perhaps clearer meaning to endurance, and develop for ourselves the means of expressing the suffering within us and its conquest more precisely and clearly than is possible to those who have to apply their powers to something else.' Compare Yeats's contrast, already quoted, of the discipline from within with the discipline from without.

Secondly, Rilke, though admitting that his theme is the invisible world, holds that the artist must find equivalents for this inner vision in the world of external *appearance*. His ideal, the 'Angel', represents the fusion of the two. I suspect that Yeats in his later poems was feeling for the same ideal —

> What can be shown?
> What true love be?
> All could be known or shown
> If Time were but gone.

Thirdly, Rilke, like Yeats, is obsessed and depressed by the opposition to this ideal of the world of Here and Now. But, like Yeats, he refuses to abdicate his position in Here and Now. Thus in the Ninth *Duino Elegy* he questions the strange paradox of life —

> oh why
> *have* to be human, and, shunning Destiny,
> long for destiny?

> warum dann
> Menschliches müssen — und, Schicksal vermeidend,
> sich sehnen nach Schicksal?

and   answers that our liability, as human beings, can be converted into an asset. This conversion is an artistic process. A thing becomes more than itself when it is given a name; from being relative it becomes absolute —

> *Here* is the time for the Tellable, *here* is its home.
> Speak and proclaim.

> Hier ist des Säglichen Zeit, hier seine Heimat.
> Sprich und bekenn.

In his own note on the meaning of the Elegies Rilke wrote: 'Nature, the things we move about among and use, are provisional and perishable; but, so long as we are here, they are our possession and our friendship, sharers in our trouble and gladness, just as they have been the confidants of our ancestors.' Our business is to comprehend fully the significance of these perishable things and so transform them. This transformation (*Verwandlung*) which takes the things of Here and Now into ourselves and digesting them, so to speak, translates them into the invisible, can be better effected if the particular things we meet are, through long acquaintance and tradition, congenial to us from the start—if they have been the confidants of our ancestors. Rilke laments that such things are now becoming rare: 'Now there come crowding over from America empty, indifferent things, pseudo-things, dummy-life. . . . A house, in the American understanding, an American apple or vine, has nothing in common with the house, the fruit, the grape into which the hope and meditation of our forefathers had entered. . . . The animated experienced things that share our lives are coming to an end and cannot be replaced.' Yeats would have endorsed this lament; his prose and verse are full of similar, nostalgic passages. Compare *A Prayer on Going into My House*:

> grant
> That I myself for portions of the year
> May handle nothing and set eyes on nothing
> But what the great and passionate have used
> Throughout so many varying centuries
> We take it for the norm . . .

Fourthly, Rilke related the conception of Love to the conception of Death: 'every one of our deepest raptures makes itself independent of duration and passage; indeed, they stand vertically upon the courses of life, just as death, too, stands vertically upon them; they have more in common with death than with all the aims and movements of our vitality. Only from the side of death (when death is not accepted as an extinction, but imagined as an altogether surpassing intensity), only from the side of death, I believe, is it possible to do justice to love.' Thus in the Ninth Elegy he addresses the Earth:

> I've now been unspeakably yours for ages and ages.
> You were always right, and your holiest inspiration's
> Death, that friendly Death.

Yeats too, in his later poems, denies that death is an extinction, and, what is more, sometimes writes as if death contained the formal cause that gives motive and significance to our actions in life—

> what disturbs our blood
> Is but its longing for the tomb.

Lastly, both Yeats and Rilke (and herein they are distinguished from Eliot) insist, for all their recognition of misery and bewilderment and frustration, that the mainspring of Art, and even of Life, is *joy*. In the Tenth *Duino Elegy* it is, by a basic paradox, the personified Lament that leads the newly dead youth to the source of Joy, *die Quelle der Freude*, and tells him:

> Bei den Menschen
> ist sie ein tragender Strom.

> Among men
> it's a carrying stream.

Yeats too held that a Lament can lead to the source of Joy and in a late poem makes the very true paradox that 'Hamlet and Lear are gay' (Cleopatra's suicide was after all an assertion of the values of life—and of the joy of life also). Where Rilke, in spite of his loneliness, has to admit that 'Hiersein ist herrlich', Yeats has progressed through a series of disappointments to the conclusion:

> Out of Cavern comes a voice
> And all it knows is that one word 'Rejoice'.

CHAPTER IX

Dramatist and Prose-Writer

Players and painted stage took all my love
And not those things that they were emblems of.

W. B. YEATS

I

There are many people better qualified than I am to assess Yeats's dramatic achievement, which cannot be isolated from the history of the Abbey Theatre. Yeats was the cause of drama in other men but he does not seem to me to have been properly a dramatist himself. I wish however briefly to examine his verse plays—and, still more briefly, his prose-writings—for the light they throw on his poetry in general. On the whole the poetry of the plays is less interesting, less powerful, and less original than that of the lyrics, but it is always the same man writing.

His plays can be divided into different groups, according to content or according to technique. A classification by content will place together the early tapestry-like fantasies—*The Countess Cathleen* (1892), *The Land of Heart's Desire* (1894), *Deirdre* (1907), *The Shadowy Waters* (verse version 1906, acting version 1911). Then there is the Cuchulain group which contains, in the order of the legend, At the Hawk's Well (1917), *The Green Helmet* (1910), *On Baile's Strand* (1904), *The Only Jealousy of Emer* (1919), and his very late little play, *The Death of Cuchulain*. Thirdly, there are those plays which are near to fable or which might be called parable-plays—*The Kings Threshold* (1904), *The Hourglass* (1914), *The Cat and the Moon* (1926), *Calvary* (1920), and *The Resurrection* (1931); also *A Full Moon in March* and the play which it superseded, *The King of the Great Clock Tower*. Certain plays stand alone, for instance *Cathleen ni Houlihan* (1902), a vivid piece of nationalist propaganda, and *The Words upon the Windowpane*, a study, through the medium of spiritualism, of the problems of Swift. If the plays are regrouped according to technique, all those will fall together which were deliberately constructed after the model of the Noh plays of Japan—*At the Hawk's Well, The Only*

Jealousy of Emer, The Dreaming of the Bones, Calvary, The Cat and the Moon; possibly also, though much less true to type, *The Resurrection*.

The most obvious characteristic of nearly all these plays is their remoteness from ordinary life; the characters either come from the world of legend or are simplified nursery-rhyme figures like the Lame Beggar and the Blind Beggar in *The Cat and the Moon*. Yeats deliberately avoided psychological characterization. The theme and the words were the two things all-important; like Eliot he held that poetry was the mother, not the handmaid, of drama. And this poetry, in reaction from Ibsen's 'leading article sort of poetry', was to be unsullied by psychology or contemporary problems, uncompromised with comedy. Thus in an essay on *The Theatre* (1899) he wrote: 'The theatre began in ritual, and it cannot come to its greatness again without recalling the words to their ancient sovereignty.' In an essay on *The Tragic Theatre* (1910), he argued that character is 'continuously present in comedy alone'; in most tragedy 'its place is taken by passions and motives'. (Aristotle also had subordinated character but subordinated it to plot; Yeats, who was an admirer of Maeterlinck, would subordinate it to the unity of feeling or of mood, or even to the words themselves). Shakespeare, according to Yeats, wrote tragi-comedy; 'in mainly tragic art,' he goes on, 'one distinguishes devices to exclude or lessen character' and he compares the experience of being in love where the lover must forget all his psychology. We may compare the advice that Michael Robartes gave to the Dancer:

> bear in mind your lover's wage
> Is what your looking-glass can show,
> And that he will turn green with rage
> At all that is not pictured there.

In *Estrangement* he gives a congenial account of what happens to a play when it is being written: 'At first, if it has psychological depth, there is a bundle of ideas, something that can be stated in philosophical terms; my *Countess Cathleen*, for instance, was once the moral question: may a soul sacrifice itself for a good end? but gradually philosophy is eliminated until at last the only philosophy audible, if there is even that, is the mere expression of one character or another. When it is completely life it seems to the hasty reader a mere story.' (A parallel can be found in Jean Cocteau with his emphasis on 'poème agi', his elimination of the message from the symbol.) Yeats disliked conversation plays where the thought is the important thing. 'Thought', he wrote in *On the Boiler*, 'is not more important than action,' and he went on to find a 'mediaeval man of action' in Hamlet. This is the Yeats of Crazy Jane speaking: 'Our bodies are nearer to our coherence because nearer to the "unconscious" than our thought.'

Wishing to eliminate character, moral discussions, circumstantial realism, he naturally made his plays short. He found the model he wanted in the Noh plays of Japan, a narrow traditional genre practised for the pleasure of a small aristocratic circle and without commercial machinery or naturalism. The Japanese players' movements, Yeats explained with approval in 1916, are founded on those of puppets: 'It is a child's play become the most noble poetry, and there is no observation of life, because the poet would set before us all those things which we feel and imagine in silence.' The Japanese dramatist, on this assumption, is emulating *in drama* what the French *Symbolistes* attempted in lyric. Yeats, in adopting this elusive aim, turned his back not only on Shakespeare and Ibsen but on Racine and the Greeks; there was observation of life, and also moral argumentation, in Aeschylus as well as in Euripides. Yeats with his distrust of observation, of rhetoric, of 'a leading article type of poetry', preferred the Japanese game of 'listening to incense'.

In the plays which he wrote on the Noh model, the cast in each case contains three musicians, 'their faces made up to resemble masks.' These musicians act as a chorus, singing or reciting verses at the beginning and the end of the play and sometimes also in the course of it. In *The Only Jealousy of Enter* one of the musicians performs the function of a Euripidean prologue and explains what the trouble is about. In *The Dreaming of the Bones* the players go round the stage once and the musician, like an Elizabethan stage placard, explains that they are going up a mountain. In *The Cat and the Moon* the musician speaks by proxy for an invisible saint (a device used more thoroughly in *A Full Moon in March*). The musicians therefore are used to dispense with naturalism and to give the whole proceedings an air of ritual. Unlike the Greek chorus they do not serve as a bridge between players and audience. Their function is primarily lyrical and they draw the characters of the play up with them on to a lyrical plane remote from the world of everyday conflicts. It is significant that when physical violence is to be represented in these plays, Yeats represents it in a stylized manner with dance-steps and drum-beats. Every device—and lack of device—is employed to keep the play inside a crystal. For instance, he admired and copied the Noh dramatists' habit of 'playing upon a single metaphor', a habit which, like the refrain in a lyric poem, is incantatory or ritualistic rather than dramatic. The most notable example in his own work is in Calvary where the musicians' introductory song depicts a symbolic heron standing in a moon-crazed trance. During the play we hear, first of 'a flute of bone Taken from a heron's thigh'; later there is a comparison of love to 'a drowned heron's feather'; later still Judas says that when he planned the betrayal

> There was no live thing near me but a heron
> So full of itself that it seemed terrified.

The last song of the musicians mentions, instead of the heron, other birds symbolic of self-contained loneliness—the sea-bird, the geier-eagle, the swan—and has for refrain what is an aphorism integral to the play—

> God has not appeared to the birds.

Browning made the lyric approximate to the drama; Yeats, working on Pater's principle that art is the removal of surplusage, makes the drama approximate to the lyric. One can apply to him the moral of a remark which he quotes from William Morris, who having compared two accounts of the battle of Clontarf, one written by a Norseman, the other by an Irishman, concluded that 'the Norseman had the dramatic temper, the Irishman the lyrical'. It is to be doubted whether Yeats could have appreciated the Icelandic sagas. His lack of the dramatic gift can be very easily seen from a comparison of his *Deirdre* with Synge's *Deirdre of the Sorrows*. Yeats's Deirdre is elegant and two-dimensional, the characters never come out at the audience, the verse is the blank verse of narrative; the whole is a charade. He himself could see in Synge's play the tug and thrust which were lacking in his own, and could see, no doubt, also that Synge's colloquial diction is not only more flexible but more heroic than his own—'Draw a little back with the squabbling of fools when I am broken up with misery.' It would be a confusion of cause and effect to attribute Yeats's failure as a dramatist to the inadequacy of his dialogue. His dialogue was inadequate because he lacked the dramatic sense.

Though undramatic, the verse of his plays has its virtues. It is fairly traditional but well controlled in its rhythms, straightforward in statement and not overburdened with decoration; it compares well with the dramatic verse of Tennyson which smacks very much of the study, as for example, Tennyson's

> Yea, and I
> Shall see the dewy kiss of dawn no more
> Make blush the maiden-white of our tall cliffs,

> Nor mark the sea-bird rouse himself and hover
> Above the windy ripple, and fill the sky
> With free sea-laughter . . .

Yeats's is preferable to this, though, like Tennyson's, it is too like his narrative verse, which, again like Tennyson's, is inferior to his lyric. Recent experiments in verse drama suggest that blank verse in the Elizabethan tradition is no longer practicable, though it may be one degree less unsuitable than the Morris-like couplets of Murray's translations from the Greek. There are at least greater possibilities in the resolved blank verse of Archibald MacLeish or T. S. Eliot. The verse of *The Family Reunion by* Eliot is verse written to be spoken and elastic enough to accommodate widely varied characters and to express a wide range of feelings from the trivial to the mystically intense; Eliot manages to retain what Yeats desired, a combination of simple statement with the feeling of ritual, Yeats in his last verse plays, *The Herne's Egg and Purgatory*, tried to break from the grooves of the traditional metric but, lacking experience, proved awkward in the absence of formal limits.

The same themes, as I have said, and the same *personae* appear in the plays as in the lyrics. Apart from the figures of Irish legend, Cuchulain in particular, we meet in the plays a set of what may be called fable-types, who correspond to the beggars and fools and hermits of the lyrics. There are the Fool and the Blind Man in *On Baile's Strand*, there are the Lame Beggar and the Blind Beggar in *The Cat and the Moon*, there is the Fool in *The Hour-glass*, and there are the Roman soldiers in *Calvary*. All these stand outside the world of heroism and are foils to it. The Roman soldiers attendant on the Crucifixion are typical with their hail-fellow-well-met nihilism—

Second Roman Soldier:

> Whatever happens is the best, we say,
> So that it's unexpected.

Third Roman Soldier:

> Had you sent
> A crier through the world you had not found
> More comfortable companions for a deathbed
> Than three old gamblers who have asked for nothing.

First Roman Soldier:

> They say you're good and that you made the world
> But it's no matter.

The Fool and the Blind Man in *On Baile's Strand*, one of the more attractive of the earlier plays, are a double foil to Cuchulain. Up to a point the Blind Man is type of the crafty sage while the Fool, as always, is the Fool pitting an indolent, arrogant faith against every one—

> When you were an acorn on the tree-top,
>   Then was I an eagle-cock;
> Now that you are a withered old block,
>   Still am I an eagle-cock.

But they are also walking metaphors as is shown by a remark of one of the characters while they are offstage—

> Life drifts between a fool and a blind man
> To the end, and nobody can know his end.

Thirdly, they are vehicles for Yeats's irony. Cuchulain at the end of the play, maddened by the discovery that he has killed his son, rushes into the sea. The fool tells the blind man that all the people are leaving their houses to watch Cuchulain drown. The play ends with a hypnotic repetition and a final deliberate bathos—

Fool:
   There, he is down! He is up again. He is going out in the deep water. There is a big wave. It has gone over him. I cannot see him now. He has killed kings and giants, but the waves have mastered him, the waves have mastered him!
Blind Man:
   Come here, Fool!
Fool:
   The waves have mastered him.
Blind Man:
   Come here.
Fool:
   The waves have mastered him.
Blind Man:
   Come here, I say.
Fool [coming towards him, but looking backwards towards the door]:
   What is it?

Blind Man:
> There will be nobody in the houses. Come this way; come quickly!
> the ovens will be full. We will put our hands into the ovens. [They go
> out.]

The *persona* of the Poet, sometimes wild, sometimes dignified, is used in *The Countess Cathleen*, *The King's Threshold*, *The Shadowy Waters*, and burlesqued in *The Player Queen*. Aleel in *The Countess Cathleen* is typical of the early Yeats, love-lorn, hysterical, and atavistically possessed by Aengus and the gods. Forgael with his harp in *The Shadowy Waters* is the poet *qua* magician, guided by man-headed birds to some supernatural world—

> and dreams,
> That have had dreams for father, live in us.

Seanchan in *The King's Threshold* caused some indignation when it was first produced in Dublin. A legendary court poet dying on hunger strike because of an infringement of his priveleges, he is a mouthpiece for Yeats's doctrine that the poet is a pillar of society. Yeats also speaks through Seanchan when he asserts that poetry in *all circumstances* is an affirmation of joy of life—

> And I would have all know that when all falls
> In ruin, poetry calls out in joy,
> Being the scattering hand, the bursting pod,
> The victim's joy among the holy flame,
> God's laughter at the shattering of the world.

The themes of his plays naturally reflect Yeats's dominant ideas and moods at the time of writing. Thus *The Land of Heart's Desire* (1894) is in key with early lyrics such as *The Man who Dreamed of Fairyland*. He wrote about this play to A.E. in 1904 that it has 'an exaggeration of sentiment and sentimental beauty which I have come to think unmanly. The popularity of *The Land of Heart's Desire* seems to me to come not from its merits but because of this weakness'. *Deirdre* (1907) is orientated not to the fairy world but to ancient Irish history. It is significant that Naoise and Deirdre themselves self-consciously echo the actions of an earlier pair of lovers, antiquity in itself being, in Yeats's eyes, a virtue; similarly Dectora in *The Shadowy* Waters finds herself keening a legendary lover who died a thousand years ago. *At the Hawk's Well* (1917) and *The Only Jealousy of Enter* (1919) show some of the bitterness of *Responsibilities*. *The Dreaming of the Bones* (1919) shows the influence of those speculations which had begun two years before and which were later formulated in *A Vision*; the 'dreaming back' of Dermot and Dervorgilla is true to the definition given in *A Vision*—'In the *Dreaming Back*, the Spirit is compelled to live over and over again the events that had most moved it.' The same idea inspired *Purgatory*, and most of the later plays in some form or other reflect Yeats's later esoteric philosophy; thus *The Resurrection* and *The Words upon the Windowpane* embody his philosophy of history.

Yeats said that he took to drama because he hankered for 'clean outline'. The plays as plays are little more than charades but his exercise in this genre undoubtedly had valuable effects upon his lyric. His very latest dramatic verse shows him breaking down the traditional metric and aiming, promisingly if not quite successfully, at a new tougher and starker kind of verse which might have rung true on the stage. I quote part of a speech from *Purgatory*:

> Great people lived and died in this house;
> Magistrates, colonels, members of Parliament,
> Captains and Governors, and long ago
> Men that had fought at Aughrim and the Boyne.
> Some that had gone on government work
> To London or to India, came home to die,
> Or came from London every spring
> To look at the May-blossom in the park.
> They had loved the trees that he cut down
> To pay what he had lost at cards
> Or spent on horses, drink and women;
> Had loved the house, had loved all
> The intricate passages of the house,
> But he killed the house; to kill a house
> Where great men grew up, married, died,
> I here declare a capital offence.

II

Yeats's prose has a closer relationship to his verse than is the case with some other poets—Meredith, for example, or Hardy or Kipling. The same principles governed his composition in verse and prose and he never treated prose as a mere means of getting somewhere quickly; sometimes, however, in his later days he wrote his 'poems' first in prose and then versified them. His prose has been much praised but such praise should be qualified. In a period where the best prose writing—with a few exceptions such as Joyce and Virginia Woolf—was bleakly functional, Yeats stood out as a writer with a style. While his prose style is fascinating, we should remember that he sometimes used it rather meretriciously to make the reader accept statements which were unsound or prejudiced or merely careless. Thus he was not a good literary critic (if criticism means the scientific assessment of literary values) but he passes himself off as one by his flair for aphorism and picturesque statement and his mastery of cadence. He began in prose as a follower of Pater who was also far from being a true critic. Later he pruned or purged his prose in the same way that he pruned or purged his verse but this new simplicity he used none the less to trick and beguile the reader. Often I get the impresssion, when reading his prose, that this is the art of revealing that one is concealing art.

In narrative fictional prose he suffered from lack of observation and lack of psychological insight. Consequently his very early short novel, *Sherman*, is flat and unconvincing, while his stories of peasants, fairies, heroes and sages, and the stories of Red Hanrahan, have a certain charm but are no more significant than the prose stories of Morris which he so much admired. Influenced by the aesthetes of the Nineties, he felt he should appeal to the eye, but as he had not a good eye, his visual effects are usually conventional or merely decorative. His earliest prose was rather clumsy but a little later it became too elaborate; the puppet figure Robartes complains in one of his poems—

> He wrote of me in that extravagant style
> He had learnt from Pater . . .

When however he started to make his verse less 'poetic', he applied the same canons to his prose and attained the same control over it, writing for the most part simply, sometimes almost naïvely, then flashing out an epigram or a sudden picture or a sonorous or glamorous name. The parallel here between his prose and verse is fairly close.

I have already quoted his adverse comment on A.E.' s prose. Remarks which he makes on George Moore's style, or lack of style, complement this. As Moore is still over-praised as a stylist, Yeats's indictment is salutary: 'Because Moore thought all drama should be about possible people set in their appropriate surroundings, because he was fundamentally a realist . . . he required many dull, numb words. [Yeats readily admits that such words are often necessary; he made artistic use of them himself!] But he put them in more often than not because he had no feeling for words in themselves, none of their historical associations. . . . Our worst quarrels, however, were when we tried to be poetical, to write in what he considered my style.' He goes on to say that their dramatic collaboration 'was unmixed misfortune for Moore, it set him upon a pursuit of style that made barren his later years. . . . Style was his growing obsession, he would point out all the errors of some silly experiment of mine, then copy it. It was from some such experiment that he learnt those long, flaccid, structureless sentences, "and, and, and". . . . Charm and rhythm had been denied him. Improvement makes straight roads, he pumice-stoned every surface because will had to do the work for nature.'

Yeats, like Moore, wrote prose with great difficulty but weighing it by the ear rather than by any theory, and following his instinctive taste in regard to words' associations; his simplicity is pregnant where Moore's is barren. His tricks are fairly easily discernible but they usually succeed. In his prose, as in much of his verse, there is often a crafty alternation of vagueness and precision (we can compare Shakespeare's habit of joining two words, the one general or abstract; often of Latin derivation, the other particular and physical, often Anglo-Saxon). Yeats is addicted to indefinite pronouns which excuse a bad memory or a lack of knowledge, and to parentheses which, like Pater's, beguile the reader from the point He often—deliberately—exhibits the charm of inconsequence. He sometimes makes a parade of learning which he did not possess and sometimes he lays on proper names with a palette knife; they had the same fascination for him that they had for Marlowe and Milton. Similarly, he is fond of historical analogies; in excusing his nationalist activities he writes: 'now I had found the happiness that Shelley found when he tied a pamphlet to a fire balloon.' He uses the same similes over and over again; he is fond of rhetorical questions and of self-quotation. He has a trick of writing a paragraph that is dry and matter of fact, the voice apparently of common sense, and then ending it off with an extravagant but beautifully phrased generalization; this is a confidence trick. In order, again, perhaps to seem natural, he leaves out conjunctions and other words conventional in formal prose; this makes the reader feel at home because he assumes— quite wrongly—that the author is speaking to him as the bird sings or as one man to another and not *ex cathedra*; this habit of asyndeton, which he became increasingly fond of, contributes to speed. His prose, to sum up, is the product of elaborate and sometimes underhand craftsmanship. But, whether he is writing in the short sentences of a casual notebook or inlaying his clauses like Pater, it is nearly always enjoyable.

I have already had occasion to quote many of his more critical sentences. His generalizations are excellent if they are taken not, as they were uttered, absolutely but are related to his own peculiar world-outlook. He is, in spite of his early professed hatred for rhetoric, a brilliant rhetorician—as when he writes to Lady Gregory: 'We must accept the baptism of the gutter.' His delight in pithy statement may have been inherited from his father, who was a vivid talker and whose own prose, both in content and manner, shows the same traits as his son's. Yeats's *Autobiographies* reveals other speakers and writers who inspired his emulation—Oscar Wilde, for instance, and the Irish orator, J. F. Taylor.

Many of his sentences have the ring of a remark which he quotes from Wilde: 'We Irish are too poetical to be poets; we are a nation of brilliant failures, but we are the greatest talkers since the Greeks.' One can also notice echoes of Taylor who, speaking at a Dublin debating society, found an analogy for the Irish nationalists in Moses at the court of Pharaoh: 'I see a man at the edge of the crowd; he is standing there, but he will not obey. Had he obeyed he would never have come down the mountain carrying in his arms the Tables of the Law in the language of the outlaw.'

A.E. declared himself disappointed by *Autobiographies*, finding in it too much anecdote and too little about Yeats's own soul; no one, A.E. argues, really can give useful information about any human being except himself. Without going so far as this we might agree that Yeats is not the man to look to for information about others. Yet, however unsound his judgement of men may have been, *Autobiographies* is a most valuable book. It is partial, partisan, full of gaps, and the presentation of its characters may be one-sided but the presentation is memorable. Take his picture of William Morris which stresses those paradoxes in Morris which fitted in with Yeats's scheme of human individuality:'a never idle man of great physical strength and extremely irascible—did he not fling a badly baked plum pudding through the window upon Christmas Day?—a man more joyous than any intellectual man of our world, he called himself "the idle singer of an empty day", created new forms of melancholy, and faint persons, like the knights and ladies of Burne-Jones, who are never, no not once in forty volumes, put out of temper. A blunderer who had said to the only unconverted man at a Socialist picnic in Dublin, to prove that equality came easy, "I was brought up a gentleman, and now, as you can see, associate with all sorts," and left wounds thereby that rankled after twenty years, a man of whom I have heard it said "He is always afraid that he is doing something wrong and generally is," he wrote long stories with apparently no other object than that his persons might show to one another, through situations of poignant difficulty, the most exquisite tact.'

Here, from the same book, is a typical passage of rhetorical generalizing: 'Without intellectual freedom there can be no agreement, and in Nationalist Dublin there was not—indeed there still is not—any society where a man is heard by the right ears, but never overheard by the wrong, and where he speaks his whole mind gaily, and is not the cautious husband of a part; where phantasy can play before matured into conviction; where life can shine and ring, and lack utility. Mere life lacking the protection of wealth or rank, or some beauty's privilege of caprice, cannot choose its company, taking up and dropping men merely because it likes, or dislikes, their manners and their looks, and in its stead opinion crushes and rends, and all is hatred and bitterness: wheel biting upon wheel, a roar of steel or iron tackle, a mill of argument grinding all things down to mediocrity.' From these two passages it will be seen that, if Yeats lacked the virtues of the novelist, he had the virtues of the anecdotist and the pamphleteer. And the anecdote and the pamphlet are as near to poetry as the novel is.

His later prose was largely occasional and he is at his best in *Dramatis Personae* where, in the carefree tones of a clubman, he pours out personal gossip and generalizations about life and art and Ireland with equal ease and point. W. H. Auden has said that the poet necessarily contains the journalist. One might think that Yeats was the last poet who could be accused of journalism, but this book shows brilliant journalistic qualities (qualities implicit also in his later poetry). Witness his rhetorical description of Moore: 'he was Milton's lion rising up, pawing out of the earth, but, unlike that lion, stuck halfway.' Moore also inspired him to many easy but incisive anecdotes; thus he begins a new section of the book with an insidious simplicity—'In the early autumn Zola died, asphyxiated by a charcoal stove. Innumerable paragraphs and leading articles made Moore jealous and angry; he hated his own past in Zola. He talked much to his friends on Saturday nights. "Anybody can get himself asphyxiated."'

On the Boiler, which contains his last prose writings, is impudently occasional. It shows the same salt and vigour and the same pig-headed extravagance that enliven his later poetry. One may not take very seriously what he says but, like other Irishmen on platforms or boilers, he is a joy to watch. Thus it is exhilarating to hear him attacking the later architectural accretions to Dublin's eighteenth-century Mansion House: 'All Catholic Ireland, as it was before the National University and a victory in the field had swept the penal laws out of its bones, swells out in that pretentious front. Old historic bricks and window panes obliterated or destroyed, its porch invented when England was elaborating the architecture and interior decoration of the Gin Palace, its sole fitting inhabitant that cringing firbolg Tom Moore cast by some ironmonger—bronze costs money—now standing on the other side of Trinity College near the urinal.' This is journalism but it is magnificent. And a little further on he makes a lazy but pungent comparison of the old type of politician with the new: 'My imagination sets up against him some typical elected man, emotional as a youthful chimpanzee, hot and vague, always disturbed, always hating something or other.'

His prose is punctuated with aphorisms; I quote a few at random—'In daily life one becomes rude the moment one grudges the clown his perpetual triumph.' 'In Christianity what was philosophy in Eastern Asia became life, biography, and drama.' 'Women . . . give all to an opinion as if it were some terrible stone doll.' 'Nobody running at full speed has either a head or a heart.' 'A good writer should be so simple that he has no faults, only sins.' As statements of fact few of these generalizations can be defended. A study of his prose will show that there, nearly as much as in his verse, he treated fact as soft putty. In his prose he appears to be dealing, more than in his verse, with everyday fact; in his later prose he became increasingly colloquial, introducing more and more unpoetioc properties, writing short, apparently careless sentences, sometimes using slang; on the face of it he was increasing in realism. This realism was partly, though not wholly, illusory. Yeats often maintained that the artis is concerned with the particular moment, the unique experience, the individual person—with the streaks on the tulip that failed to excite Dr Johnson. Actually he was a great generalizer. The same passion for neat ness that produced *A Vision* produces in his autobiographical writings a world that is too good to be true, a cartoon world drawn in a few hard black lines. Both his rhetoric and, more unexpectedly, his use of anecdote contribute to this. He tells you one story or quotes one remark from Mr A. and that fixes Mr A. in the pattern; the rest of him is discounted. At all costs Yeats avoided flux, the sphere of the realist proper.

A.E. indulged in the interesting speculation 'whether James Joyce was not made inevitable by W. B. Yeats, is not in a sense the poet's creation'; he was assuming, however, that Joyce is Yeats's opposite. If we are not so stupid as to lock Joyce up in the category of realists, we shall see that they have a good deal in common. Joyce, like Yeats, has a flair for incantation. He too began with a passion for elaborate style, in his earliest prose out-Patering Pater. His early poems were written in the Celtic twilight. And he too at times appears to accept Yeats's early dictum: 'Words alone are certain good.' The mystical obsession with words which dominates *Finnegan's Wake* had appeared long before, here and there, in the *Portrait of the Artist.*

Apart from his fanatical devotion to style, Joyce resembles Yeats in his habit of cranky speculation (see the discussion of Hamlet in *Ulysses*) and in his disproportionate eagerness to square the Here-and-Now with the There-and-Once (witness the fantastically elaborate Homeric analogy in *Ulysses* which has little more direct effect on the reader than the esoteric doctrines of *A Vision* have on the reader of *The Winding Stair*). The earlier Joyce, again, resembles the *later* Yeats in his debt to Dean Swift, in his habit of sharp juxtaposition of dissimilars. They both, moreover, rely largely for their vitality upon an Irish idiom, an Irish background, or Irish *personae*. They both, finally, are spoilt priests, aiming in their writings at a blend of mysticism and dogma which they could not achieve in their lives.

On a surface view—the view taken perhaps by A.E. — Yeats represents idealism and Joyce realism, Yeats belongs to the Land of the Ever Young and Joyce to the 'kips' of Dublin. Joyce indeed, like other younger Irish novelists, was in conscious reaction against the Celtic Twilight—not because he thought it refined but because he thought it vulgar. Yeats on the other hand, especially the later Yeats, cannot—as I hope I have shown—be reduced to mere twilight. The hard sense which he showed in balancing the accounts of the Abbey, the malicious wit which he showed in private conversation, the shrewdness, courage and rhetoric which he showed in public controversy, these are by no means unrepresented, though they may be disguised or transmuted, in his poetry. It is no more difficult to demolish the thesis that Joyce is primarily a realist. He is full of passages of sensuous or emotional romantic writing, from the conclusion of his short story, *The Dead,* to *Anna Livia Plurabelle,* and while large sections of *Ulysses* are an attempt at a more or less scientific definition of facts, other sections, such as the chapter of parodies and the Walpurgis-nacht in the brothel quarter, are an escape into fantasy; Joyce uses his huge erudition, his extraordinary ear, his Rabelaisian humour, to create a new world for himself. He differs from Yeats in his morality; the creator of Poldy Bloom remains a Catholic puritan, possessed by a sense of guilt and a fear of the flesh.

CHAPTER X

Some Comparisons

You were silly like us; your gift survived it all.

W. H. AUDEN

I have already, in Chapter IV, compared Yeats with A.E. Housman. Of a later generation than Housman's, the finest poets in England, in my opinion, were T. S. Eliot, Wilfred Owen, D. H. Lawrence, and, within narrower limits, Robert Graves. All of these poets, as having escaped the Nineties, inevitably approached their world from a different angle from Yeats but it was still in many respects the same world and Yeats for his part did not remain in the Nineties. Apart from the time difference, however, there was the important difference of local background. Yeats, with Ireland at his elbow, was in a position to ignore large tracts of industrialized, commercialized, and internationalized life and was not very sympathetic to those (and they are the majority) who were not in the same position. As a result of this he found Eliot essentially prosaic (he would not have recognized what G. K. Chesterton called 'the poetry of the beauty of refuse') and excluded Owen from his anthology on the ground that 'passive suffering is not a theme for poetry'. He preferred poets who compromised only up to a point with the contemporary world, who admitted, though with disgust or irritation, its existence, but attempted to spike its guns, not by a faith in humanity (a vulgar liberal error), but by an old-fashioned faith in the soul.

In both Dorothy Wellesley and W. J. Turner he found two things that he looked for—faith and an elegance of phrase. To me it seems that their phrasing, like their rhythms, is sometimes uncertain and that both these poets are hampered by some of those facile poeticisms (in particular, grammatical inversion) which Yeats himself outgrew. Among other astonishing statements, Yeats wrote in the Introduction to *The Oxford Book of Modern Verse* that 'but for a failure of talent' he would have been in the school of Turner and Dorothy Wellesley. What he meant by this, unless it was merely a compliment, it is hard to say. He may, feeling in his heart his own philosophical inadequacy, have suspected that their philosophy was better grounded than his own; both of them, in a loose sense, are philosophical poets and excited by their own speculations. Yet, though their thought may have much in common with Yeats's own, it burns in comparison low and fitfully; in any case poems are made with words rather than with 'thoughts'.

Dorothy Wellesley in a poem, *Fire*, spoke after Yeats's own heart when she argued that, once man loses immediate contact with the four elements, he has sold his birthright—

> The pride of science stands, and the final desolation.

Turner spoke after Yeats's own heart here and there in *The Seven Days of the Sun*; his lines—

> But now I know that the solar system and the
>   constellations of stars
> Are contained within me.
> Nothing exists outside me . . .

are, in thought, very like Yeats's lines—

> Whatever flames upon the night
> Man's own resinous heart has fed.

There is an affinity also in Turner's attitude to women, as when he describes mannequins—

> The violence of supernatural power
> Upon their faces,
> White orbits
> Of incalculable forces.

Yeats as a critic of poetry was partisan, as is patent from his anthology. He seems, for instance, to have preferred Edith Sitwell to Eliot because her surface qualities were more congenial to him; on a deeper analysis he might have found himself more properly aligned with Eliot.

Before comparing him with any other English poets I would go back to Ireland. From his early days he had expressed a hope that he might found a school of Irish poetry. Superficially he succeeded; since 1890 there has been a steady and remarkable output of poetry by Irishmen, most of which would never have appeared had it not been for his example or encouragement. A 'school', however, implies more than this. Most of his

Irish successors followed him in eschewing the industrial world and in writing their verses carefully, but they followed him in little else. There is rarely much meat on their poems. Yeats himself seems at times to have felt impatient with them, to have turned away towards English poets who were breaking his own rules.

Of the Irish poets of his own generation A.E. is by far the most interesting. It is difficult with A.E. to say wherein he influenced Yeats and wherein he was influenced by him; we know, however, that he anticipated Yeats in the exploration of Indian thought and possibly also in the cult of the ancient Irish gods. Yeats seems to have had only a moderate opinion of A.E. as a poet; he writes of him in *Autobiographies* that 'He wrote without premeditation or labour,' an account endorsed by A.E. himself in *Song and its Fountains* where he describes his own poems as being 'fashioned by an art with which the waking brain had but little to do'. Yeats, whose brain was nearly always awake, found this poetry too easily poetic—neither hard enough or sharp enough nor earthy enough. Envying A.E. his visions he deplored the fact that he neither criticized them nor formulated them precisely. He wrote in *Discoveries* (1906): 'If it be true that God is a circle whose centre is everywhere, the saint goes to the centre, the poet and artist to the ring where everything comes round again.' Perhaps the explanation of A.E.' s comparative failure as a poet was that he was sitting at the centre.

His poems, as Yeats suggests somewhere, contained much poetical commonplace. The music is sometimes insipid, sometimes even a little vulgar. There are, however, affinities to Yeats as in one of his better poems, *Dark Rapture*, which is written in alexandrines—

> Ah, did he climb, that man, nigher to heaven than I,
> Babbling inarticulately along the road
> His drunken chaotic rapture, lifting to the sky,
> His wild darkness, his hands, his voice, his heart that glowed;
> Gazing with intoxicated imagination on
> The dance the tireless fiery-footed watchers make
> Through unending ages on the blue, luminous lawn.

Both in diction, movement, and the final image, this is reminiscent of Yeats but Yeats would have written 'nearer' instead of 'nigher' and would not have allowed the drunkard to lift so many things to the sky at once. Yeats compared A.E. with George Herbert, but a comparison of their poetry will show that Yeats was probably also right when he wrote that it would have been better for A.E. 'had he, instead of meeting as an impressionable youth with our modern subjective romanticism, met with some form of traditional belief' which 'would have kept him a religious teacher'. Herbert was fortunate enough to have a traditional belief which, itself precise, precluded romantic impreciseness in his writing.

Of the other Irish poets whose work first appeared in print in the late Eighteen Eighties or early Nineties, Todhunter and Rolleston wrote one memorable poem each, Katherine Tynan's work was pretty but very slight, William Larminie, who experimented in assonance, is now hardly readable. A later generation, less conscious of being pioneers, wrote more naturally, looking less to the idealized Ireland of the past than to the everyday Ireland of the present though they could only treat the latter in miniature. Seumas O'Sullivan, Padraic Colum and Joseph Campbell did not copy the broad sweep of Yeats and their poetry lacks brainwork but they succeeded better than Yeats himself in some of the objects which he had proposed for Irish poets. Thus Colum and Campbell, as did Douglas Hyde in Gaelic, expressed much more truly than Yeats does the folk elements of Ireland. Campbell's short poems, fairly free from literary consciousness, are a matter of delicate music and vivid, simple pictures—

> The ploughman ploughs the fallow—
> Smoking lines
> Of sunset earth
> Against a clump of pines.
>
> A flock of rooks and seagulls
> Wheel and cry
> About him, making music
> In the sky.
>
> Wings black and silver
> In a sky of grey,
> Like shadows folding
> Between night and day.

Both Colum and Campbell can at times be accused of facile prettiness and their refinement of the folk manner became insipid when overworked. Unfortunately, it was the only manner they could use with much success; Colum becomes pompous when he forsakes the folk as in *Fuchsia Hedges in Connacht*. Similarly, O'Sullivan and a younger poet, Frank O'Connor, when they try the grand manner, fall into clichés.

Whatever the deficiencies of these poets, Yeats's insistence on craftsman-ship had borne its fruit and the slapdash verse of 'Young Ireland' was gone apparently for ever. It was no longer assumed that not to take trouble is a Celtic privilege. The modern example of Yeats was supported here by the examples of the ancient Irish poets who were now more familiar to the public. Sigerson in his Introduction to *Bards of the Gael and Gall* had explained in detail the subtleties of ancient Irish verse—the use of assonance, alliteration, and internal rhymes—and had even claimed that these inspired the intricate schemes of mediaeval Latin verse, instancing the Latin poems of the Irish saint Columbanus. This early Irish poetry appears to have combined two virtues usually divorced, to have been unusually elaborate in pattern and at the same time to have been direct and clear-cut. Thomas MacDonagh in *Literature in Ireland* (1916) maintains that even its rhythms remained natural, that the intonations were those of prose or ordinary speech, and that grammatical inversions were avoided. It is interesting that Yeats, who did not know Irish, should have, working independently, achieved the same blend of naturalness and subtlety.

MacDonagh in the same book gives a very interesting account of Anglo-Irish poetry as a genre distinct from English poetry, assessing in particular the 'effect of Irish rhythm, itself influenced by Irish music, on the rhythms of Anglo-Irish poetry'. Maintaining that in Ireland, as contrasted with England, there is a more uniform stress over the syllables, a 'less pronounced hammering of the syllables', he goes on to argue that Yeats owes the 'peculiar musical quality of his early verse to that Irish chant, which at once saves Irish speech from too definite a stress and from an utterance too monstrous and harsh'. (In illustration of his point I would suggest again a comparison of Housman's poem, *When I was one-and-twenty*, with Yeats's *Down by the Salley Gardens*.) MacDonagh finds the same rhythmical effects in Dowson's *Cynara* where the influence, as he admits, is French. If this is granted, it means that Yeats in his youth was exposed to two distinct technical influences tending in the same direction.

It is probable that the fresh output of original Gaelic verse during the last fifty years has had effects both on the manner and the matter of much recent poetry written by Irishmen in England. (Mr F. R. Higgins main-tains that Yeats himself benefited from indirect contact with the Gaelic.) Technically, the Gaelic influence has encouraged a music of hovering stresses combined with a careful patterning of vowels and consonants. As far as matter goes, it seems to have kept the range of Irish poetry unduly narrow, imposing upon educated authors the outlook of the Gaedhal

Tacht. The great pioneer in modern Gaelic poetry was Douglas Hyde of whom Yeats wrote: 'He had the folk mind as no modern man had it. . . . He wrote in joy and at great speed because emotion brought the appropriate word. Nothing in that language of his was abstract, nothing worn out; he need not, as must the writer of some language exhausted by modern civilization, reject word after word, cadence after cadence; he had escaped our perpetual, painful, purification.' Yeats envied him, but knew that for himself he must continue purifying. Others were not so wise.

Of Synge's importance to Yeats and to Ireland and to poetry, I have written already. A younger generation than that of Synge or Stephens or O'Sullivan has put some of Synge's theory into practice; poets like F. R. Higgins and Frank O'Connor have realized that it is more important for their poetry to be strong than to be pretty. Higgins's verse, which to start with was conventionally pretty, has steadily acquired more body and its elegances have become more subtle—

> Here, drowned within their dewy depths of June,
> The fields, for graziers, gather evening silver;
> And while each isle becomes a bush in tune,
> The Boyne flows into airy stillness.

An excellent craftsman, he owes his technique partly to Gaelic sources (as for example his habit of assonance) and partly to Yeats from whom he has also accepted much poetic doctrine. Other Irish poets of his generation such as E. R. Dodds and Austin Clarke are equally careful craftsmen; Yeats had stamped upon the literary circles of Dublin at least a respect for words.

There is, however, a group of young poets in Ireland who have abandoned Yeats and whose mainly revolutionary verses have been assembled by Mr Leslie H. Daiken in an anthology called *Goodbye, Twilight*. The revolutionary proletarian poet works on the maxim of Marx, 'Philosophers have previously offered various interpretations of the world. Our business is to change it,' substituting the word 'poets' for 'philosophers'. Of recent years there has been much discussion about poetry and propaganda and the question merits discussion, for if the poets of *Goodbye, Twilight* are right, Yeats took all his trouble for nothing.

More often than not the opponents and defenders of propaganda poetry have no common ground. The opponent will say: 'If you consider the evidence of the world's poetry you cannot maintain that it is essentially propaganda.' The defender will merely deny that the evidence is any longer cogent; times have changed. Sometimes the defender is less wise and goes further, arguing, firstly, that good poetry has *always* been propaganda, and, secondly, that poetry can only be judged by its success as propaganda. Many communists argue that poetry is only of value as a means, deliberately or directly employed, to a political or social end. They would be better advised to qualify this argument and argue that *at the present moment* poetry used as a means to such an end is *socially* more useful than poetry written for its own sake, and that, as the poet is included by and subordinate to the man, it is the poet's business—as he is a man first and a poet second—to write propaganda. This is a tenable position but it is bad logic to infer from it that the values of poetry and the values of propaganda are identical. The Marxist historian is also employing bad logic if, having proved that poetry in any period is *conditioned* by the social and economic background, he goes on to assume that either the *cause* or the function or the end of poetry can be assessed in sociological or economic terms.

I have already stated, as my own opinion, that the poet is subordinate to the man and that poetry cannot be assessed purely in terms of itself. I take 'the man', however, to mean something wider and more complex than he means to those Marxists who, in spite of Marx's warnings on the subject, recognize *only* his economic conditioning. Much Marxist criticism seems to rest on a fallacy—on the confusion of the motivation to an activity with the form which that activity takes (a fallacy which is also found among psychologists). No doubt there were social—and so, at a second remove, economic—reasons why the ancient Greeks took to studying mathematics, but the development of that science was governed by principles which were not economic or political or social but which were mathematical. Poetry, as I have already said, has not the objectivity of a science, because a poem is a personal utterance, but this does not disprove the possibility of poetic truth, for the humanity of persons is a fairly constant factor; though the personal element is not *sufficiently* constant to be scientifically formulated, it is unjustifiable to conclude that, because poetry is personal, it is therefore irresponsible. .

The propaganda poets claim to be realists—a claim which can only be correct if realism is identical with pragmatism. Truth, whether poetic or scientific, tends as often as not to be neither simple nor easily intelligible, whereas the propagandist is bound by his function to give his particular public something that they can easily swallow and digest. Realism, in the proper sense of the word, takes account of facts regardless of their propaganda value and records not only those facts which suit one particular public but also those facts which suit another public and even those facts which suit no one. The propagandist may have his 'truth' but it is not the truth of the scientist or of the realist; it is even further removed from these than poetic truth is. He is only interested in changing the world; any use of words therefore which will lead to that end—lies, distortions, or outrageous over-simplifications—will, from his point of view, be true. This again is a tenable position but it does not prove either that the poet will write better poetry by substituting propagandist truth for poetic truth or even that it is the poet's duty as a man to write propaganda poetry.

Even if the poet believes in the end of the propagandist he can have legitimate doubts whether that *end* will be in the long run usefully served by a prostitution of poetry. Poetry is to some extent, like mathematics, an autotelic activity; if bad poetry or bad mathematics is going to further a good cause, let us leave this useful abuse of these arts to people who are not mathematicians or poets.

There is in Marxist theory a basic paradox—perhaps a basic fallacy. Marx wrote: 'It is not the consciousness of men that determines their existence, but on the contrary their social existence determines their consciousness.' Many of his successors have narrowed this doctrine into a very stringent determinism; any individual, it is assumed, is *entirely* conditioned by brute material circumstances, any cerebration he may do is merely an epiphenomenon; the brute circumstances, however, change of themselves through the inexorable laws of history; when these have changed, the individual will automatically change also. But why then all the trumpeting, the slogan-shouting, the argumentation, the crate-loads of pamphlets and polemics and strategical and theoretical writings? Why does the revolutionary write or orate at all? Because he hopes to convert people to his creed? That answer is inconsistent with his determinist doctrine; to persuade, or even to browbeat, people is an unmaterialistic activity, it is consciousness setting out to affect existence. And Marx, we are told, considered such activity futile (Marx whose own consciousness of social history so infected the consciousness of his contemporaries and successors that it has changed the history of Europe). The everyday communist, however, is not worried by inconsistency; he still keeps his faith in the magical value of slogans, still holds that if he repeats a statement often enough it will turn into a fact, and *at the same time* denies the practical value of any spiritual faith, of any intellectual ideal, of any absolute or universal judgement. Whether it is true or not that Yeats was reactionary and communism is progressive, there are comparatively few communists who are in a position to accuse Yeats of a mumbo-jumbo idealism.

Goodbye, Twilight is a collection of proletarian poems—some communist, some Irish republican, and all written in a defiant spirit of opposition. Mr Daiken's introduction shows clearly that this poetry represents a violent reaction against Yeats and all that he stood for, though he has the sense not to contend that it is better poetry than Yeats's. 'Nobody dreams', he admits, 'that Ireland has yet a peasant and proletarian poetry' that can be compared with the plays of Sean O'Casey or certain prose writings by Peadar O'Donnel and Liam O'Flaherty; such poetry, however, is evolving and will become the dominant type. Quite possibly he is right but, if so, proletarian poetry will have to become a great deal less bourgeois; at the moment it relies upon clichés, and is trying to fight the bourgeois with his own discarded weapons.

Some of the poems in *Goodbye, Twilight* are marked by a deliberate irreverence towards the Celtic renaissance; one poet writes 'we, feet firm, plod out on the naked hills that do not care about being holy', and another writes 'I prefer a Grand Piano to a Harp'; such poems, being conditioned by Irish dislikes, are still specifically Irish. Other poems here are the conventional utterance of the international working class—

> I indict the ruling class
> With words of dynamite,
> The smashing inky bombs of words
> Will be my way of fight.

Many, however, are still blatantly nationalistic and some are even devoutly Roman Catholic. Compared with these young men, whether they are communist or nationalist or anarchist, Yeats no longer appears as an isolated figure; he shares the same doomed cell with Joyce, Eliot, and Pound and even—I suspect—with Bernard Shaw.

Over in England there is a similar tentative growth of proletarian poetry, examples of which can be found in the now dead *Left Review* and in a monthly periodical called *Poetry and the People*. I shall not discuss this type of poetry further because the great gulf between it and Yeats makes comparison fruitless. I shall, however, say a little about Auden and Spender who have also sometimes been called communist poets but in whose work Yeats could find 'no trace of the recognized communist philosophy'. Many communists would agree with Yeats on this point; certainly, if communist poetry can only be written by proletarians and must primarily be propagandist, Auden and Spender are not, and never have been, communist. It is possible, however, that both Yeats and the disapproving communists are wrong, not only about the relation of poetry to communism, but about the nature of communism itself. Before considering further these problems of a younger generation I would compare Yeats with two older poets, D. H. Lawrence and T. S. Eliot; he has more in common with either of them than appears at first sight

Eliot himself in *After Strange Gods* has grouped Lawrence and Yeats together as writers who have suffered from the lack of an established religion and a traditional moral code and who have invented for these things Robinson Crusoe substitutes. Mr Edmund Wilson has grouped Eliot and Yeats together with Joyce, Paul Valéry, and others, as aesthetic individualists, members of the Ivory Tower. Mr Stephen Spender in *The Destructive Element* has found that Eliot and Yeats are united in a tendency towards fascism. We might say of Yeats that he approximates to Lawrence in so far as he is eclectic, and to Eliot in so far as he is authoritarian. Lawrence, declassed, took to an eclectic pursuit of physical sensations; Yeats took to an eclectic aestheticism. We have seen Yeats making believe that the 'Ancient Gods' are still with us. Lawrence, a devotee of a mystical religion of sex, trekked the world from Etruria to Mexico, making believe that he was finding survivals of some Golden Age when this religion was universally practised. Like Yeats he lives half in the past; the Mediterranean still reveals to him a 'Minoan distance'. Like Yeats he hated machines and wanted to stop the clock or even smash it; one of his poems which Yeats chose for the *Oxford Book* is a violent, nostalgic expression of this hatred—

At last, for the sake of clothing himself in his own leaf-like cloth tissued
    from his life,
and dwelling in his own bowery house, like a beaver's nibbled mansion
and drinking from cups that came off his fingers like flowers off their
    fivefold stem
he will cancel the machines we have got.

But if Lawrence is, like Yeats, an eclectic, he is also like Yeats a one-minded one; he is always looking for the same thing. Whether he is writing about women or tortoises or cyclamens or schoolboys or death or the bourgeoisie or Italy or coal-mines, he is always the religious seeker who finds God everywhere or, failing to find him, is obsessed by his absence. Lawrence's instinctive mysticism is a more physical thing than

Yeats's elaborated faith in mystical values. Lawrence can see the world in a grain of sand but at the same time can convey with an almost unique perceptiveness the physical impression of sandiness. Beside Lawrence's animals and flowers the physical images of Yeats are merely heraldic. Yet a natural object is for neither of them self-contained; it is referred back, by Yeats to a world-system, by Lawrence to a world instinct.

It may be pertinent to comment on Lawrence's verse technique. He was less successful in regular forms than in free verse, which was more consonant with his whole mentality. His more regular verse is often clumsy and forced and the diction and syntax unnatural. In free verse he found his own voice; he uses the cumulative effects of Whitman but his phrases and cadences are his own. Most poets, perhaps, require definite formal limits since the structural problem helps them to clarify and organize their content; Lawrence most probably did not need this assistance; his vision was immediate; he looked at Nature like a clairvoyant. Yeats, like most poets, did not have this immediate vision and so was aware of the value of limits but he also knew that technical limits are liable to disorganize as well as to organize; as early as 1902 he pointed out, in an essay on Spenser, the dangers of rhyme; 'rhyme is one of the secondary causes of that disintegration of the personal instincts which has given to modern poetry its deep colour for colour's sake, its overflowing pattern, its background of decorative landscape, and its insubordination of detail.'

Eliot's poetry overlaps Yeats's at a different point. Both Eliot and Yeats are essentially *literary* poets. They both hanker for a hierarchic social system. They both combine speculative and sceptical habits with a somewhat frustrated urge to religion. They both dislike the liberal conceptions of progress and democracy; Eliot described the modern world as 'worm-eaten with liberalism' (A.E. Housman, it might be remembered, had already maintained that slavery is necessary to civilization). Mr Spender's imputation of fascist tendencies might be supported by a comparison with Mr Roy Campbell, a poet who starting with a nostalgia for the old régime, for the heroism and ritual of bull-fighters and for the supposed idyllic qualities of a rural, priest-ridden community subject to a land-owning caste, ended by finding in General Franco the patron saint of Christianity, chivalry, and beauty.

Yeats who, as I have said before, failed to see the peculiar virtues of Eliot, must almost certainly have failed to see his own affinities with him. He admired Eliot in much the same way that he admired Shaw, that is as a sort of anti-Christ whose gospel and methods were repugnant but whose honesty and skill were beyond question. But Eliot does not, in fact, represent a reaction against Yeats and Yeats's poetry. Yeats's account of Eliot's poetry is inadequate and incorrect: 'Eliot has produced his great effect upon his generation because he has described men and women that get out of bed or into it from mere habit; in describing this life that has lost heart his own art seems grey, cold, dry. He is an Alexander Pope working without apparent imagination, producing his effects by a rejection of all rhythms and metaphors used by the more popular romantics rather than by the discovery of his own, this rejection giving his work an unexaggerated plainness that has the effect of novelty.' Ignoring the implication that Pope had no imagination, I would merely point to Eliot's poems themselves; if they are what Yeats says they are, how did it happen that many people besides myself found them, after one or two readings only, both more memorable and more vivid than the bulk of the poetry we knew?

There have been modern poets, including many writers of free verse, who have produced work which is merely flat and grey—an inventory of the dreary world of habit. Eliot is not among them; his poetic world may be sombre but it is heightened with strange lights. He is a subtle and imaginative craftsman using many devices—metaphysical wit, symbolist imagery, delicate syntax, rapid transition, and, above all, an exact sense of rhythm—to convey his themes in an appropriate, concentrated, and memorable form. And it cannot be said that he represents a break from the English tradition, or even a complete break from the Romantic tradition; witness his use of lilac and hyacinths. He also, like Yeats, is full of echoes of the Past, and the Past for him, as for Yeats, is something irrecoverably glamorous. The echoes come in even when his eye is on the squalid and boring present; a brittle satirical poem about modern Venice contains an echo from *Antony and Cleopatra*; broken coloured threads from Dante and *The Tempest* run through the web of *The Waste Land*. And he likes, like Yeats, to suggest that past tragedies repeat themselves—

> You who were with me in the ships at Mylae!

Even *Prufrock*, which is social criticism (and that, according to Yeats, is not a poet's business) ends with a nostalgia reminiscent of some of the poems in *Responsibilities*:

> I have seen them riding seaward on the waves
> Combing the white hair of the waves blown back
> Where the wind blows the water white and black.

> We have lingered in the chambers of the sea
> By sea-girls wreathed with seaweed red and brown
> Till human voices wake us, and we drown.

Eliot's English admirers have often admired him uncritically, but some of Yeats's admirers reject Eliot even more uncritically, inheriting from their master the belief that Eliot is a poet who sold his birthright, who jettisoned imagery and rhythm. This belief is false. Eliot's poetry is a very fine example of what Dr Johnson called Wit—something 'at once natural and new'. Not only is Eliot a master of the startling but inevitable image; he can also wed image and rhythm in such a way as to represent simultaneously in picture and sound the appropriate shade of meaning or mood—

> My life is light, waiting for the deathwind
> Like a feather on the back of my hand.

This is something that Yeats can also bring about. They resemble each other too in their use of diction; Eliot takes ordinary words and poises them in such a way, by syntax or rhythm or both, as to enlarge or heighten their meaning and fuse it into the poem as a whole; sometimes too Eliot, like Yeats, shows a Marlovian fondness for exotic names; his poem *Animula* has the exciting sequence—Guiterriez, Boudin, Floret. They are even alike in their weaknesses; Eliot tends to over-work images with a private significance and to employ figures that come from a private, archaic, and slightly affected mythology—as, in *Ash Wednesday*, for instance, the three white leopards and the garden god in the stained glass window.

In their critical utterances they are often diametrically opposed, poetry appearing essentially impersonal to one and personal to the other; in practice all that this amounts to is that Eliot avoids saying 'I'. There is a more basic difference in their gloom, Eliot's tending to be defeatist where Yeats's is heroic, Eliot's involving the abasement of the individual, Yeats's enhancing his individuality—'Hamlet and Lear are gay.' Eliot chose as a caption for *Sweeney Agonistes* a quotation from St John of the Cross: 'Hence the soul cannot be possessed of the divine union, until it has divested itself of the love of created things.' Yeats wrote in his introduction to *Gitanjali* by Rabindranath Tagore: 'it is our own mood, when it is furthest from a Kempis or John of the Cross, that cries, "And because I love this life, I know I shall love death as well."'

Other poets of an older generation than my own, for instance Edwin

Muir and Robert Graves, provide certain parallels with Yeats, though they were in no way directly influenced by him. Thus, where Yeats began in the Celtic twilight, then moved on to a period of occasional and disillusioned poetry, and finally took to expressing an esoteric philosophy in verse that is symbolic but hard, Graves began with the romanticism of the nursery, moved on to a period of occasional and disillusioned poetry, and is now writing poetry that is bleakly metaphysical. The chief difference is that, whereas Yeats's poetry became increasingly human, Graves's poetry has moved further and further from humanity.

In England about 1930 a school of poets appeared who mark more or less of a reaction against the influence of Eliot. Curiously, in spite of their violently 'modern' content, they were not so much in reaction against Yeats, who for his part found them, on occasions, sympathetic, and discovered in them a 'concentrated passion' which, according to him, distinguished their poetry from Eliot's. This distinction is fallacious but they can be grouped with Yeats rather than with Eliot on the following grounds. Eliot, in the essay already quoted from, had maintained that the poet must adapt himself to his world; if his world is difficult and complex, his poetry must be difficult and complex (a theory exemplified by *The Waste Land*). Poets like Auden and Spender abandoned this feminine conception of poetry and returned to the old, arrogant principle—which was Yeats's too—that it is the poet's job to make sense of the world, to simplify it, to put shape on it. The fact that these younger poets proposed to stylize their world in accordance with communist doctrine or psychoanalytical theory (both things repugnant to Yeats) is comparatively irrelevant. Whatever their system was, they stood with Yeats for system against chaos, for a positive art against a passive impressionism. Where Eliot had seen misery, frustration, and ruins, they saw heroic struggle—or, sometimes, heroic defeat—and they saw ruins rebuilding. The two earlier English poets who chiefly influenced my generation were Donne and Blake; it is significant that, whereas we shared Donne with Eliot, we shared Blake with Yeats; our aim was to use our brains, as Donne and Eliot had done, but to follow Blake in not abjuring life or the world of 'created things'. Eliot has deplored the 'diabolic influence' in modern literature; we may remember that Blake wrote of Milton: 'he was a true Poet and of the Devil's party without knowing it.'

Yeats found much of this new poetry exasperatingly obscure and ostentatiously experimental. He distrusted *deliberate* originality and had written in Per *Amica Silentia Lunae* (1917): 'It is not permitted to a man, who takes up pen or chisel, to seek originality, for passion is his only business, and he cannot but mould or sing after a new fashion because no disaster is like another.' But, if the younger poet sometimes seemed wilfully original, he recognized also that they had their own disasters, that they could not be expected to write to his own recipe. He must have considered their content too heterogeneous and must have disliked Auden's guide-book curiosity; if Auden had written poems about the Rosses he would never have left out Metal Man who stands in the harbour.

On the other hand he welcomed their vigour of thought, being tired no doubt of the spineless elegance of some of his own imitators. He approved also their return, though 'with a new freedom', to the traditional metres and to the personal lyric. And he liked their zest, a quality which, except in his own poetry, had been notably lacking in English verse for some time.

I will not push these comparisons any further. It is fashionable in some circles in England to-day to dismiss Yeats as a mere reactionary, a man who wrote elegantly in an outmoded manner and preached a gospel which was not only obsolete but vicious. This very superficial view has been well combated in an article by Auden entitled The Public v. the late Mr W. B. Yeats (published in *The Partisan Review*), which takes the form of a speech for the prosecution and a speech for the defence. The defence argue—quite rightly—that a work of art cannot be assessed merely by its political reference. Auden, however, as was natural in a poet who had abruptly abandoned the conception of art as handmaid of politics for the conception of art as autotelic, overstates his case; he says that the case for the prosecution rests on the fallacy that art never makes anything happen. The case for the prosecution does rest on a fallacy but it is not this. The fallacy lies in thinking that it is the *function* of art to make things happen and that the effect of art upon actions is something either direct or calculable. It is an historical fact that art *can* make things happen and Auden in his reaction from a rigid Marxism seems in this article to have been straying towards the Ivory Tower. Yeats did not write primarily in order to influence men's actions but he knew that art can alter a man's outlook and so indirectly affect his actions. He also recognized that art can, sometimes intentionally, more often perhaps unintentionally, precipitate violence. He was not sentimentalizing when he wrote, thinking of *Cathleen ni Houlihan*:

> Did that play of mine send out
> Certain men the English shot?

Conclusion

Safe from the wolves black jaw, and the dull asses hoofe.

BEN JONSON

This survey of Yeats's poetry has, I hope, made it clear that he is a less simple and a more substantial poet than many of his detractors and some of his admirers think him. In considering poetry we are not yet free from the bugbear of Beauty. When a reader talks about Beauty, he more often than not means either that a poem is *about* something which he thinks beautiful in life or merely that he likes the sound or shape of the poem for its own sake; both these are very inadequate criteria. By a bastard reasoning, to use Aristotle's phrase, we can consider a poem valuably in two ways; we can assess its self-coherence and we can assess its correspondence to life. Every poem, to be good, must correspond (in some way) to life and must be self-coherent, and either of these facts involves the other. A poem which fulfils both these requirements can, if one wishes, be called beautiful; it can equally well be called true. Neither its beauty nor its truth, however, is identical with the beauty we find in nature or the truth we find in science. The only safe epithet is tautological; a good poem is in the truest sense poetic just as a healthy animal is undeniably animal. To speak of Yeats as a servant of Beauty is misleading because Beauty, in the popular sense, was irrelevant to his main function. Truth, in the popular sense, was also something irrelevant to him. What he was concerned with was Poetry.

I do not mean that Yeats remained a disciple of Art for Art's sake; we have already seen how he deviated from that conception. Art for Art's sake defeated its own end because Art was thought of almost solely in terms of form, whereas the material of art is life and matter conditions form; the Aesthetes themselves were inconsistent in laying so much stress on passion. The paradox of poetry is like the paradox of individual freedom. An individual is not less free but more free, if he recognizes the factors which condition him and adjusts himself to his context; a poem is not less of a poem, but more of a poem, if it fulfils its business of corresponding to life. The necessity of circumstance does not destroy either the individuality of a man or the poetry of a poem. The exponents of Art for Art's sake were either sentimentalists or bad logicians; art is autotelic in so far as its value (except incidentally) is non-utilitarian; it is not autotelic if that is taken to mean that it neither comes from life nor affects it, and that therefore it can be understood without reference to life. A poem is a self-contained entity but an organic one; it is not a lone comet. Any particular animal is himself and no other animal but it is the stream of life running through him from outside of himself that keeps him alive and allows him to affect other lives. A poem too, is specifically itself but it has a stream of life running through it, otherwise it could not communicate with us; the poet has given it legs with which it leaves him behind and treks the world on its own.

Yeats's view of poetry, as we have seen, underwent modifications during his life. As most poets do, he throve on theoretical half-truths. He began by requiring 'beauty' in the popular narrower sense and 'passion' in the Romantic sense, abjuring the intellect and rhetoric and everyday moods and ideas and contemporary subjects. Yet, whatever he may have thought himself, he was never merely a poet of passion; his intellect was always involved in a Platonic search for universals. During his nationalist period he maintained that the nationalist poet is concerned with permanent values whereas the 'contemporary' poet is concerned only with the ephemeral and the irrelevant. Later he admitted that nationalism can sidetrack the poet into narrowness, aridity, and even hypocrisy, while he conceded that the contemporary world must be faced, for 'every man everywhere is more of his time than of his nation'. Theoretically, he believed in revelation; in practice he was exceptionally deliberate in selecting and arranging his material. He made himself a poet and, as poet, he was essentially a maker. Some might suggest that he made his bricks without straw or, at least, out of very odd mixtures of clay and grit and rubbish. The great fact is that he made them.

His doctrine of poetry may have been unsound but it does not compare too badly with the doctrines of his contemporaries or immediate predecessors. With that, for example, of the Symbolists and their English disciples who turned their backs at once upon society and statement. Or with that of the American Imagists who renounced all use of generalities. Or with that of A.E. Housman who in *The Name and Nature of Poetry* renounced the element of meaning. Or with that of the Surrealists who, following Housman's trend still further, made the poet a 'modest registering machine' modestly registering the Unconscious. Or with that of T. S. Eliot who renounced personal enthusiasm and implied that a dislocated world required dislocated poetry. Or with that of Miss Laura Riding who, more logical than earlier advocates of 'pure poetry', would purge it not only of description and rhetoric and moralizing but of emotions and sense-imagery also. Or with that of W. H. Auden who, in rightly impugning the divorce between poetry and life, went on to infer that there was *no* difference in kind between poetry and other human activities. Or with that of the Communists who demand that poetry shall be propaganda first, foremost, and for ever.

Yeats, as we have seen from his practice (and I have also quoted critical statements of his in support of this), did not do these things—not, at least, if we consider his work as a whole. He did not turn his back on either society or statement; he did not renounce generalities and confine himself to 'shots' of the particular; he was not ashamed of personal enthusiasm; he did not believe in dislocation; he repudiated the flux of the Unconscious; he did not attempt Miss Riding's rarefaction; unlike Auden, he thought of poetry as a specialized activity; unlike the Communists, he refused to think of it as advertising.

In the first chapter I raised the question whether Yeats was sincere. In succeeding chapters, I have conceded, as Yeats conceded himself, that in many respects he was a poseur. Owing, for example, to a belief in aristocracy he faked a legend about his family. Owing to a belief in mysticism he pretended to mystical experience. Owing to a belief in Ireland he— at times—misrepresented her. His distortions of fact, it will be seen, were accounted for by a belief; believing that things ought to be so, he wrote as if they were so. This was not, on his premises, sharp practice, since it can be referred back to another, more fundamental belief of his—that the artist's world is what the artist makes it. (The fact that he is thinking primarily of the *artist's* world absolves him at least to some extent from the fallacy implicit in propaganda poetry.)

It could be argued that while it is one thing for a poet to distort his facts when he is writing within a convention not dependent on himself (as was the case with the Troubadours and the poets of the Roman Empire), it is quite another thing for a poet to distort his facts when he insists, as Yeats did, that poetry is personal utterance. When the Troubadour professes extravagant love for a lady he hardly knows, we accept this as deliberate dramatization—hardly even self-dramatization—for in the Troubadour's poetic world the particular facts of self are entirely subordinated to a convention; both he and his readers, consequently, know where they stand. Yeats, on the other hand, denied that he accepted any such set of values or conventions from outside himself; his outlook was to be conditioned by his own personal emotions; each poem was to embody a unique experience. This leads us to consider whether Yeats's emotions were genuine. If he misrepresented facts in order to square them with his belief, if he even faked his beliefs because he so much *wanted to believe*, is it not possible that he sometimes faked his passion because he so much wanted to be passionate?

Perhaps sometimes he did fake his passion but certainly not always. That he may have done so can be to some extent excused if we refer back his pseudo-passions to a 'passion for passion' just as we have referred his pseudo-beliefs back to a 'belief in belief'. Every poem cannot be taken at its surface value. I would not contend that pseudo-passions are just as good—even in poetry—as real passions; Yeats's would-be mystical reactions to external objects cannot be compared, even as ingredients for poetry, with the more genuine mystical reactions of Rilke or D. H. Lawrence. I would maintain however, that they do not necessarily falsify his poetry—any more than the poet who recollects emotion in tranquillity falsifies his poetry because the emotion itself is past. A great deal of poetry can be explained as a sort of emotional *couvade*; the poet makes believe that he is bearing the sufferings of the world, or at least those select sufferings which interest him. Such make-believe is not sentimental if the poet himself takes it seriously. Though Yeats may not always have felt what he said he felt, he did not make such statements with his tongue in his cheek. The actor playing Lear in his madness does not have his tongue in his cheek because he is sane.

I would say, in fact, that Yeats, as a poet, is characterized by integrity. He talks a lot of nonsense, he poses, he suppresses, exaggerates, misrepresents. Working, according to his lights, on *a priori* principles, he refused to give way to what others would consider evidence. We may consider this deplorable, but we should not call it dishonest. Who would impute dishonesty to Spinoza?

Poets of my generation, who distrust *a priori* methods, tend to found— or think they found—their own beliefs and their own moral principles on evidence. These beliefs and principles are, in their opinion, of the utmost importance to their poetry. So they are, but not necessarily because they are the 'right' beliefs. Poetry gains body from beliefs, and the more suited the belief is to the poet, the healthier his poetry; one poet can thrive on pantheism and another on Christianity; Housman *as a poet* flourished on beliefs the opposite of Browning's. It is not the absolute, or objective, validity of a belief that vindicates the poetry; it is a gross over-simplification to maintain that a right belief makes a poem good and a wrong belief makes a poem bad. First, beliefs are not so easily sorted out into merely right and merely wrong; secondly, by the time a belief is embodied in a poem, it has suffered a biochemical change, has become blended inextricably with mood, picture, and drama. We can, however, say that at certain times in certain places there are certain beliefs affecting us so widely and deeply that they are for us the right ones. This being so, we can argue that some of Yeats's beliefs were wrong and can go on to infer that better, or greater, or more 'significant' poetry than Yeats's could be made, given better ingredients. This inference, too, is possibly correct (though we must remember that a belief, in the narrow sense, is only one ingredient out of many), but we should be mistaken if we inferred that *Yeats* could have written better poetry if he had had the 'right' ingredients; he probably could not have assimilated them. Yeats, like Gerard Manley Hopkins, was a special case. Those critics are fools who lament that, if Hopkins had not been a Jesuit, he would have written much better poetry. If Yeats had been different from what he was, if he had had different beliefs, or even been capable of different beliefs, he might not have written at all. The spiritual lesson that my generation (a generation with a vastly different outlook) can learn from Yeats is to write according to our lights. His lights are not ours. *Go thou and do otherwise.*

He can serve us also, perhaps, as an example of zest. Much modern poetry has inevitably a gloomy content; so had much of Yeats's poetry, but whether it is nostalgic, love-lorn, cynical, darkly prophetic, angry over politics, or embittered over old age, there is nearly always a leaping vitality—the vitality of Cleopatra waiting for the asp. The poet kicks against life but that is because his demands from life are high. Yeats's determinist cyclic philosophy seems to my generation defeatist, but I would suggest that this determination is a bluff, perhaps an unconscious one. Knowledge and power, if we are to take him literally, are things imposed upon us from outside according to our predetermined place on the gyres of history; what is going to happen must happen. But Yeats puts the emphasis elsewhere; his point is that it is worth it, that we who are on the gyres are lucky to be in at the deaths and births of history, and that, whoever is responsible, whoever is the author of the play, it is we who hold the centre of the stage—

CONCLUSION

A shudder in the loins engenders there
The broken wall, the burning roof and tower
And Agamemnon dead.

             Being so caught up,
So mastered by the brute blood of the air,
Did she put on his knowledge with his power
Before the indifferent beak could let her drop?

Notes

Ch. II, p. 37. *Pater's worship of style*. Style, if regarded as mere décor or even mere dress, is something comparatively trivial, but before jeering at the Aesthetes for their triviality, we should do well to remember that at least they avoided the intellectualist error which the modern world inherited from the Greeks and which still vitiates literary criticism, viz. that it is the *thought* that dominates a poem and gives it its value (an error well combated by I. A. Richards in his *Principles of Literary Criticism* and censured even by a Marxist critic, Christopher Caudwell, in his penetrating study of poetry, *Illusion and Reality*). There is something in a suggestion made by Hermann Broch in his novel, *The Sleepwalkers*, where he wonders 'whether even the thought of an epoch is not a vehicle for its style, governed by that same style which attains visible and palpable expression in works of art; which amounts to the assertion that truth, the ultimate product of thought, is equally a vehicle for the style of the epoch in which it has been discovered and in which it is valid . . .' [Translation by Willa and Edwin Muir.]

Ch. II, p. 39. *Science the Tree of Death*. I should have said more about Yeats's phobia of science. He snared the error of Keats in thinking that science might come to supersede poetry. I. A. Richards in *Science and Poetry* points out that while science has made obsolete the 'Magical View' of nature, the basis of much of the poetry of the past, it can never take over the proper functions of poetry. Yeats could not be so adequate a representative of his time as say Dante was for the simple reason that he tried to build on a 'magical view' which was not acceptable to his age.

Ch. IV, p. 65. *Yeats's eye*. Yeats was very short-sighted. George Moore complained that he did not, as he walked in the open air, appreciate the beauties around him. Lady Gerald Wellesley (*Letters on Poetry from W. B. Yeats to Dorothy Wellesley*) corroborates this, recounting that he hated flowers and that 'his lack of observation concerning natural beauty was almost an active obsession . . .'

Ch. IV, p. 73. *Yeats and mythology*. Thomas Mann in a lecture on 'Freud and the Future' maintains that Freud has encouraged the creative writer in his habit of 'regarding life as mythical and typical' [one usually connects this attitude more with Jung] and of looking for 'a fresh incarnation of the traditional upon earth'. Yeats in *A Vision* (see pp. 112 ff. in this book) attempted—to the point of absurdity—to work out such a mythology of types in his classification of human individuals. Cuchulain, Clytemnestra, Parnell, Oscar Wilde, all became types for Yeats, all became myths. And his doctrine of reincarnation was intended to buttress the traditional.

Ch. VI, p. 117. *Circuits of Sun and Moon.* I. A. Richards wrote in *Science and Poetry*: 'To Mr Yeats the value of *The Phases of the Moon* [the poem of that name] lies not in any attitudes which it arouses or embodies [which according to Richards is the proper effect of a poem] but in the doctrine which for an initiate it promulgates.' I doubt this: see Yeats's own account quoted on p. 117. He wished to affect his reader emotionally, not to convert him.

Ch. VI, p. 117. *Michelangelo.* Yeats (see p. 154) considered that Michelangelo's ideal was 'profane perfection of mankind'. Michelangelo himself, an ardently religious nature, was unaware of this; see his Twenty-third Sonnet, an address to a beautiful woman, which is based on the Platonic conception of sōma-sēma, of the body as a prison or tomb.

Ch. X, p. 187. *Yeats and D. H. Lawrence.* I. A. Richards in *Science and Poetry* points out this too—that, in spite of their different modes of escape, Yeats and Lawrence were alike in 'dodging those difficulties which come from being born into this generation rather than into some earlier age'.

Index

INDEX